More Praise for *The Power of Appreciative Inquiry*

"*The Power of Appreciative Inquiry* is a practical, down-to-earth guide to a compelling and rich methodology. Through the AI process, individuals, work groups, organizations, and even communities can become engaged and empowered — which leads to positive changes not previously imagined. Anyone wishing to explore the potential of Appreciative Inquiry will find this book to be an excellent resource and an ongoing reference."

> —Darlene Van Tiem, President, International Society
> for Performance Improvement

"*The Power of Appreciative Inquiry* changed the way I approach my clients. It's been one of my best investments! It clearly describes Appreciative Inquiry's theoretical background, but it's also a practical guide on how to use AI as a powerful tool for organizational change and development."

> —Carlos Aguilera Muga, founder and Managing Director,
> Gestar Blanchard International Group, Santiago, Chile

"*The Power of Appreciative Inquiry* is sage, thorough, and practical guidance to help answer the essential question, *how do we build a more appreciative world?*"

> —Marilee Adams, PhD, author of *Change Your Questions, Change
> Your Life*

"*The Power of Appreciative Inquiry*, more than any other book, inspired positive change in our personal and professional lives. The book was the perfect resource to help us imagine and then build a future based on the best of our past. We now rely on Appreciative Inquiry to work with our clients throughout Latin America and the United States."

> —Jeff Jackson and Maurice Monette, Codirectors,
> The Vallarta Institute, Mexico

"*The Power of Appreciative Inquiry* is the best, most comprehensive book on the subject that I have encountered. It is a terrific 'handbook' for people just learning about Appreciative Inquiry, for those who want a reference book, or for those that wish to get reacquainted with the subject: a must for anyone who is interested in Appreciative Inquiry."

—Tenny Poole, former Vice President of Human Resources,
    Experian Americas

"We would like to thank Diana Whitney and Amanda Trosten-Bloom. Their book, *The Power of Appreciative Inquiry*, along with Diana's kind visit and several workshops, has greatly changed the way organization development is practiced in Japan. Many Japanese companies and the government were struggling with deficit-based approaches to change management. The members of the organizations who came to know AI are now moving forward with a lot of energy, happily and productively."

—Kunio Takama, President, Human Value Inc., Japan

"This is *the* seminal guide to the theory and application of Appreciative Inquiry. Consultants, coaches, facilitators, and change leaders all support human systems in moving toward new and positive possibilities. This influential book clearly articulates the essential principles and practices for accessing and mobilizing these possibilities."

—Doug Silsbee, author of *Presence-Based Coaching*

"In order to make real the proposition that 'a better world is possible,' we must construct new forms of social interaction, and that requires individual, group, organizational, and social transformation. Appreciative Inquiry is a very helpful tool in that endeavor. But to get beyond the affirmations, we need a guide that describes the philosophy and practice. *The Power of Appreciative Inquiry* does just that. This book has inspired us to bring together a group of people to continue and deepen the advances achieved in our social development. Thank you, Diana and Amanda, for your act of love."

—Patricia Arenas Bautista, PhD, Coordinator,
    Community of Learning on Human Change, Havana, Cuba

"I could hardly imagine anything to improve *The Power of Appreciative Inquiry*'s first edition — but here it is, even better! Its sweetness and excitement make it my first choice. Hardly a week goes by without my recommending it."

—Paul Chaffee, Executive Director, Interfaith Center at the Presidio

"Au-delà de comprendre les bases de l'AI ce livre m'a fait traverser l'Atlantique plusieurs fois pour rencontrer ses auteurs, percevoir l'AI au-delà des mots. Bon voyage au cœur de l'AI!" (Beyond understanding the basis of AI, this book made me fly over the Atlantic several times to meet its authors, to understand AI beyond words. Have a nice trip to the heart of AI!)

—Philippe Poulin, Oxigen Consulting, France

"Of all the books on Appreciative Inquiry that I use for my clients and consulting work, *The Power of Appreciative Inquiry* is the book I recommend and return to for its clarity, accessibility, and application to the real world of organizations. This book embodies core messages of Appreciative Inquiry, encouraging and enabling people to be positive, to build strong and productive relationships, and to dream about what is possible."

—Alan Briskin, author of *The Stirring of Soul in the Workplace* and coauthor of *The Power of Collective Wisdom*

"At last — the quintessential guide to Appreciative Inquiry, for the experienced practitioner or the novice."

—Jean Moore, Executive Director, Workforce Development, Verizon, and author of *Reconnecting with People*

"Amanda and Diana have cocreated, tested, and enhanced processes for positive change for many years. Such processes call people, organizations, and communities to higher ground — beyond common ground. Their work, including this revised edition, is congruent with the people they are. They don't just talk about AI; they live it! That is what makes *The Power of Appreciative Inquiry* so compelling and impactful."

—Max Hardy, Director, Twyfords, Australia

"*The Power of Appreciative Inquiry* is the best book written on the powerful change process of Appreciative Inquiry. It is easy to read and easy to use. I highly recommend it."

—Sabine Bredemeyer, consultant, Germany

"Appreciative Inquiry was the catalyst for a positive change in customer service at British Airways in North America. The use of Appreciative Inquiry transformed the entire organization in ways that we could not have imagined. Now, our managers use Appreciative Inquiry techniques in dealing with issues that confront them on a day-to-day basis. This book will be a great tool for them."

—Dave Erich, Executive Vice President, British Airways

"This book is as exciting as a brand new box of crayons — the one with sixty-four colors. As people, we become hopeful and empowered when we are connected with others around common yearnings. These are the kind of conversations we need to have — and this book will help you figure out how to do it."

—Kathleen D. Dannemiller, founder, Dannemiller Tyson Associates, and author of *Whole-Scale Change*

The Power of Appreciative Inquiry

Also by the Authors

Appreciative Inquiry
McGraw-Hill, 2010

Encyclopedia of Positive Questions, Volume 1
Crown Custom Publishing, 2005

Appreciative Team Building
iUniverse, 2004

Positive Family Dynamics
Taos Institute Publications, 2008

The Appreciative Organization, Revised Edition
Taos Institute Publications, 2008

Appreciative Inquiry: A Positive Revolution in Change
Berrett-Koehler, 2005

The Appreciative Inquiry Summit
Berrett-Koehler, 2003

Appreciative Inquiry Handbook, Second Edition (book and CD)
Crown Custom Publishing, 2008

Advances in Appreciative Inquiry (DVD)
Corporation for Positive Change, 2008

Foundations of Appreciative Inquiry: A Workshop by Diana Whitney and David Cooperrider (CD)
Corporation for Positive Change, 2007

The Power of Appreciative Inquiry

A Practical Guide to Positive Change

Diana Whitney & Amanda Trosten-Bloom

Foreword by David Cooperrider

Second Edition

Berrett–Koehler Publishers, Inc.
San Francisco
a BK Business book

Berrett-Koehler Publishers, Inc.
235 Montgomery Street, Suite 650
San Francisco, CA 94104-2916
Tel: (415) 288-0260   Fax: (415) 362-2512   www.bkconnection.com

Ordering Information

Quantity sales. Special discounts are available on quantity purchases by corporations, associations, and others. For details, contact the "Special Sales Department" at the Berrett-Koehler address above.

Individual sales. Berrett-Koehler publications are available through most bookstores. They can also be ordered directly from Berrett-Koehler: Tel: (800) 929-2929; Fax: (802) 864-7626; www.bkconnection.com

Orders for college textbook/course adoption use. Please contact Berrett-Koehler: Tel: (800) 929-2929; Fax: (802) 864-7626.

Orders by U.S. trade bookstores and wholesalers. Please contact Ingram Publisher Services, Tel: (800) 509-4887; Fax: (800) 838-1149; E-mail: customer.service@ingrampublisherservices.com; or visit www.ingrampublisherservices.com/Ordering for details about electronic ordering.

Berrett-Koehler and the BK logo are registered trademarks of Berrett-Koehler Publishers, Inc.

Printed in the United States of America

Berrett-Koehler books are printed on long-lasting acid-free paper. When it is available, we choose paper that has been manufactured by environmentally responsible processes. These may include using trees grown in sustainable forests, incorporating recycled paper, minimizing chlorine in bleaching, or recycling the energy produced at the paper mill.

Library of Congress Cataloging-in-Publication Data
Whitney, Diana Kaplin.
 The power of appreciative inquiry : a practical guide to positive change / Diana Whitney and Amanda Trosten-Bloom ; foreword by David Cooperrider. — 2nd ed.
  p. cm.
 Includes bibliographical references and index.
 ISBN 978-1-60509-328-4 (pbk. : alk. paper)
 1. Communication in organizations. 2. Customer relations. 3. Appreciative inquiry. I. Trosten-Bloom, Amanda, 1957– II. Title
  HD30.3.W52 2010
  658.4'06—dc22   2009046828

SECOND EDITION
15 14 13   10 9 8 7 6 5 4

Designer: Detta Penna
Copyeditor: Sandra Craig
Proofreader: Katherine Lee
Indexer: Joan Dickey

Contents

Tables, Figures, Exhibits

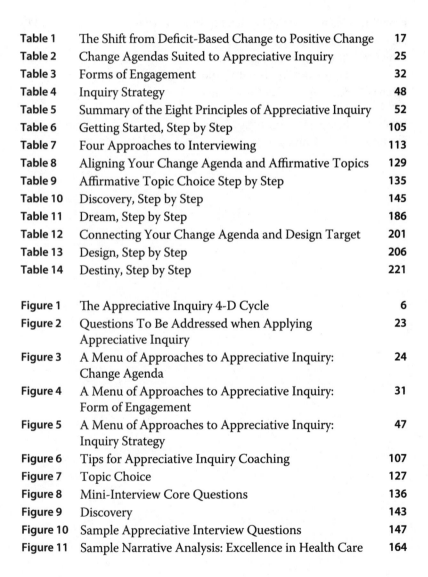

Foreword

Since the first edition of *The Power of Appreciative Inquiry* in 2003, there has been a remarkable explosion of interest, innovation, and powerful business applications of the theory and practice of what many now simply call *AI*—that is, Appreciative Inquiry. Many of the major consulting firms, such as McKinsey and PWC, have brought AI concepts not only into their client engagements but also into their own leadership and organization development work.

In 2004, Kofi Annan, then secretary-general of the United Nations, designed a world summit using the AI summit method to bring together some five hundred CEOs for the largest meeting of its kind ever held at the UN. The purpose—"to unite the strengths of markets with the power of universal ideals"—called upon the best in business to ignite economic empowerment, eradicate extreme poverty, and advance eco-innovation in greener products, services, and sustainable operations. Significantly, a very large proportion of the companies—Hewlett Packard, BP, Nokia, Phillips, Green Mountain Coffee Roasters, and others—were not new to AI, as each had already infused AI's strength-based, positive-change philosophy into many of their organization-development and change-management practices.

These results, as this new edition of *The Power of Appreciative Inquiry* demonstrate, are not atypical or singular victories. Nor are they flash-in-the-pan, unsustainable, change-program-of-the-month experiences. Perhaps the greatest additional asset of this book's Second Edition, especially for those looking for an evidence base for the long-term viability of AI, is this volume's documentation of AI's impacts over a *decade or more*. How many books on organization development do you know of that document not just the early returns but also the *long-term* staying power, the long-term *continuing* improvements or results, and all the ways in which an approach (like AI) becomes part of an organization's DNA?

If you are anything like me, you will love this Second Edition for its courage and for stepping up to the plate to engage the most complex question that everyone today seems to have: where *are* the real-life, not just the theoretical or dreamed-about, cases of successful corporate change that demonstrate precisely how change is sustained, maintained, and even elevated over time, not dissipated or discarded?

If you read nothing else in this book, you must read this volume's featured case presentation. It's the inspiring story of Hunter Douglas, the leading manufacturer and marketer of custom window coverings in North America, whose products are found in millions of homes and commercial buildings around the globe. It is a world-class case not just of AI but of long-term, sustained organization development: the authors narrate the story from its creative beginning in early 1996, then carry the analysis forward almost a decade and a half, tracing results right up to the publication deadline of this volume.

When Diana Whitney and Amanda Trosten-Bloom originally asked me to write the foreword to their exceptionally crafted book, I immediately said yes. I had worked with Diana and Amanda for years, on projects ranging from Verizon to the United Religions Initiative to Hunter Douglas, and I recognized over and over again their uncanny abilities to translate theory into practice. I knew how fully their lives and work were organized around their belief in human beings' built-in bias toward goodness, and I felt confident that they would transmit the depth of what Appreciative Inquiry has to offer to individuals, organizations, and the world.

This is a very special and important book, written with soul and deep conviction. Indeed, the writing is both graceful and joyful—the kind of writing that is destined to contribute to countless persons and institutions in positive, life-giving ways. Diana and Amanda, I am convinced, must have had a twinkle in their eyes when they wrote it. Believe it or not, this is a book about organizational change—and yes, *it makes you happy.*

Have you ever read a corporate history of organizational change with a smile on your face the whole way through? Not likely. To be sure, this positive volume is not the "same old, same old" as it relates to theories of change. By the time you have been inspired by the powerful story of Hunter Douglas and have reached Chapter 12, "Why Appreciative Inquiry Works," you realize that most of the ideas we have been sold in conventional change books are simply obsolete, finished, no longer needed. This book is *that* different. It is refreshing. Nowhere, for example, will you find references to common change management terms such as "resistance" or "gap analysis" or "burning platforms." Instead, this book explores the transformational power of positivity—and the kind of change that happens when strength touches strength, and one person's hope connects with another's hope. And while this book is primarily a business book, it easily integrates remarkable new findings in the rapidly growing field of positive psychology and the domain of social constructionist thought—all while it makes you smile. That's precisely the reason why I can easily imagine my colleagues' eyes twinkling: Diana and Amanda knew, when they wrote this gift, that they were up to something a bit mischievous.

The thesis of the book, as well as the vivid corporate stories that demonstrate the thesis, is this:

- Appreciative Inquiry transforms organizations into places that are free and alive, where people are eager and filled with positive power, and where the creativity of the whole never ceases to amaze, surprise, and innovate.

- It enhances organizations' enterprise-wide capacity for whole-system positive change—and takes the current interests in strengths management and positive psychology beyond the individual level to whole-system applications.

- And, as mentioned, it shows how AI's impacts can reverberate for decades, as in the case of Hunter Douglas, which has become a major manufacturer of architectural products as well as the world's market leader in window coverings.

Shortly before he passed away, I met with Peter Drucker and had what I call my Peter Drucker moment. He was interested in hearing about Appreciative Inquiry, and then I asked him a question: "Peter, you have written more on management thought and change leadership than anyone in history. Is there one lesson you can share, something everyone should know?" "Yes," he said, "and it is ageless in its essence: *the task of leadership is to create an alignment of strengths in ways that make a system's weaknesses irrelevant.*" I immediately wrote it down. And I thought about the words over and over. What Drucker was saying is that leading change is literally *all* about strengths—it has nothing to do with weakness—and strengths do more than perform: they *transform*. But he did not share precisely how this could be done; nor did he offer a theory of a positive, rather than deficit-based, approach to human system change. Fortunately for every one of us, this volume does both. The book is so clearly practical and direct that it can and should be given to virtually every manager or leader of change. There are strength-based tools and methods on every page.

But the volume is equally enticing conceptually. It is filled with dozens of powerful hypotheses related to the stages, vocabularies, and expansive vistas of positive change. When we look back twenty years from now, I am certain that we will find doctoral dissertations traced to this book, exploring such topics as "conversations that matter," "why wholeness brings out the best in human beings," "the narrative basis of sustaining change," and "the journey to liberation—from oppression to power."

The theory of change Diana and Amanda describe has its parallels in the sciences, which introduce us to the concept of *fusion energy.* Fusion is the power source of the sun and the stars. It results when two positively charged elements are combined into one. Throughout this book, the authors describe the powerful, positive energy that is released in organizations when we fuse those things that give life to human systems. What happens in these unifying moments when joy touches joy, strength touches strength, health touches health, inspiration combines with inspiration—and how to make the combinations happen more rapidly and frequently—is what much of this book is about. According to Diana and Amanda, Appreciative Inquiry is so thrilling and full of wonderful possibilities that "having once experienced this liberation of power and the effect it has on the world, people are permanently transformed."

My favorite story in the book perfectly illustrates this fusion energy. The story involves a machine operator who was inspired with his appreciative search for possibilities. While doing his appreciative interviews, he discovered a best practice in another business unit. A fabric press had been adapted to do double the work of the printers in his business unit. He began wondering if the printers in his own business unit might do the same thing. People at first scoffed at the idea: "Ridiculous. Impossible. We've tried it before, and it doesn't work." But the machine operator was elevated by his inquiry. He began to see his world not as a static repetition but as mobile energy capable of innumerable configurations. He felt intellectually alive, and with the persistence of a seasoned inventor, he put his whole heart into giving substance to what was, at first, a dimly lit sense of possibility. He requested Saturday overtime, and in less than a day he transformed a machine worth $110,000 into something worth double the investment. It could now do twice the work. He was filled with joy, with the thrill of the creative act, and with the experience of reshaping reality. But the organization's leaders were equally thrilled. His one discovery saved the company $220,000 that had been projected for the purchase of two new presses.

What is the one topic that deserves priority attention in the expansive and rapidly growing literature on Appreciative Inquiry? In my view, it is the topic of human freedom and the exercise of power in organizational life. And it is right here that Diana and Amanda are at their best, breaking exciting new ground in Chapter 12, "Why Appreciative Inquiry Works." Drawing on Paulo Freire's pedagogy of the oppressed, the authors call all of us to a higher-level conception of positive change. Nothing Pollyannaish—Diana and Amanda reflect directly on issues of organizing that are too frequently avoided or neglected. And they invite a reconsideration of power. I really like the questions they raise, for example:

What is the value of a naturally and comfortably powerful human being? Who knows that she personally has the power to change the world? Who chooses to exercise that power for the good of the whole? Who encourages and grooms the people around her to similarly exercise their power? What is it about Appreciative Inquiry that liberates people's power?

According to the authors, there are at least six conditions for the liberation of power, called the Six Freedoms: freedom to be known in relationship, freedom to be heard, freedom to dream in community, freedom to choose to contribute, freedom to act with support, and freedom to be positive. After lively discussion of each, the authors conclude: *"The power of Appreciative Inquiry comes from the way in which it unleashes all of the Six Freedoms over the course of just one complete 4-D Cycle."*

What I like most about this articulation is its precious attention to things not often talked about in human systems change. For example, the authors write, "Surprisingly little has been written about the experience of being heard" in organizations. Then they describe how Appreciative Inquiry creates not just organizations in which everyone has full voice but organizations in which real listening, for a deep level of meaning making, is the norm.

Similarly, they point to the fact that almost every management text celebrates the role of visionary leaders. No argument here. But again they gracefully challenge: "But what of the dreams of the people?" Hunter Douglas Window Fashions Division loved this question. Their remarkable story shows what happens when you take questions like this seriously. People love Hunter Douglas. I know because I worked there, with Diana and Amanda. The sense of pride is palpable. In the words of a woman who works on the third shift: "I'm actually seeing my wildest dreams come true."

The freedom that most intrigued me—that made me stop and think the most—was the freedom to be positive. We live in a world in which almost everything is under assault in the popular media and in a corporate world where critical, problematic, and deficit-based voices are often the loudest. Diana and Amanda offer all of us a rich vocabulary of change that helps us to shed the perceptual logic of that culture and create a center stage on which our organizations' positive revolutionaries can perform.

Perhaps this is why I said at the outset that I could easily imagine Diana and Amanda with a twinkle in their eyes. Yes, they knew when they were writing this gift that they were up to something a bit mischievous. The tools in this book will entice you. After a little testing and practice, the tools—and especially the results—will surprise you. And before you know it, this practical guide will have you taking on more daring, more important, and more expansive change management assignments than you ever imagined or felt possible.

"Fantastic. Life changing. Powerful." These are the exact words I think you will find emblematic of your experience, once you step into the opportunities offered by this wonderful volume.

David L. Cooperrider, Ph.D.
Fairmount Minerals Professor of Social Entrepreneurship
Weatherhead School of Management
Case Western Reserve University
Cleveland, Ohio
July 2009

Preface

Put Your Values into Practice

If you, like us, believe that organizations can be a source of community and meaning, a vehicle for creating a better world, and a place where human beings can thrive and grow, read on. You may be an executive, a manager, a consultant, a social activist, a human resources professional, or an informal leader in your own organization. You are part of a new generation of leaders, seeking tools and methods to put your values into practice.

This book is a practical guide to a new way of working—a way to achieve exceptional financial performance, leadership at all levels, and extraordinary employee performance and loyalty. That way is called Appreciative Inquiry.

Welcome to the Second Edition

Appreciative Inquiry has come of age. This book, described by readers as the most accessible text on Appreciative Inquiry, has played a significant role as a practical guide for those who wished to design and lead Appreciative Inquiry initiatives. We are delighted to introduce the Second Edition. New tools and information about Appreciative Inquiry have been woven into each chapter, and the book's most important case—Hunter Douglas Window Fashions Division—has been updated. This edition also includes a short but sweet addition to Chapter 10, a new section called Sustainability: The Enduring Capacity for Positive Change, which responds to one of the most frequently asked questions: How do you sustain the positive momentum that Appreciative Inquiry creates? Finally, we are excited to include an entirely new Chapter 11, "Appreciative Inquiry: A Process for Community Planning," which showcases three powerful cases and includes ten practical tips.

In keeping with the spirit of the original book and unanimous input from readers and reviewers, we have strengthened *The Power of Appreciative Inquiry* as a book for learning how to *do* Appreciative Inquiry. All in all, we believe we have made a great book even better. We look forward to your reflections on how you use it to create positive change in your organization or community.

How This Book Can Help You

By reading this book, you will learn the principles and practice of Appreciative Inquiry. You'll learn how to use Appreciative Inquiry to build the kind of organization you've always wanted.

This book provides three kinds of information. Chapters 1 through 4 introduce Appreciative Inquiry, describing what it is and how it works. Chapters 5 through 10 explain how to do Appreciative Inquiry. Chapter 11 is the new chapter dedicated to community planning applications of Appreciative Inquiry. And finally, Chapter 12 tells the story of why Appreciative Inquiry works.

Throughout the book, theory and practice are illustrated with stories of successful Appreciative Inquiry initiatives around the globe. In particular, the "how-to" chapters feature the powerful case of Hunter Douglas Window Fashions Division. This case study demonstrates that organizations can build leadership and achieve significant increases in productivity, profitability, innovation, and employee loyalty when they engage all of their stakeholders by using Appreciative Inquiry to build more positive futures.

By reading this book, you will learn to apply the power of Appreciative Inquiry in unique and creative ways to transform organizations into centers of creativity, innovation, and life that can benefit the world and all living beings.

Acknowledgments

This book is a rich testimony to thirty years of friendship, professional partnership, and collaborative learning. Along the way we have met many creative people with intellectual courage, whose love of humanity inspires constructive action and whose generosity of spirit opens doors for others to walk through. One such person is David Cooperrider. To David and his colleagues at Case Western Reserve University, especially Suresh Srivastva and Ronald Fry, we say a heartfelt thank you for your seminal research and thought leadership. Similarly, we thank the founders of the Taos Institute for their innovative contributions, and we recognize the ongoing contributions of our Corporation for Positive Change colleagues to the growing field of positive change.

This Second Edition of *The Power of Appreciative Inquiry* came to life because thousands of people around the world read and loved the original book. Thank you especially to Paul Chaffee, Barbara Child, Tenny Poole, Anita Sanchez, Kit Tennis, Francisco Gomes de Matos, Milt Markewitz, Joy Salmon, Ruth Seliger, Ray Wells, Sherene Zolno, Kathy Carmean, Larry Dressler, Marc Fine, Bill Godfrey, Bob Hedrick, Chris Hoffman, Bea Mah Holland, Howard Lambert, Mike Neal, Bob New, and Helene Sugarman, who read, reviewed, and provided thoughtful reflections on the earlier edition, helping us make a good book even better.

We deeply appreciate the people of Hunter Douglas Window Fashions Division for their willingness to embrace Appreciative Inquiry as a radically new way of working and for helping us understand how and why Appreciative Inquiry works. We especially thank Rick Pellett (president), along with HR heads Mike Burns and Diana Sadighi.

Thank you as well to the many other people and organizations whose stories and spirit enliven this book, including: British Airways, Verizon, Nutrimental Foods, the United Religions Initiative, Roadway

Express, Lovelace Health Systems, John Deere Harvester Works, and IHS, along with the three communities featured in our newest chapter, Boulder County Aging Services Division; the Sisters of the Good Shepherd, Province of Mid-North America; and the city of Longmont, Colorado. To our friend and teacher Howard Bad Hand, our spiritual family, and our United Religions Initiative community around the world, we say thank you for your prayers and dedication to peace.

From Diana: Many people made this book possible by their presence in my life. To my son and daughter, Brian and Shara Kaplin, global citizens whose love, support, and sharing give essential meaning to my life, thank you for inspiring me with your courage, wisdom, integrity, and humor. To my mom, Eleanor Stratton, thank you for a lifetime of love and for reading the manuscript and giving us your clear and helpful input. Thank you to colleagues and friends who over the years have brought out the best of me, my thinking, and my idealism: Kenneth and Mary Gergen, Judith Schuster, Tom Kaney, Jim Grady, Jim Ludema, Allan Holman, Charles Gibbs, Marge Perry, and David Cooperrider. To my brother, Louis Cocciolone, who worked on the "second edition" of my home while I worked on the Second Edition of this book, thank you for your integrity, your commitment to family, and for just being you. I am especially grateful for the brilliant design and exceptional beauty you have added to my life through the renovation of my home. And to Amanda, thank you for a long and loving journey together as friends, spiritual sisters, colleagues, and authors. Your presence elevates my being and my work.

From Amanda: I am so grateful to all those whose support helped birth this book. To my husband, Barry, and my daughter, Hannah Joy, thank you for your love, devotion, and playfulness—and for twice giving up so much of me. Your presence in my life makes everything else possible. To my sister, Jessica Lewis, and all the "old ladies," thank you for always being there and for always believing in me. To my parents, Arthea, Leonard, and Jane, thank you for teaching me that it's never too late to look for the light. To my friends Suzanne and John Mariner and my extended community, thank you for the behind-the-scenes support. Your curiosity about and belief in my work has inspired me to share it with others. Thank you also to those along the way who helped me learn my trade, find my voice, and know my strength: Tom Kaney, Bob Possanza, my ACI community, and my many clients, colleagues, and students. Most especially, Diana, thank you for all the years of friendship, family, collaboration, and mentoring. Thank you for your breadth of vision and for all the ways in which that has expanded my life and work.

Together: We acknowledge the creativity, commitment, and collaboration of the four readers who helped bring this Second Edition to life: Cindi Bergen, Peggy Holman, Perviz Randeria, and Jackie Stavros. We further acknowledge our editor, Johanna Vondeling, and the Berrett-Koehler staff for their sage counsel and professionalism. Finally, we thank Berrett-Koehler's president, Steve Piersanti, for his courage to create and lead an "appreciative publishing company" that through exemplary collaboration serves all of its stakeholders—customers, authors, and shareholders alike—in their quest for a world that works for all.

It is with great delight and humility that we offer you this book. Appreciative Inquiry has become a way of life for us—the practical expression of our deepest spiritual beliefs. We have been transformed through our consulting and teaching of Appreciative Inquiry and, more recently, through the writing of this Second Edition of *The Power of Appreciative Inquiry*. We hope you find it a useful, inspiring, and challenging call to bring out the best in yourself, your colleagues, and your organizations.

Diana Whitney	Amanda Trosten-Bloom
Chapel Hill, North Carolina	Golden, Colorado
June 2009	June 2009

CHAPTER 1

What Is Appreciative Inquiry?

We are no longer surprised when clients ask, "Appreciative what? What do you mean by Appreciative Inquiry?" After all, the words are a somewhat unusual, if not paradoxical, addition to a business vocabulary that revolves around strategy, structure, problems, and profits. After learning more about the power and potential of Appreciative Inquiry, however, our clients declare, "We want to do Appreciative Inquiry, but we will definitely have to call it something different for it to catch on in our organization."

Appreciative Inquiry is the study of what gives life to human systems when they function at their best. This approach to personal change and organization change is based on the assumption that questions and dialogue about strengths, successes, values, hopes, and dreams are themselves transformational. In short, Appreciative Inquiry suggests that human organizing and change at its best is a relational process of inquiry, grounded in affirmation and appreciation. The following beliefs about human nature and human organizing are the foundation of Appreciative Inquiry:

- People individually and collectively have unique gifts, skills, and contributions to bring to life.

- Organizations are human social systems, sources of unlimited relational capacity, created and lived in language.
- The images we hold of the future are socially created and, once articulated, serve to guide individual and collective actions.
- Through human communication—inquiry and dialogue—people can shift their attention and action away from problem analysis to lift up worthy ideals and productive possibilities for the future.

Words create worlds, and the words Appreciative Inquiry are no exception. Clients have named their Appreciative Inquiry initiatives The Zealots Program, The Power of Two, Value-Inspired People, and in the case of Hunter Douglas, Focus 2000. In each case the company brand has endured—along with the words Appreciative Inquiry. As people understand more about the principles of Appreciative Inquiry and begin to experiment with its practices, they realize how radically positive and subtly different it is from business as usual. To fully describe and understand Appreciative Inquiry, consider the meaning of each of the two words.

Appreciation: Recognition and Value Added

Appreciation has to do with recognition, valuing, and gratitude. The word appreciate is a verb that carries a double meaning, referring to both the act of recognition and the act of enhancing value. Consider these definitions:

1. To recognize the best in people and the world around us.
2. To perceive those things which give life, health, vitality, and excellence to living human systems.
3. To affirm past and present strengths, successes, assets, and potentials.
4. To increase in value, as in "the investment has appreciated in value."

Indeed, organizations, businesses, and communities can benefit from greater appreciation. Around the globe, people hunger for recognition. They want to work from their strengths on tasks they find valuable. Executives and managers long to lead from their values. They seek ways to integrate their greatest passions into their daily work. And organizations strive regularly to enhance their value to shareholders, employees, and the world. But Appreciative Inquiry is about more than appreciation, recognition, and value enhancement. It is also about inquiry.

Inquiry: Exploration and Discovery

Inquiry refers to the acts of exploration and discovery. The spirit of inquiry is the spirit of learning. It implies a quest for new possibilities, being in a state of unknowing, wonder, and willingness to learn. It implies an openness to change. The verb inquire means:

1. To ask questions.
2. To study.
3. To search, explore, delve into, or investigate.

Inquiry is a learning process for organizations as well as for individuals. Seldom do we search, explore, or study what we already know with certainty. We ask questions about areas unfamiliar to us. The act of inquiry requires sincere curiosity and openness to new possibilities, new directions, and new understanding. We cannot "have all the answers," "know what is right," or "be certain" when we engage in inquiry.

To continue to succeed, organizations need more inquiry. They need less command and control by a few and more exploration of possibilities among many. They need less certainty in their usual plans and strategies and a greater capacity to sense and adapt quickly as their world changes. They need leaders who can acknowledge what they don't know and who will enthusiastically ask provocative and inspiring questions.

For Appreciative Inquiry to be effective, however, not just any questions will do. Questions must be affirmative, focused on topics valuable to the people involved, and directed at topics, concerns, and issues central to the success of the organization. When appreciation sets the direction for inquiry, the power of Appreciative Inquiry is released.

The Catalytic Effect of Appreciative Inquiry

Like the elements hydrogen and oxygen—which combine to make water, the most nurturing substance on earth—appreciation and inquiry combine to produce a vital, powerful, and catalytic effect on leadership and organization change. By tapping into accounts of organizations that are functioning at their best, Appreciative Inquiry unleashes information and commitment that together create energy for positive change.

Hierarchies all too often exclude those people most significantly impacted. Appreciative Inquiry turns those hierarchies into knowledge-rich, relationally inclusive, self-organizing enterprises. This change is powerfully illustrated by British Airways. After September 11, 2002, most airlines needed to cut costs and reduce headcount as demand for air travel declined drastically. British Airways Customer Service in North America was no exception. However, their prior experience using Appreciative Inquiry led them to involve people in determining how best to reduce the workforce. People explored one another's career hopes and dreams, suggested options, and volunteered for sabbaticals, job sharing, and part-time positions. Appreciative Inquiry created a context for people to be included and heard throughout the difficult and challenging time.

Appreciative Inquiry turns command-and-control cultures into communities of discovery and cooperation. For example, a year into our work with one long-term client, we asked an employee to tell what had happened. This is what he said:

> Before Appreciative Inquiry if the R&D group wanted to run a prototype on my machine, they would go to my supervisor, who would review the schedule and tell me when to do it. Now, they come to me directly and together we work out the best time to do it.

This organization moved beyond authoritarian styles of management, liberating people to create together what they knew was best for their customers, the business, and themselves.

When we began working with GTE, an organization that had earlier laid off thousands of employees, morale was at an all-time low. Conversations at all levels in the organization were about "ain't it awful," "what's wrong around here," and "why it won't get any better." We created a process that invited employees to use Appreciative Inquiry to make the organization a better place to work—and they did. Thousands of employees were trained in the Foundations of Appreciative Inquiry, Front-Line Leadership Using Appreciative Inquiry, and Appreciative Union-Management Relations. After their training, front-line employees at GTE self-organized a wide range of initiatives, including changes in customer satisfaction surveys, studies of call center best practices, and appreciative processes for employee recruitment, orientation, and retention. After the many organic changes that took place, GTE won the American Society for Training and Development Excellence in Practice Award (Managing Change) in 1997.

Finally, Appreciative Inquiry renews leaders as well as organizations and communities. Rick Pellett, president and general manager of Hunter Douglas Window Fashions Division, describes profound personal shifts in perception as a result of leading the Hunter Douglas initiative:

> The work I did here began to change me, almost right away. It got me asking questions—not just about the company but about my life.
>
> The questions we were asking and the dreams we were dreaming opened doors for me. They invited me to consider where I was heading, and whether it was the future I really wanted to live. They compelled me to take action to correct things that I'd simply chosen to live with for years and years and years.
>
> I recognize that this experience wouldn't create the same kind of "awakening" in everybody that it touched. But for me, it was revolutionary. And for many of the other hard-core, quick-deciding, bottom-line leaders that rise to the top in corporate America, it just might be life changing, for the better.

The 4-D Cycle

How does Appreciative Inquiry work? The process used to generate the power of Appreciative Inquiry is the 4-D Cycle—Discovery, Dream, Design, and Destiny (Figure 1). It is based on the notion that human systems, individuals, teams, organizations, and communities grow and change in the direction of what they study. Appreciative Inquiry works by focusing the attention of an organization on its most positive potential—its positive core—and unleashing the energy of the positive core for transformation and sustainable success. This is the essential nature of the organization at its best—people's collective wisdom about the organization's tangible and intangible strengths, capabilities, resources, and assets.

The 4-D Cycle can be used to guide a conversation, a large group meeting, or a whole-system change effort. It can serve as a framework for personal development or coaching, partnership or

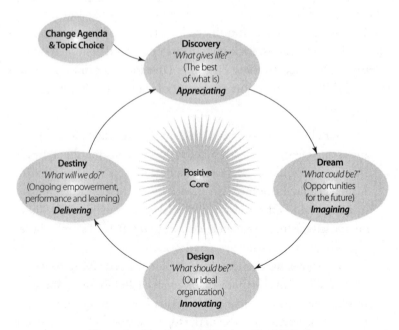

Figure 1. The Appreciative Inquiry 4-D Cycle

alliance building, and large-scale community or organization development. Whatever the purpose, the Appreciative Inquiry 4-D Cycle serves as the foundation on which change is built.

Affirmative Topic Choice

The 4-D Cycle begins with the thoughtful identification of what is to be studied—Affirmative Topics. Because human systems move in the direction of what they study, the choice of what to study—what to focus organizational attention on—is fateful. The topics that are selected become the organization's agenda for learning and innovation.

Affirmative Topics are subjects of strategic importance to the organization. They may be aspects of the organization's positive core that if expanded would further the organization's success. They may be problems that if stated in the affirmative and studied would improve organizational performance. Or they may be competitive success factors the organization needs to learn about in order to grow and change.

Once selected, these affirmative topics guide the 4-D Cycle of Discovery, Dream, Design, and Destiny. A thorough explanation of how to choose affirmative topics, criteria for good topics, and many sample topics can be found in Chapter 6, "Affirmative Topic Choice."

Discovery

Discovery is an extensive, cooperative search to understand the "best of what is and what has been." It is typically conducted via one-on-one interviews, though it may also include focus groups and large-group meetings. In any form, Discovery involves purposefully affirmative conversations among many or all members of an organization, including external stakeholders, "best-in-class" benchmark organizations, and members of the organization's local community. A detailed description and comprehensive guide for the Discovery phase is provided in Chapter 7, "Discovery: Appreciative Interviews and More."

The Discovery process results in:

- A rich description or mapping of the organization's positive core.

- Organization-wide sharing of stories of best practices and exemplary actions.

- Enhanced organizational knowledge and collective wisdom.

- The emergence of unplanned changes well before implementation of the remaining phases of the 4-D Cycle.

Dream

Dream is an energizing exploration of "what might be." This phase is a time for people to collectively explore hopes and dreams for their work, their working relationships, their organization, and the world. It is a time to envision possibilities that are big, bold, and beyond the boundaries of what has been in the past. The Dream phase is both practical and generative. It amplifies the positive core and challenges the status quo by helping people envision more valuable and vital futures, better bottom-line results, and contributions to a better world. Typically conducted in large-group forums, Dream activities result in alignment around creative images of the organization's most positive potentials and strategic opportunities, innovative strategic visions, and an elevated sense of purpose. A detailed description and comprehensive guide for the Dream phase is provided in Chapter 8, "Dream: Visions and Voices of the Future."

Design

Design is a set of Provocative Propositions, which are statements describing the ideal organization, or "what should be." Design activities are conducted in large-group forums or within a small team. Participants draw on discoveries and dreams to select high-impact design elements, then craft a set of provocative statements that list the organizational qualities they most desire. True to the principles of Appreciative Inquiry, Provocative Propositions are written in the affirmative. They expand the organization's image of itself by presenting clear, compelling pictures of how things will be when the organization's positive core is boldly alive in all of its strategies, processes, systems, decisions, and collaborations. A detailed description and comprehensive guide for the Design phase is provided in Chapter 9, "Design: Giving Form to Values and Ideals."

Destiny

Destiny is a series of inspired actions that support ongoing learning and innovation, or "what will be." This is the final phase of the 4-D Cycle. The entire cycle provides an open forum for employees to contribute and step forward in the service of the organization, and change occurs in all phases of the Appreciative Inquiry process. The Destiny phase, however, focuses specifically on personal and organizational commitments and paths forward. In many cases, Appreciative Inquiry becomes the framework for leadership and ongoing organization development. Therefore, in the Destiny phase, many organizations begin the Appreciative Inquiry 4-D Cycle anew.

Destiny activities are often launched in large-group forums and continue as small-group initiatives. The result of destiny is generally an extensive array of changes throughout the organization in areas as diverse as management practices, HR processes, measurement and evaluation systems, customer service systems, work processes, and structures. A detailed description and comprehensive guide for the Destiny phase is provided in Chapter 10, "Destiny: Inspired Action and Improvisation."

What Is Distinctive About Appreciative Inquiry?

As an approach to organization change, Appreciative Inquiry borrows from the strengths of many other practices in the field of organization development. From Harrison Owen, creator of Open Space Technology, we learned about the power of self-organizing processes. From the groundbreaking work of the "mother" of Whole-Scale® Change, Kathleen Dannemiller, and her colleagues at Dannemiller Tyson Associates, we borrowed many practices for designing and facilitating large-scale meetings.

From organizational learning guru Peter Senge—and his colleagues in the Society for Organizational Learning—we came to value the practice of dialogue for awakening the flow of collective meaning making and enhancing organizational learning. And from Marvin Weisbord and Sandra Janoff, creators of Future Search, we understand the importance of bringing all the stakeholders together to focus upon and create the future.

While honoring the contributions made by these and other leaders in the field of organization development, we believe that Appreciative Inquiry offers the field a radically new direction in principle and in practice. Grounded in the theory and practice of social construction, Appreciative Inquiry is an invitation to a positive revolution in change. It is distinctive in three significant ways: it is fully affirmative, it is inquiry based, and it is improvisational.

It Is Fully Affirmative

As a process of positive change, Appreciative Inquiry is fully affirmative. Moving through the 4-D Cycle builds upon the organization's track record of success and inspires positive possibilities for the future to be expressed and realized. Unlike other change methodologies, Appreciative Inquiry does not include deficit approaches to organizational analysis, such as root cause of failure, gaps, barriers, strategic threats, or resistance to change. All Appreciative Inquiry activities, practices, and processes focus on the organization at its best—past, present, and future.

Too often, organizations are prevented from fully knowing or drawing upon their positive potential because of their habit of focusing on problems rather than possibilities. The result, according to David Cooperrider and Diana Whitney, is decreased organizational capacity:

> Problem analytic methodologies are based on deficit discourse. Over time, they fill the organization with stories, understandings, and rich vocabularies of why things fail. Compulsive concern with what's not working, why things go wrong, and who didn't do his or her job demoralizes members of the organization, reduces the speed of learning, and undermines relationships and forward movement.[1]

A classic example of AI's commitment to the affirmative is the case of British Petroleum's ProCare, a U.S. auto repair business. At the end of its first year of operation, ProCare's customer surveys showed that 95 percent of all customers were 100 percent satisfied—an astonishing statistic, as anyone in the auto repair industry will confirm. ProCare was not satisfied, however. They decided to conduct customer focus groups. Unfortunately, they asked only the 5 percent of dissatisfied customers about their dissatisfaction. Then, on the walls in every station, they posted vivid descriptions of the identified causes of dissatisfaction. Within a short time customer satisfaction ratings dropped, along with employee morale and retention.

After hearing about the success gone astray, a team of Appreciative Inquiry consultants made suggestions to help the failing business. They recommended that focus groups be conducted with the customers who were 100 percent satisfied. With great skepticism and a moderate amount of curiosity, the leaders of ProCare agreed. The results were stunning. Customer satisfaction ratings reversed once again, this time for the better, as people began to learn and replicate the root causes of their success. The fully affirmative stance of Appreciative Inquiry created a rich learning environment and paid off by restoring high levels of customer satisfaction.

It Is Inquiry Based

At the heart of Appreciative Inquiry is the "art of the question"—the ability to craft unconditionally positive questions and to interview tens, hundreds, even thousands of people with questions of organizational relevance and vitality.

Organizational life is a continuous stream of questions and analysis. What caused this downturn in productivity? How can we reduce overtime? Why did you do it that way? Who needs to be involved in this decision? How can we increase revenue while containing costs? Appreciative Inquiry confirms that all questions are important, but the nature of our questions is particularly important. Appreciative Inquiry posits that organizations move in the direction of what they consistently ask questions about, and that the more affirmative the questions are, the more hopeful and positive the organizational responses will be.

The starting point and essential component of any Appreciative Inquiry process is the appreciative interview. Appreciative Inquiry would not be Appreciative Inquiry without appreciative interviews. Without appreciative interviews there is no inquiry, no openness to learn, and little potential for transformation. There is only an appreciative perspective. There is an important distinction between an appreciative perspective and Appreciative Inquiry. An appreciative perspective focuses on recognition, values, and affirmation, whereas Appreciative Inquiry implies a search, a willingness to discover, and an openness to learn.

To understand the difference, let's look at the processes two organizations used to establish employee alignment on shared values. The first organization is actually a composite of many. We would describe it as having an appreciative perspective. A small group of people, consisting of the executive team and several employees with high potential, met and articulated the company's values. They printed a beautiful document defining the values and describing their importance to the business. They wanted all employees to be informed, to understand, and to be rewarded for performance in alignment with the values. To roll out the values, they launched a communication campaign and implemented a values-based recognition system. Employees were given "values cards" to carry in their wallets and posters of the "values statements" for their office walls.

Most employees hung the posters, but few learned or felt valued in the process.

The second organization, the American Red Cross, decided to use Appreciative Inquiry to seek out and identify their living values. They were sincerely interested in discovering and learning about the values enacted on a daily basis by their members. To learn what values guided the service provided by their members, they conducted over three thousand appreciative interviews about values in action. They collected thousands of heartwarming and inspiring stories about the challenging, committed, and compassionate work of the American Red Cross. The stories were clustered, and the ten most frequently lived values were identified. At a national conference, two thousand members heard stories of the Red Cross's living values and saw videos of themselves and their colleagues telling stories of their values in action. As members shared stories and watched the videos, the organization's collective knowledge increased.

In the spirit of inquiry, all members had the opportunity to be interviewed and share their stories in this living values process. Thousands participated and were inspired, recognized, and honored for their values-based work on behalf of the American Red Cross.

It Is Improvisational

As an approach to change with endless variation, Appreciative Inquiry is improvisational. It is not a singular methodology because it is not based on one firmly established way of proceeding. Like great jazz improvisation—a metaphor proposed by consultant Frank Barrett—each Appreciative Inquiry is a new creation, an experiment that brings out the best of human organizing. It begins with a clear purpose. But from there, who knows precisely what will happen? In many cases, the most remarkable outcomes are unplanned and unexpected—they emerge as the organization's unique version of Appreciative Inquiry unfolds.

And like musical improvisation, Appreciative Inquiry is loosely structured, based on a set of principles and generally following the framework of the 4-D Cycle. This book is filled with stories that illustrate a variety of ways that individuals and organizations have used the 4-D Cycle to meet their unique goals, with surprising and positive results. But even the 4-D Cycle itself can be adapted to different cultures and situations. For example, social activist Mac Odell—whose work with thousands of women throughout rural Nepal demands great improvisation—added three more Ds: Do It Now, Drumming, and Dancing. Similarly, the international consulting firm Cap Gemini Ernst & Young's Appreciative Inquiry process, branded ePositive Change, has five Ds: Define, Discover, Dream, Design, and Deliver.

As an improvisational approach to change, Appreciative Inquiry is guided by a series of questions:

- What is your overall Change Agenda?
- What Form of Engagement will best suit your needs?
- What is your overall Inquiry Strategy?
- What steps will you take at each phase of the 4-D Cycle?

In Chapter 2, "A Menu of Approaches to Appreciative Inquiry," we expand upon these questions and highlight some of the many ways Appreciative Inquiry has been used.

Green Mountain Coffee Roasters' (GMCR) answers to these questions led them through a highly successful experiment with Appreciative Inquiry. What was their Change Agenda? To increase the effectiveness of existing business process teams—and in turn reduce overall operating costs. What Form of Engagement did they choose? They created a new approach to inquiry. They trained five intact business process teams in Appreciative Inquiry and set them loose to initiate their own process-related inquiries. Several times during their three-month period of Discovery, one or more of the inquiries seemed to veer off their original course. Each time this happened, a mixed group of executives and operations staff adapted and revised the process, ensuring its continued relevance and success. In the end, using Appreciative Inquiry, GMCR achieved a 25 percent reduction in operating costs as well as organization-wide input on ongoing strategic initiatives.

The improvisational character of Appreciative Inquiry makes invention and continual learning imperative. Professor and Appreciative Inquiry thought leader David Cooperrider believes that only 5 percent of the possible practices, applications, models, methodologies, and approaches to Appreciative Inquiry have been created. We hope this book helps you learn the basics so you will be able to design your own Appreciative Inquiry initiatives and add to the growing body of knowledge on positive change.

From Deficit-Based Change to Positive Change

Appreciative Inquiry is a bold shift in the way we think about and approach organization change. The ultimate paradox of Appreciative Inquiry is that it does not aim to change anything. It aims to uncover and bring forth existing strengths, hopes, and dreams—to identify and amplify the positive core of the organization. In this process, people and organizations are transformed. With Appreciative Inquiry, the focus of attention is on positive potential—the best of what has been, what is, and what might be. It is a process of positive change.

In contrast, most other approaches to change are deficit based—focused on problems and how to overcome them. Success depends on a clear identification and diagnosis of the problem, the selection of an appropriate solution, and the implementation of that solution. In our experience, deficit-based change can work—it has for years—just not as effectively as positive change.

Appreciative Inquiry is an invitation to shift from a deficit-based approach to change to a positive approach to change. Our experiences, spanning twenty-five years of organizational consulting, reflect this shift. Early in our careers, we confidentially gathered information about our client systems, diagnosed organizational problems, and designed processes whereby our clients would correct what was wrong. Periodically, while employing these well-established approaches to change, we would see glimpses of alternatives. And so we experimented.

We experimented with engaging organizational members in their own action research. While consulting on the merger of SmithKline Corporation and Beckman Instruments, we established research teams made up of line managers, front-line employees, and HR staff to study the best practices of each organization. Sixty people conducted interviews and focus groups with thousands of participants. We facilitated their sharing of stories and data and the identification of five core competencies. We took the experiment further by having them design and lead a week-long workshop on the five core competencies. Three thousand employees worldwide participated in these workshops as part of the merger integration.

At the same time, we began to focus people and organizations on possibilities—on what they wanted to do and to be, and on the collaborative creation of their work processes and services. At the Visiting Nurse Service of New York we brought teams of administrators, nurses, medical assistants, social workers, and patient advocates together to learn from each other and collectively envision and define their processes for service delivery. We facilitated their success by keeping their eyes and their conversations focused on what worked and what they hoped and wished could be.

The positive results of these experiments guided us toward new assumptions and new ways of working that we now describe as positive change. This transition from deficit-based change to positive change is illustrated in Table 1.

As you can see, the move from deficit-based change to positive change alters what is studied—from problems to the positive core. The shift alters who is involved and who has access to information—from some of the people to all of the people. Finally, it alters the results—from a best solution to the problem to the boldest dream of positive possibility. And it shifts the capacity gained in the process—from the capacity to implement and measure a specific plan to the capacity for ongoing positive change.

For us—as for many of our colleagues—there is no going

Table 1. The Shift from Deficit-Based Change to Positive Change		
	Deficit-Based Change	*Positive Change*
Intervention Focus	Identified problem.	Affirmative topics.
Participation	Selective inclusion of people.	Whole system.
Action Research	Diagnosis of the problem.	Discovery of positive core.
	Causes and consequences.	Organization at its best.
	Quantitative analysis.	Narrative analysis.
	Profile of need.	Map of positive core.
	Conducted by outsiders.	Conducted by members.
Dissemination	Feedback to decision makers.	Widespread and creative sharing of best practices.
Creative Potential	Brainstormed list of alternatives.	Dreams of a better world and the organization's contribution.
Result	Best solution to resolve the problem.	Design to realize dreams and human aspirations.
Capacity Gained	Capacity to implement and measure the plan.	Capacity for ongoing positive change.

back. Having made the transition from deficit-based change to positive change, we are committed to working from our strengths, to helping people around the globe discover and work from their strengths, and to building vibrantly successful organizations in which the human spirit soars.

But What About Problems?

Isn't it unrealistic to deny them? Aren't you asking us to ignore problems or to act as if they don't exist? These are some of the most frequently asked questions about Appreciative Inquiry. Let us be clear. We are not saying to deny or ignore problems. What we are saying is that if you want to transform a situation, relationship, organization, or community, focusing on strengths is much more effective than focusing on problems. In Chapter 4, "Appreciative Inquiry in Action: From Origins to Current Practice," we offer numerous stories about organizations and communities that benefited significantly by using Appreciative Inquiry to shift their attention from problems to possibilities.

We often work in situations fraught with anxiety, tension, and stress: union-management relations, merger integration, and cross-functional conflict. Frequently, when we turn people's attention from "what is wrong around here" to "who are we when we are at our best," conflict turns to cooperation.

We do not dismiss accounts of conflict, problems, or stress. We simply do not use them as the basis of analysis or action. We listen when they arise, validate them as lived experience, and seek to reframe them. For example, the problem of high employee turnover becomes an inquiry into magnetic work environments or a question of retention. The problem of low management credibility becomes an inquiry into moments of management credibility or inspired leadership. The problem of sexual harassment at work becomes a question of positive cross-gender working relationships.

The capacity to reframe problems into affirmative topics is central to Appreciative Inquiry. Chapter 6, "Affirmative Topic Choice," offers a description of how to do this, along with several compelling examples.

Why Does Appreciative Inquiry Work?

The Buddha once said, "Life is suffering." Problems are like suffering—they're always present. But suffering and problems are not the only qualities present in life or organizations. In addition to suffering, there is joy. In addition to problems, there are successes, hopes, and dreams. Appreciative Inquiry redirects the focus of analysis. This simple shift in attention allows people and organizations to rise above and move beyond the conditions in which the problems originally existed.

Appreciative Inquiry works because it treats people like people, not like machines. As humans, we are social. We create our identities and our knowledge in relation to one another. We are curious. We like to tell stories and listen to stories. We pass on our values, beliefs, and wisdom in stories. We like to learn and use what we learn to achieve our best. And we delight in doing well in the eyes of those we care about and respect. Appreciative Inquiry enables leaders to create natural human organizations—knowledge-rich, strength-based, adaptable learning organizations.

We know this in part through experience and in part through our research. We wondered why Appreciative Inquiry had worked so well—so we did an inquiry. We interviewed people and conducted focus groups. We asked them to tell us stories of Appreciative Inquiry at its best—how it influenced them and why it worked. What we discovered surprised and delighted us. Appreciative Inquiry works because it liberates power. It unleashes both individual and organizational power. It brings out the best of people, encourages them to see and support the best of others, and generates unprecedented cooperation and innovation.

The people we interviewed told us that Appreciative Inquiry works for six reasons, briefly outlined here and described in detail in Chapter 12, "Why Appreciative Inquiry Works":

- *It builds relationships, enabling people to be known in relationship rather than in roles.* As one participant put it, "Appreciative interviews are energizing every time you do them. They build relationships and give you a chance to connect. This tells people that they are important and that they belong." Many people told us of the satisfying and productive friendships they made in the process of Appreciative Inquiry—among co-workers, among managers and line employees, and among customers and members of the organization.

- *It creates an opportunity for people to be heard.* Recognition, mutual respect, and morale all go up when people feel heard. One manager described his experience by saying, "My people were finally recognized as contributors. We'd been considered the black hole in the organization for years. Through our work with Appreciative Inquiry, we were really seen and heard for the first time."

◆ *It generates opportunities for people to dream, and to share their dreams.* Repeatedly people were glad to be asked to describe their dreams. And they got even more excited when they discovered that their dreams were shared by others. In the words of one Appreciative Inquiry enthusiast, "Sharing our stories and our dreams is the best vehicle for positive change that I have ever experienced. I will retire now knowing that I helped create a better company and a better world."

◆ *It creates an environment in which people are able to choose how they contribute.* When people are free to volunteer based on their interests and passions, their capacity to learn and contribute is significantly increased. Understanding the value of free choice, one director sent the following memo to his staff: "As you know, Appreciative Inquiry is not mandatory. On the other hand, if it does not fit your style, do not obstruct what others are choosing to do. We need to be talking about the process and sharing our approaches so we can all keep learning and gain confidence."

◆ *It gives people both discretion and support to act.* One participant commented, "We had always had support to take action on behalf of the organization, but now—suddenly—people were making resources available and paying attention to what we were doing. They backed us up and made it possible for us to follow through on—and finally do—the things that we knew needed to be done."

◆ *It encourages and enables people to be positive.* As one employee commented, "It isn't always popular to be positive! People make fun of you and tell you that you're Pollyannaish. Appreciative Inquiry turned my positive attitude into an asset rather than a liability. It gave me things to look forward to here at work."

Throughout this book, we illustrate our explanations of Appreciative Inquiry with the story of one company—Hunter Douglas Window

Fashions Division (Hunter Douglas)—and its use of Appreciative Inquiry. The company is introduced in Chapter 4, "Appreciative Inquiry in Action: From Origins to Current Practice." The story continues in Chapters 5 through 10. At the end of each of these chapters you will find vignettes about Hunter Douglas, describing how they carried out each phase of the Appreciative Inquiry 4-D Cycle. Together with other case studies and examples, the Hunter Douglas story provides clear and substantial evidence that Appreciative Inquiry works. More importantly, perhaps, it shows you how it works.

CHAPTER 2

A Menu of Approaches to Appreciative Inquiry

Most Appreciative Inquiry processes follow the general flow of the 4-D Cycle. However, the reasons for using Appreciative Inquiry vary, as do the approaches taken and the ways in which key steps in the process are carried out. As a result, no two Appreciative Inquiry processes are ever exactly the same. Given that Appreciative Inquiry is an approach rather than a single methodology, how do you go about applying it? You do so by considering—and then answering—a series of questions. Figure 2 illustrates three broad questions that must be addressed when applying Appreciative Inquiry.

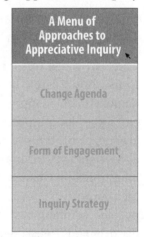

Figure 2. Questions To Be Addressed when Applying Appreciative Inquiry.

- What is your Change Agenda? What are you trying to accomplish? What is your purpose?

◆ What is the most appropriate Form of Engagement, given your Change Agenda, your organization's culture, time frame, and resources?

◆ What is your Inquiry Strategy? Having identified the purpose and form of engagement, what decisions and steps must you take along the way to ensure the project's success?

This chapter will help you answer these questions and more. By describing a wide variety of purposes for which Appreciative Inquiry has been used, it will help you determine your Change Agenda. By providing an overview of the eight most frequently used forms of Appreciative Inquiry, it will guide your choice of an appropriate Form of Engagement. And finally, by introducing a framework for creating an inquiry strategy, it will help you get the right people involved, in the right ways, to accomplish your unique goals.

Let's now explore each point on the Menu of Approaches to Appreciative Inquiry—its definition and its implications for your Appreciative Inquiry process.

Change Agenda: What Are You Trying to Accomplish?

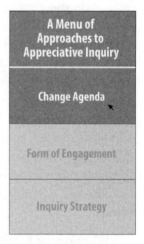

There are many reasons you might choose to use Appreciative Inquiry. As this book demonstrates, Appreciative Inquiry is employed for purposes of organizational change, global transformation, and personal development. In short, it can be used for many different Change Agendas. Whatever the purpose, Appreciative Inquiry helps people, communities, and organizations discover and realize their highest potential.

Table 2 lists some of the many Change Agendas to which you might apply Appreciative Inquiry.

Figure 3.   A Menu of Approaches to Appreciative Inquiry: Change Agenda

Table 2. Change Agendas Suited to Appreciative Inquiry	
Change Agenda	*Examples*
Organizational change.	Culture transformation.
	Customer satisfaction.
	Morale and retention.
	Organization design.
	Leadership development.
	Business improvement.
Organizational and community planning.	Strategic business planning.
	Participatory community planning.
Interorganizational capacity building.	Merger integration.
	Alliance building.
	Union-management partnership.
	Strategic resource sharing.
Community development.	Asset mapping.
	Economic development.
	Educational reform.
	Peace building.
Global transformation.	Global organizing.
	Multilocal planning.
	Consciousness raising.
Team and small-group development.	Team building.
	Business development.
	Meeting management.
	Instructional design.
Intergroup change.	Conflict resolution.
	Process improvement.
Personal/relational transformation.	Leadership development.
	Coaching.
	Performance appraisal.
	Employee orientation.
	Career planning.
	Relationship enrichment.
	Spiritual development.

Organizational Change

This book is largely about organizational change. In either business or not-for-profit settings, Appreciative Inquiry is a powerful vehicle for whole-system organizational change. Many organizations have benefited from using Appreciative Inquiry for organizational change. Eight of these are described in detail in Chapter 4, "Appreciative Inquiry in Action: From Origins to Current Practice."

Interorganizational Capacity Building

The interorganizational change agenda involves bringing together two or more organizations to build a relationship, create a common identity, or achieve a shared purpose. For example, Appreciative Inquiry has been used to create an innovative union-management partnership among two national unions—the IBEW and the CWA—and GTE, to merge the Nevada State and Clark County Child Welfare services, and to merge the Traffic Engineering and Traffic Operations departments in the city of Denver.

Community Development

Appreciative Inquiry is a proven tool for international community development. Beginning with the work of Case Western Reserve University's GEM (Global Excellence in Management) and SIGMA (Social Innovations in Global Management) programs, Appreciative Inquiry has been used around the world for such purposes.

Hundreds of community projects have been inspired by the landmark Imagine Chicago initiative, which is described in detail later in this chapter. For example, a Swedish consulting team led by Sven Sandstrom and Lisen Kebbe conducted an Appreciative Inquiry called Imagine Gotland to help the community of Gotland envision its future without the military base that had been the community's largest employer. In addition, Appreciative Inquiry has been used by organizations such as Save the Children, Lutheran World Relief, and UNICEF to enhance the quality of life for people around the world. Similarly, in the early twenty-first century, international consultant Ravi Pradhan used Appreciative Inquiry in communities throughout Southeast Asia to reduce the incidence of maternal mortality.

Beginning in the late 1990s, Appreciative Inquiry was adopted for planning purposes by a number of municipal and county governments, including the city and county of Denver; the city of Buckeye, Arizona; Larimer County, Colorado; and the Maricopa Association of Governments. Two of the most noteworthy of these initiatives— Focus on Longmont and Greeting Our Future, both in Colorado— garnered local, regional, national, and international attention and awards and are prominently featured in Chapter 11, "Appreciative Inquiry: A Process for Community Planning."

Global Transformation

The more we work with Appreciative Inquiry, the more we see its capacities for promoting global change. Appreciative Inquiry has been used successfully to create several global organizations, including the Mountain Forum, an organization dedicated to the care and preservation of mountain cultures and environments worldwide, and the United Religions Initiative, a global interfaith organization existing now in 179 locations around the world.

Appreciative Inquiry is currently being used as a vehicle for several global inquiries intended to raise awareness and transform life on the planet, including Case Western Reserve University's Business As an Agent of World Benefit project, the United Religions Initiative's Global Peace Inquiry, and Valeo, a project to create an epidemic of optimal health.

Small-Group/Team Development

Appreciative Inquiry is a proven process for instructional design, meeting management, and team building. It has been used for business leadership development, high school curriculum development, and graduate education. Organizational consultant and educator Charlese Pratt conducted a life-changing experiment with Appreciative Inquiry as a learning process for high school students. It went something like this. Shaw High School in Cleveland had been declared an educational emergency. More students were failing the basic proficiency exams than were passing. After introducing Appreciative Inquiry to the school, Charley decided more had to be done, and fast. She created a three-week summer camp for students using Appreciative Inquiry. There were three criteria for attending: students had to have failed the proficiency exam three times; their teachers had to believe they had no chance at college; and the students had to freely choose to participate.

The process was simple. Students conducted interviews with teachers, administrators, parents, and other people who were academically successful. Their interviews explored how other people study and learn, what kinds of job opportunities exist for college graduates, and what college is like. After their interviews, the students shared stories and data, prepared and made presentations, and taught one another. Thirty-one students were selected; twenty-nine completed the program; and twenty-eight passed the proficiency exam at the end of the program and were determined to go to college. In the process, both the students' self-esteem and their academic proficiency improved significantly.

When supervisors and managers learn the principles of Appreciative Inquiry, they too are changed. For example, they find that opening a meeting with one unconditionally positive question sets the tone for the entire meeting's success. And they begin asking questions such as, "What have we done well in the past week?" and "What was the most inspiring customer service you experienced, saw, or heard about in the department since our last meeting?"

Finally, intact work groups and teams experience profound changes when they discover the benefits of Appreciative Inquiry. Basic activities, such as creating team identity, aligning people's strengths, building camaraderie and trust, establishing team norms, and creating project visions and goals are all more effective when grounded in Appreciative Inquiry processes. Our book *Apprecia-tive Team Building: Positive Questions to Bring Out the Best of Your Team* offers specific tools and examples for applying Appreciative Inquiry in this environment.[2]

Intergroup Change

Similarly, Appreciative Inquiry is a proven tool for enhancing inter-group cooperation and trust. For example, Ruth Seliger, a leading European consultant, was asked to help an organization that was being pulled apart as the founder and CEO prepared to retire. The fear of the future was palpable. As a result, the outgoing leader was not getting the recognition he deserved. Ruth suggested Apprecia-tive Inquiry to bridge the gap, and the outgoing CEO thought it was a great idea. Although some members of the new leadership team were not so convinced, they went along with the interviews. To their own and everyone else's surprise, during the two-day Appre-ciative Inquiry summit, they were the most vocal and appreciative about the company's past leadership and accomplishments. Day 1 of the summit focused on the best of the past—the organization and its leadership. Day 2 focused on the future. At the end of the two days, the organization had a clear vision for its future and a clear understanding of what it wanted to continue, even as it grew and changed.

Personal Relationship Transformation

Appreciative Inquiry can be a powerful vehicle for personal trans-formation in coaching, mentoring, and even therapy. Many orga-nizations have built Appreciative Inquiry into their processes for recruitment, performance appraisal, employee orientation, and career planning. McDATA Corporation, for example, designed and implemented an Appreciative Inquiry–based mentoring program to address some of the human resources challenges associated with their rapid growth. Within the first few weeks of employment, every new hire was invited by a mentor to share a meal. During that meal, mentor and mentee participated in two-way appreciative interviews. Mentors interviewed to collect positive first impressions of the organization and to get to know their mentees' strengths, hopes, and dreams for their future. New employees interviewed their mentors to learn about the company's core culture and values. New relationships were forged as the most positive aspects of the company's culture were reinforced and amplified.

Indeed, the fields of coaching and leadership development have been among the fastest-growing applications of Appreciative Inquiry over the past decade, with workshops, articles, and books abounding. In particular, the books *Appreciative Coaching*[3] and *Appreciative Leadership*[4] provide practical examples and tools for doing this important work. Similarly, the Appreciative Leadership Development Program©[5] is a forum for discovering and building upon their positive core—their unique strengths, skills, and talents. We have used these skills and others as we have provided one-to-one coaching with executives and managers, helping them find ways of cultivating appreciative cultures and bringing out the best in others.

Appreciative Inquiry can also be used in a wide variety of ways to enrich spiritual development, heal wounds among diverse groups, and enhance personal relationships. For example, theologian Peggy Green uses Appreciative Inquiry as the vehicle to bring gay and evangelical Christians together in dialogue. Her courageous project, First Be Reconciled, has paved the way for healing and cooperation among these highly divided populations.

For personal use, Appreciative Inquiry can serve families for such purposes as family reunions, anniversaries, retirements, and birthday celebrations. For example, we have created videotapes and scrapbooks of testimonials from friends and family members, describing moments when someone has made a difference in their lives, together with their hopes and dreams for that person's future. Such documents celebrate people's lives and nurture personal growth.

Form of Engagement: What Approach to AI Is Best Suited to Your Needs?

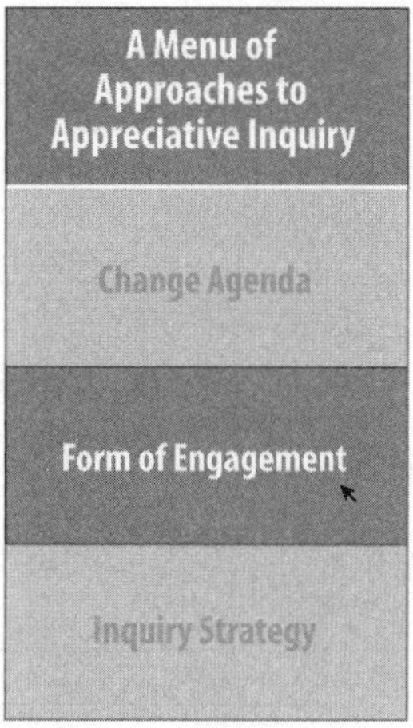

Some Appreciative Inquiry processes take place over a period of days or even hours, and others unfold over an extended period of time. Some require significant resources and coordination, and others become an invisible, self-managed approach to work already being performed. Whatever the circumstances, you will always want to choose an Appreciative Inquiry Form of Engagement that is appropriate for your Change Agenda, timeline, resources, and other circumstances.

A Menu of
Approaches to
Appreciative Inquiry

Change Agenda

Form of Engagement

Inquiry Strategy

Figure 4. A Menu of Approaches to Appreciative Inquiry: Form of Engagement

At the time of this writing, we know at least eight Appreciative Inquiry Forms of Engagement. These have been developed over a period of years as practitioners around the globe experiment, reflect, and refine the practice of Appreciative Inquiry in the face of new and unexpected circumstances. Table 3 summarizes the eight Forms of Engagement. A more detailed description of each process follows. Although they are presented as distinct and separate, these Forms of Engagement often overlap each other.

Some of the descriptions that follow are long and detailed, reflecting the relative complexity of the process, while others are relatively short and straightforward. Regardless of the length or detail, the descriptions are offered as sparks to stimulate imagination, creativity, and the invention of new and meaningful approaches to positive change.

Whole-System 4-D Dialogue

A Whole-System 4-D Dialogue is an Appreciative Inquiry process in which the entire organization, along with many of its stakeholders,

Table 3. Forms of Engagement	
Form of Engagement	**Summary Description**
1. Whole-System 4-D Dialogue.	All members of the organization and some stakeholders participate in an AI 4-D process. It takes place at multiple locations over an extended period of time.
2. Appreciative Inquiry Summit.	A large group of people participate simultaneously in a two-to-four-day AI 4-D process.
3. Mass-Mobilized Inquiry.	Large numbers of interviews (thousands to millions) on a socially responsible topic are conducted throughout a city, a community, or the world.
4. Core Group Inquiry.	A small group of people selects topics, crafts questions, and conducts interviews.
5. Positive Change Network.	Members of an organization are trained in AI and given the resources to initiate projects and share materials, stories, and best practices.
6. Positive Change Consortium.	Multiple organizations collaboratively engage in an AI 4-D process to explore and develop a common area of interest.
7. AI Learning Team.	A small group of people with a specific project—that is, an evaluation team, a process improvement team, a customer focus group, a benchmarking team, or a group of students—conduct an AI 4-D process.
8. Progressive AI Meetings.	An organization, small group, or team goes through the AI 4-D process over the course of ten to twelve meetings that each last two to four hours.

works through a complete 4-D Cycle—Discovery, Dream, Design, and Destiny—over an extended period of time. Some members of the organization select Affirmative Topics and craft the Interview Guide(s). Some serve on an Advisory Team. Others conduct interviews, make meaning, and communicate their findings. Still others join in to envision the future and design the ideal organization. And still others participate in creating transformational projects to realize the Dream and Design. Some people choose to contribute to the entire process, while others prefer to help out with just one part of the process. No matter what the contribution, in the course of the 4-D Cycle, everyone is involved.

Typically, a Whole-System 4-D Dialogue takes place within two months to one year. It involves inquiry at multiple sites—all the locations where the organization and its customers do business—and it involves activities that integrate the inquiry across business units, departments, and functions. Other Appreciative Inquiry Forms of Engagement—such as the Appreciative Inquiry Summit and Appreciative Inquiry Learning Teams (descriptions follow)—are generally incorporated into a Whole-System 4-D Dialogue to ensure integration and learning across the whole organization.

Regardless of the time frame or location, each phase of the Whole-System 4-D Dialogue uses appreciative interviews to connect newcomers and old-timers to a single powerful group with a common story line, shared vision, and collective wisdom. This allows people to come and go over the life of the initiative—making way for new people and ideas, while honoring and building upon the work that has taken place along the way. To further understand how a Whole-System 4-D Dialogue occurs over time and location, consider the example of British Airways Customer Service NA. Forty people met for two days to select Affirmative Topics and draft an Interview Guide. Within two months, one hundred people were trained to be interviewers. Within six months, nine hundred employees were involved in interviews. At the end of the interview process, data synthesis and dreaming took place at all eighteen airport locations. One month later a ninety-person AI Summit drafted organization Design Statements and launched cross-location, cross-functional Innovation Teams. These teams worked for three months making significant contributions to the organization in the areas of Happiness at Work, Continuous People Development, Harmony Among Work Groups, and Exceptional Arrival Experiences.

When might your company initiate a Whole-System 4-D Dialogue? This approach is particularly effective when organizations are attempting to accomplish any or all of the following:

- *Build leadership capacity.* Whole-System 4-D Dialogues strengthen existing leadership while beginning to identify and develop future leaders. They exercise people's leadership muscles, teaching them skills that enable them to engage as positive and productive leaders—both within and outside the AI engagement.

- *Dissolve or transcend communication barriers.* Whole-System 4-D Dialogues put people in touch with people, helping them build positive relationships that transcend titles, functions, tenures, and other social barriers to communication. They mobilize collaborative efforts across the organization and foreshadow systems and structures that are well suited to life-centered organizations.

- *Create a learning culture.* Whole-System 4-D Dialogues establish webs of relationships through which organizational information and learning can be transmitted. They create a forum for sharing best practices. They reinforce people's willingness to modify practices and approaches, using what has worked in the past as a template for positive change.

- *Liberate the best in people.* Whole-System 4-D Dialogues liberate human potential and power—and in so doing, liberate the best of what's possible in organizations. For organizations to be the best they can be, they must be composed of individuals and groups that are also operating at their best.

- *Enhance capacity for positive change.* Whole-System 4-D Dialogues create opportunities for people to feel safe, to participate, and to be heard, which in turn enhances the organization's overall capacity for positive change, a competitive advantage.

Appreciative Inquiry Summit

An Appreciative Inquiry (AI) Summit is a large-scale meeting designed to cover the 4-D Cycle in two to four days. Participation in an AI Summit is diverse and inclusive of all the organization's stakeholders—employees, customers, suppliers, community members, government agencies, and others. The number of people who attend can range anywhere from fifty to more than two thousand.

The AI Summit gets its name from the idea that together large groups of people can achieve extraordinary heights of success—well beyond those of which any small group is capable. Going to an AI Summit means lifting up positive possibilities that serve the highest good of people, the organization, and the world.

Although each summit has its own design, successful AI Summits share common characteristics. Each is clearly focused on a topic of strategic business relevance. Each brings together all the people who have an interest and influence in the topic, who are often in the same room for the first time. Each summit flows through the Appreciative Inquiry 4-D Cycle—Discovery, Dream, Design, and Destiny. Each involves a combination of one-to-one interviews, together with small- and large-group processes. And each gives an equal voice to everyone present.

Organizations that have embraced Appreciative Inquiry and its principles routinely hold AI Summits for strategic planning, capacity building, and organization change. For example, Roadway International has hosted a series of AI Summits to enhance margins and business literacy. Nutrimental Foods SA similarly conducts annual summits, bringing the whole organization together to redesign the way they do business. And the United Religions Initiative hosted seven regional summits within one year to lift up the purpose, principles, and design of its newly chartered organization.

When might you host an AI Summit? AI Summits are often an essential part of a Whole-System 4-D Dialogue. In addition, they are an effective stand-alone Appreciative Inquiry Form of Engagement that is particularly effective for the following:

◈ *Accelerating planning, decision making, and innovation.* Traditional approaches to planning and decision making that are based on small-group processes and communication rollouts take time. And it is time that most organizations don't have when faced with rapidly changing markets and business environments. By bringing all the stakeholders together at once, an AI Summit enables rapid decision making and ensures a shared focus going forward.

- *Crafting inspiring and generative visions of the future.* Images compel action. Many organizations suffer poor performance because they lack inspiring visions for the future. AI Summits are one of the best ways to lift up new possibilities and visions. When large groups of people share their dreams, collective capacities are mobilized and new directions inspired.

- *Forging mergers, alliances, and partnerships.* The greatest challenge faced by merging organizations is the challenge of building relationships and bonds among people. One of the greatest strengths of an AI Summit is its capacity to bring together diverse groups of people. During the course of one 4-D Cycle, strangers become partners, and unprecedented levels of cooperation emerge.

- *Designing or building momentum for a new organization or initiative.* When organizations or initiatives first begin, their future success depends upon the depth and breadth of their initial designs and plans. AI Summits can mobilize the necessary people to think through all aspects of the new organization, purpose and principles, strategy and structure, people and policies. This involvement in the beginning leads to commitment and follow-through in the future.

Mass-Mobilized Inquiry

Mass-Mobilized Inquiry is a waterfall-like process for engaging large numbers of people in face-to-face conversations. An initial group of interviewers completes a series of interviews; for example, fifty people each conduct ten interviews. At the end of each interview, each invites the person interviewed to become an interviewer. Those who agree receive a phone number to call for training and a packet of Interview Guides. This way, fifty people doing ten interviews each can, in relatively short order, turn their five hundred interviews into thousands. When multiplied by a hundred, a thousand, or a million, Mass-Mobilized Inquiry can foster evolutionary transformation within an organization, a community, or the world.

In the mid-1990s, Bliss Brown, a corporate executive from First Chicago Bank, quit her job to initiate and organize a program called Imagine Chicago. This became one of the earliest and most successful experiments with Mass-Mobilized Inquiry. Using Appreciative Inquiry as "a catalyst for civic innovation," she designed the initiative around a radical set of questions and assumptions:

> What might happen if all of Chicago's citizens were mobilized to give public expression to their imagination about a healthy future for the city? What if they were invited to claim their role in bringing that vision to life? Is it possible that the creation of positive collective images in our three-million-person city might be the most prolific activity that individuals and organizations can engage in, to help bring to fruition a positive and significant future?[6]

Hundreds of intergenerational interviews were conducted, most successfully with children interviewing the city's elders—priests, CEOs, school principals, parents, entertainers, artists, activists, and scientists. Subsequent studies showed that the interviews profoundly affected all of the parties involved. One adult who was interviewed was deeply moved by the experience:

> You know, during that interview I was literally looking into the face of the future, exploring the essential elements of the good society. This conversation mattered.[7]

At the same time, children who conducted interviews improved at school in all areas, including math, reading, and writing.

The success of the original Imagine Chicago initiative spawned an entire Imagine movement: seventy projects in more than twenty countries, spanning six continents, at the time of this printing.[8] In addition, it put into motion many other Mass-Mobilized Inquiries, including the United Religions Initiative's Global Peace Inquiry and two of the three community inquiries described in Chapter 11, "Appreciative Inquiry: A Process for Community Planning." In each of the cases, hundreds, thousands, or millions of interviews were conducted to bring communities together, inspire positive images of the future, and create a better world.

When might you initiate a Mass-Mobilized Inquiry? When you want to involve large numbers of people in a single organization or an entire community or industry, Mass-Mobilized Inquiry is the way to go. Specifically, you would use this approach for:

- *Transforming a community's image of itself.* When a community's habitual story lines include poverty, corruption, drugs, violence, and worse, it needs a process to rediscover its positive core. Mass-Mobilized Inquiry can help a community transmit the best of who they have been from generation to generation, person to person, and group to group.

- *Building relationships among diverse and even conflicted groups.* Often, large and diverse communities serve as stages for tragic misunderstanding and pointless, self-perpetuating conflict. Mass-Mobilized Inquiry builds relationships across differences. It awakens possibilities for these diverse and even conflicted communities to become melting pots of wonder and joy.

- *Creating a positive revolution or an epidemic of good.* Mass-Mobilized Inquiry inspires individual goodwill and it is contagious. It fosters improbable alliances between otherwise unconnected people. It is a process through which people can meet, consider possibilities, and take action together in service of their hopes and dreams for the future.

Core Group Inquiry

Sometimes you need to start quickly or on a small scale. Other times you need a process to introduce AI and open the door for a larger engagement. In these situations a Core Group Inquiry might be useful.

This Form of Engagement is similar to a Whole-System 4-D Dialogue, but it occurs on a smaller scale and in less time. A Core

Group is assembled, consisting of from five to fifty people who represent the organization. The Core Group identifies topics, crafts questions, and conducts appreciative interviews. Additional people may join the Core Group in the Dream, Design, and Destiny phases—or the Core Group may continue to operate independently throughout the process.

At a time of major change in the nature and funding of their work, Engender Health launched a strategic planning process using Appreciative Inquiry. This organization works worldwide to improve the lives of individuals by making reproductive health services safe, available, and sustainable. It provides technical assistance, training, and information with a focus on practical solutions that improve services where resources are scarce. It works in over thirty countries and has offices in twenty of these countries. They chose to use a combination of Core Group Inquiry and AI Summit as their Forms of Engagement. In preparation for a sixty-person AI Summit, their Advisory Team commissioned a Core Group called an Internal Environmental Scan Team. This Core Group's purpose was to conduct interviews with a sample of staff, produce a written summary of the interview themes, and present their findings at the summit.

After discussing the results of the Core Group's inquiry and completing the 4-D Cycle, summit participants identified initiatives to include in the current budget cycle. In addition, they launched a broader round of inquiry. New Core Groups were formed to conduct interviews—this time with every staff member worldwide, external colleagues, donors, and other organizations that were potential partners and competitors.

The use of Core Group Inquiry enabled this organization to get started quickly, see benefits, and build commitment for a more inclusive Appreciative Inquiry process. This in turn led to widespread support for a new strategic plan, which called for a significant expansion in the organization's focus and a diversified funding strategy.

When is a Core Group Inquiry appropriate?

◆ *Quick start-up or turnaround.* Core Group Inquiry enables a small group of people to act quickly in service of the whole. Particularly when the inquiry culminates with a summit, a relatively small group of interviewers can educate, inform, and influence the whole by bringing other voices into the room.

◆ *Establish a base of enthusiasm.* Core Group Inquiry begins at a manageable level and then expands from there. It establishes a base of enthusiasm, which can serve as the foundation for a larger, more inclusive effort.

Positive Change Network

A few years ago, while working with GTE (now Verizon), we recognized the transforming power of training front-line employees in Appreciative Inquiry. Our charge was to bring Appreciative Inquiry to sixty-seven thousand employees. Rather than begin with the selection of topics and launch a company-wide inquiry, we began with a training program. The goal was to create a critical mass of employees who were familiar with Appreciative Inquiry in preparation for a company-wide inquiry. To our surprise, after a two-day Appreciative Inquiry workshop, people began initiating their own inquiries, introducing Appreciative Inquiry to their departments and changing the way they did business.

This initiative gave birth to what we now call a Positive Change Network—a process for systematically introducing Appreciative Inquiry to an organization and supporting its application in all aspects of the business and organization. Following an initial two to four days of training in Appreciative Inquiry, participants create initiatives in their own areas of interest and expertise. For example, one person does an inquiry on best recruiting practices, while another looks at ways of enhancing a particular business process. They select their own topics, craft their own questions, conduct their own interviews, and make meaning of their own data. They may or may not organize others in their particular areas to participate in the process. At some point, they design and deliver organizational innovations that are consistent with what they have learned through their individual inquiries.

Three things distinguish a Positive Change Network from pure and simple training in Appreciative Inquiry:

1. Participants are encouraged during the training to imagine ways they might apply Appreciative Inquiry to their regular jobs. Through the training, they are offered a philosophy and methodology to bring out the best in their work.

2. Participants are given opportunities to stay connected with one another, to share best practices and inspirations, and to expand their knowledge and understanding of the theory and practice of Appreciative Inquiry. This is often accomplished through an online knowledge network—a Positive Change Knowledge Exchange—through which people exchange questions and stories, kick around ideas for more inquiry, and share guides and project designs.

3. Participants are periodically brought back together for AI Summits or other face-to-face meetings to share the results of their inquiries and imagine the future of the organization.

Positive Change Networks have been successfully deployed in a variety of settings beyond the former GTE (Verizon). For example, Front Range Community College in Westminster, Colorado, established a Positive Change Network as a standing committee in its college system. Members of the group used their AI skills to provide internal consulting and support to the larger community in areas such as turnover reduction, recruiting, facilities design, and strategic planning. They also introduced AI and its applications to other institutions within and outside their state.

As a grassroots approach to organization change, a Positive Change Network can make a significant positive impact on an organization and its culture. It can engage an entire workforce to liberate employees' ideas and initiatives, to enhance strategic organizational learning, or simply to link people who are working in diverse disciplines at dispersed locations. Because it initially involves smaller groups of willing participants, it can be an easier process for introducing and sustaining AI over time, particularly in very large or complex systems. When might you implement a Positive Change Network?

- To *stimulate improvisational positive change.* Positive Change Networks begin the process of positive change by nurturing individual and grassroots efforts. They harness people's natural goodwill by providing them with tools for making systematic differences in their own jobs and in the organization as a whole.

- To *enhance strategic organizational learning.* Positive Change Networks unleash the spirit of inquiry and discovery throughout the system. In addition, they formally link people in diverse disciplines from dispersed locations. By providing these people with a common language, common skills, and creative methods for communication, Positive Change Networks encourage people to share and transport discoveries, questions, and best practices across traditional boundaries.

Positive Change Consortium

A Positive Change Consortium is a highly cooperative Appreciative Inquiry Form of Engagement that brings together teams of people from five to eight different organizations or communities to collaborate on a 4-D Cycle. The focus of their joint Appreciative Inquiry is a Change Agenda of shared strategic interest, such as exceptional call-center management or improved community health care.

Over a period of six to nine months, the teams from various organizations work as a larger, cross-organizational inquiry team. Together, they select topics of mutual relevance, craft questions, and create Interview Guides. They then conduct appreciative interviews at one another's sites in a kind of mutual benchmarking. Weeks or months later, they return to an AI Summit to make meaning of their data, write Provocative Propositions, and self-organize into company-specific teams to apply what they have learned.

Positive Change Consortia have a number of advantages over organization-specific initiatives. They allow the consulting costs for large change initiatives to be spread out over several organizations. They enhance creativity and innovation because they engage people with different points of view from potentially different industries in thinking about issues of mutual concern. Finally, they build ongoing communities of learning.

When would you sponsor a Positive Change Consortium? A Positive Change Consortium offers opportunities to build internal systems and structures that are based on industry-leading insights and innovations. In particular, it can be used to do the following:

- *Liberate the voice of the customer.* The Positive Change Consortium gives voice to the customer by bringing internal, external, and cross-company stakeholders into shared processes of Appreciative Inquiry. It creates a vehicle for customer voices to be solicited, heard, and built upon through Dream and Design activities.

- *Transform an industry.* The Positive Change Consortium offers the gift of fresh eyes that can be used to explore an individual organization's positive core, to create new models for doing business, and to reinvent the way that an industry's work is defined, imagined, and implemented.

- *Align a value chain.* By bringing together customers, suppliers, and providers within a particular industry, the Positive Change Consortium provides opportunities to redefine roles and responsibilities, realign handoffs and work processes, and generally design life-centered ways of achieving exceptional results.

Appreciative Inquiry Learning Team

The Appreciative Inquiry (AI) Learning Team is one of the simpler Appreciative Inquiry Forms of Engagement. It is known by a variety of names, such as Innovation Team, Action Group, Improvement

Team, Implementation Team, or Project Team. The AI Learning Team is a small group of people, well trained in Appreciative Inquiry, that uses the 4-D Cycle to achieve a specific goal. It is a particularly effective Form of Engagement for groups seeking to integrate Appreciative Inquiry into their ongoing work or change initiatives. AI Learning Teams have been used for process improvement, program evaluation, customer satisfaction evaluation, benchmarking, and product innovation.

It is in the Destiny phase of a Whole-System 4-D Dialogue that AI Learning Teams are most often formed. After the Discovery, Dream, and Design phases, self-organized teams are formed to carry out projects and create innovations consistent with the organization's newly articulated positive core, Dream, and Design. In addition, the teams can be used as a separate and unique Form of Engagement. In this case, teams are formed and trained in Appreciative Inquiry and then use it to stimulate improvement and innovation within their own areas of responsibility.

When might you initiate AI Learning Teams? This Form of Engagement provides a particularly useful focus to do the following:

- *Stimulate innovation.* AI Learning Teams provide front-line employees with information, skills, and resources to organize proactively in service of their business's changing needs.

- *Foster employee development.* AI Learning Teams educate people by exposing them to business information and best practices, and they develop people by providing them with skills, resources, and opportunities to meet people in different functions and businesses.

- *Enhance cross-functional, cross-departmental teamwork.* AI Learning Teams give people an opportunity to work together well on projects of mutual interest and concern, to enhance capacities for teamwork, and to build a sense of belonging to a larger system or organization.

- *Business process improvement.* AI Learning Teams help organizations redesign work processes and positively transform the way work gets done. In addition, they are a fulfilling and effective way to uncover and deploy the organization's positive core in the service of a particular process.

Progressive Appreciative Inquiry Meetings

Progressive AI Meetings are another small-scale Form of Engagement. In this application of Appreciative Inquiry, a group or team works through the 4-D Cycle over the course of several months in a series of ten to twelve short meetings that are each two to four hours long. The meeting agenda might look something like this:

- Meeting 1: Introduce AI and conduct mini-interviews.
- Meeting 2: Select topics.
- Meeting 3: Craft questions.
- Meeting 4: Identify stakeholders, plan the inquiry process, and initiate interviews.
- Meeting 5: Share results from interviews and map the positive core.
- Meeting 6: Envision possibilities.
- Meetings 7 and 8: Redesign the organization.
- Meetings 9 and 10: Self-organize for action.
- Meetings 11 and 12: Follow up, support, and improvise.

Progressive AI Meetings create opportunities for groups of people to engage in inquiry and change without significant disruption to the day-to-day operation. These meetings take discipline, however, and particular attention to continuity. It is easy to lose momentum as people inevitably miss meetings and become absorbed in other priorities.

The Inner London Courts Magistrates Office engaged their organization in this iterative process of progressive AI meetings. Consultants Adrian McLean and Marsha George built Appreciative Inquiry into a series of prescheduled management training days. In the first meeting, participants learned about AI, selected topics, and crafted Interview Guides. Following the first session they conducted interviews. They then brought their data to the second meeting, where they shared what they learned in their interviews, mapped the positive core, then dreamed and designed their ideal organization. Following the second session they launched projects that were in keeping with their designs. And then finally, in a third meeting, they returned to share the results of their efforts and learn from the process.

When would you use Progressive Appreciative Inquiry Meetings? The answer to this is easy. This Form of Engagement can be adapted to any purpose at any scale. Anytime you have a group of people dedicated to creating change whose time together is limited but ongoing, consider using Progressive Appreciative Inquiry Meetings.

Reflecting on the Forms of Engagement

The eight Forms of Engagement we have just summarized are only a starting point. Appreciative Inquiry is still in its infancy. Within the next several years, we expect to see an explosion of new approaches to Appreciative Inquiry.

As you consider using Appreciative Inquiry, choose a Form of Engagement that seems to best suit your Change Agenda and organizational context. And then experiment. As you apply Appreciative Inquiry, adapt it, alter it, and let it unfold in ways that are appropriate to your organization.

Inquiry Strategy: What Decisions and Steps Will Ensure the Project's Success?

As we have already said, Appreciative Inquiry engagements are full of choices. Decisions about what to change and how to change are two macro-level choices in a process that continually evolves over time. There is also a wide variety of micro-level choices at the heart of what we call an Inquiry Strategy.

An Inquiry Strategy is a carefully thought out plan for the way an initiative will unfold over time. It describes who will do what, when, in order to achieve the overall Change Agenda.

Table 4 (following) provides a brief summary of the choices that must be made at each phase of the 4-D Cycle in order to determine your Inquiry Strategy. Chapters 5 through 10 provide more detailed information about these choices.

Figure 5.   A Menu of Approaches to Appreciative Inquiry: Inquiry Strategy

The Appreciative Inquiry Menu:
A Frame for Improvisation

Now that you have read the menu, it is time for you to make your selections. Reflect upon your organization and its current strengths, opportunities, and business challenges and ask yourself: For what purposes might Appreciative Inquiry serve your organization? How might it help you personally? Which Appreciative Inquiry Forms of Engagement seem best suited to your organization and leadership style? And, of course, who else will you involve in the process? By answering and acting upon these questions, you begin a bold experiment in positive change. Keeping in mind the improvisational nature of Appreciative Inquiry, use the menu described in this chapter as a framework for planning and decision making, not a formula.

Table 4. Inquiry Strategy	
Phase in 4-D Cycle	**Decisions to Be Made**
Getting Started. Involves introducing decision makers to Appreciative Inquiry as a process for change, establishing a supporting infrastructure, and engaging participants in the process.	Is Appreciative Inquiry appropriate for us?
	What is our Change Agenda?
	Who will serve on our Advisory Team?
	What training does our Advisory Team need?
	What Form of Engagement will we use?
	What will our Inquiry Strategy be?
	How and when will we introduce the process throughout the organization?
Affirmative Topic Choice. Involves selecting the topics that establish the organization's course for learning and transformation.	Who will select the topics?
	Which topics will we study?
Discovery. Involves crafting the Appreciative Inquiry Interview Guide(s), conducting interviews, and making meaning of what has been learned.	Who will craft the questions? The Interview Guides?
	Whom will we interview?
	Who will conduct interviews? How many each?
	What training will our interviewers need?
	Who will make meaning of the data? How?
	How will we communicate stories and best practices?
	Whom should we involve?
	What experiential activity will we use to reveal our images of the future?
	What will be the outcome of our dream?
Design. Involves collaborative identification of the organization's social architecture and crafting Provocative Propositions—descriptions of the ideal organization.	What are we designing?
	Who needs to be involved?
	How do we describe our ideal organization?
Destiny. Involves unleashing self-organized innovation, through which the future will be made real.	How will we gather stories about what we have achieved?
	How will we celebrate?
	What are our parameters for self-organized action?
	How shall we self-organize?
	How will we support ongoing success?

CHAPTER 3

Eight Principles of Appreciative Inquiry

When it comes to Appreciative Inquiry, principles and practice go hand in hand. The practice of Appreciative Inquiry is informed by a series of eight principles—essential beliefs and values about human organizing and change. These principles, in turn, evolve as successful practice reveals new and different understandings of how positive change works.

The eight principles of Appreciative Inquiry are as unique as the practices to which they have given birth. Derived from three generalized streams of thought—social constructionism, image theory, and grounded research—the principles suggest that human organizing and change is a positive, socially interactive process of discovering and crafting life-affirming, guiding images of the future. Let's briefly consider these three streams of thought and their implications for Appreciative Inquiry.

Social constructionism posits that human communication is the central process that creates, maintains, and transforms realities. Initially introduced by sociologists Peter Berger and Thomas Luckmann in their classic work, The *Social Construction of Reality*,[9] it is

49

more recently developed by founders of the Taos Institute: Kenneth Gergen, Mary Gergen, Diana Whitney, David Cooperrider, Suresh Srivastva, Sheila McNamee, and Harlene Anderson. This tradition serves as the theoretical foundation for appreciative interviews, many Appreciative Inquiry small-group activities, and the notion that bringing all the stakeholders together is essential to constructive organization change.

Image theory, according to Elise and Kenneth Boulding in *The Future: Images and Processes,*[10] suggests that the images we hold of the future influence the decisions and actions we take in the present. Their work and that of Dutch sociologist Frederik Polak, in his book *The Image of the Future,*[11] give Appreciative Inquiry its unique focus on images and stories of the future. Image theory implies that one of the most untapped resources for organizational change is the collective images held in the stories and dreams of members of an organization.

Grounded research methodology is based on an openness to understanding a culture, society, or organization through the eyes of its inhabitants. It suggests that participant observation is the best means of data gathering for those who wish to understand and describe living cultures. It puts forth the idea that all research is intervention. Building on the notion that inquiry is intervention, Appreciative Inquiry engages members of an organization in their own research—inquiry into the most life-giving forces in their organization, the root causes of their success, and discovery of their positive core.

As you begin working with Appreciative Inquiry, you will find the principles helpful in two important ways. First, when introducing or teaching Appreciative Inquiry, they will help you describe the subtle differences between Appreciative Inquiry and other approaches to organization change. Second, when designing Appreciative Inquiry initiatives, they will guide you in inventing activities and processes that both meet the needs of your organization and maintain the integrity of Appreciative Inquiry.

In Table 5 (following) you will find a summary of the eight

principles. A quick scan of the summary will give you a general understanding. Following the table is an in-depth view, with each principle defined and its meaning and significance illustrated with rich quotes. The first five principles are derived directly from the early writing of Srivastva and Cooperrider.[12] We have added three principles, which evolved from the experience of applying Appreciative Inquiry to large-scale organization and community change efforts.

Principle #1: The Constructionist Principle

Words Create Worlds

The Constructionist Principle places human communication and language at the center of human organizing and change. It posits that meaning is made in conversation, reality is created in communication, and knowledge is generated through social interaction. In essence, it states that knowledge is a subjective reality—a social artifact resulting from communication among groups of people.

Further, the Constructionist Principle suggests that words, language, and metaphors are more than mere descriptions of reality. They are words that create worlds. Toltec teacher and shaman Don Miguel Ruiz writes that words are the vehicle through which the world is manifest:

> Your word is the power that you have to create. Your word is the gift that comes directly from God. The Gospel of John in the Bible, speaking of the creation of the universe, says, "In the beginning there was the Word, and the Word was with God, and the Word was God." Through the word you express your creative power. It is through the word that you manifest everything. Regardless of what language you speak, your intent manifests through the word.[13]

Similarly, Joseph Jaworski, chairman of the American Leadership Forum, reflects upon the power of language to create social change and ultimately reality itself:

Table 5.   Summary of the Eight Principles of Appreciative Inquiry

Principle	Definition
1. The Constructionist Principle.	*Words Create Worlds* Reality as we know it is a subjective rather than objective state. It is socially created through language and conversations.
2. The Simultaneity Principle.	*Inquiry Creates Change* Inquiry is intervention. The moment we ask a question, we begin to create a change.
3. The Poetic Principle.	*We Can Choose What We Study* Organizations, like open books, are endless sources of study and learning. What we choose to study makes a difference. It describes—even creates—the world as we know it.
4. The Anticipatory Principle.	*Images Inspire Action* Human systems move in the direction of their images of the future. The more positive and hopeful the images of the future are, the more positive the present-day action will be.
5. The Positive Principle.	*Positive Questions Lead to Positive Change* Momentum for large-scale change requires large amounts of positive affect and social bonding. This momentum is best generated through positive questions that amplify the positive core.
6. The Wholeness Principle.	*Wholeness Brings Out the Best* Wholeness brings out the best in people and organizations. Bringing all stakeholders together in large group forums stimulates creativity and builds collective capacity.
7. The Enactment Principle.	*Acting "As If" Is Self-Fulfilling* To really make a change, we must "be the change we want to see." Positive change occurs when the process used to create the change is a living model of the ideal future.
8. The Free-Choice Principle.	*Free Choice Liberates Power* People perform better and are more committed when they have freedom to choose how and what they contribute. Free choice stimulates organizational excellence and positive change.

As I considered the importance of language and how human beings interact with the world, it struck me that in many ways the development of language was like the discovery of fire—it was such an incredible primordial force. I had always thought that we used language to describe the world—now I see this is not the case. To the contrary, it is through language that we create the world, because it's nothing until we describe it. And when we describe it, we create distinctions that govern our actions. To put it another way, we do not describe the world we see, we see the world we describe.[14]

According to the Constructionist Principle, the power of language is not as an individual tool but rather as the vehicle by which communities of people create knowledge and meaning. According to leading social psychologist Kenneth Gergen, "What we take to be knowledge of the world grows from relationship, and is embedded not within individual minds but within interpretive or communal traditions."[15] Knowledge—that which is considered good, true, and meaningful—is a broad social agreement created among people through communication.

In *An Invitation to Social Construction,* Gergen explains the theory and practice of social constructionism, offering four assumptions that further describe the relational nature of meaning making:

- The terms by which we understand our world and our self are neither required nor demanded by "what there is."

- Our modes of description, explanation, and/or representation are derived from relationship.

- As we describe, explain, or otherwise represent, we also fashion our future.

- Reflection on our forms of understanding is vital to our future well-being.[16]

Words matter—they not only make a difference, they literally bring things to life, creating the world as we know it.

The Constructionist Principle in Practice

Organizations first emerge through language. They reside in stories and come to life in conversations. And organizational change occurs through language, storytelling, and human communication. The practice of Appreciative Inquiry is notably a constructive approach to change in that it brings people—all stakeholders—together to collaborate and discover, dream, and design the organization they most value and desire. It is a highly interactive process, sometimes described as both top-down and bottom-up. It brings together people from all levels and functions of an organization to learn from one another and with one another; to build relationships for going forward and expanding their collective wisdom.

The many specific ways people come together through the practice of Appreciative Inquiry include selection of affirmative topics, appreciative interviews, meaning-making sessions, dream dialogues and activities, crafting provocative propositions, and selection of inspired actions. In essence, each step in the Appreciative Inquiry process affords opportunities for people who do not generally come together to do so—and in the process to transform the nature of organizing.

A Story About the Social Construction of Reality

Recognizing that meaning is made through relationships, leaders in Nevada decided to use Appreciative Inquiry to merge state and county child welfare services. Their goals were to build positive, cooperative relationships among people who had previously competed for resources, and to collaborate to design an integrated service delivery system. They engaged all of their stakeholders— social workers, secretaries, foster parents, grandparents and youth, counselors, legislators, lawyers and judges, adoptive parents, and group home managers—in the dialogue through a series of AI Summits. As people who seldom talked to one another connected via appreciative interviews, the path to integration became ever more apparent. As they shared their dreams, the image of one organization and an integrated service delivery system became clear. And together they designed an integrated service delivery system based on their shared values of family preservation, child well-being, and one-stop service delivery. In this case, words created worlds. They made a positive difference in the lives of thousands of children and their parents.

Principle #2: The Simultaneity Principle

Inquiry Creates Change

The Simultaneity Principle holds that change occurs the moment we ask a question. In the words of therapist Marilee Goldberg, "The moment of questioning is also the moment of choice, which usually holds the greatest leverage for effective action and positive change."[17] This suggests that inquiry and change are simultaneous, that inquiry is intervention—and perhaps the most effective means to transformation.

Questions, whether they are posed to oneself or to another, can create identities and give hope where none existed before. Therapists have long recognized the provocative potential of questions to give form to identities, relationships, and patterns of living. According to Goldberg:

> Questions are the primary means by which doing, having, accomplishing, and growing are catalyzed—and often even made manifest—in our lives. Because questions are intrinsically related to action, they spark and direct attention, perception, energy, and effort, and so are at the heart of the evolving forms that our lives assume.[18]

Viktor Frankl, noted psychiatrist and concentration camp survivor, attributes his capacity for survival in part to the internal questions that beset him. While others were asking, Will we survive? Frankl was caught by the question, Has all this suffering, this dying round us, a meaning?[19] As a result of this question, Frankl inhabited a very different world from that of many of his comrades. Even in a concentration camp, his was a world of meaning and possibility, while theirs was one of life and death.

Likewise, Goldberg suggests that the questions held by clients, articulated in their stories and enacted in their relationships, hold the key to their change. Question-centered therapists work with this awareness, listening to understand and help clients reframe their life-organizing questions:

> These therapists appreciate that clients' questions—internal and
> external, conscious and unconscious—exert a profound influence
> on confining them to the worlds they want to leave, and hold keys to
> help them move into the worlds they desire to inhabit.[20]

Questions can stimulate ideas, innovation, and invention. New knowledge, theories, and inventions have frequently evolved from unusual questions—questions that require persistent reflection, consideration of paradoxical possibilities, and synthesis across diverse disciplines. Many scientists and inventors tell of the question that haunted them, begging for resolution until the answer emerged and along with it a new idea or invention.

Gutenberg's invention of the printing press, for example, resulted from consideration of what seemed at the time to be an inconceivable, even paradoxical, question: How can sacred texts be produced in large numbers to be made available to the masses? Familiar with block printing (an advanced yet slow and costly process for reproducing handwritten texts), Gutenberg continued to ponder his question day and night. When concerned friends insisted that he take a break and join them at the annual wine festival, he agreed to go. With the question still in the forefront of his thinking, he found the answer when he saw a wine press. Within days he had created the first prototype printing press. History tells the rest of this story.

The Simultaneity Principle in Practice

Contrary to the common belief that organizational change occurs through planned, long-term intervention, the Simultaneity Principle posits that inquiry is intervention. Human systems—organizations and people—move in the direction of what they study, ask questions about, inquire into, and explore with curiosity.

The practice of Appreciative Inquiry is based on the idea that the seeds of change are implicit in the first questions we ask. Given this, in Appreciative Inquiry we no longer concern ourselves with the reliability of a question to produce right or wrong answers. Instead, we consider the direction indicated in the question, and its capacity to enhance lives. As William Martin, modern interpreter of the Tao Te Ching, states:

> Your conversations help create your world. Speak of delight, not dissatisfaction. Speak of hope, not despair. Let your words bind up wounds, not cause them.[21]

Thus, the practice of Appreciative Inquiry involves the art of crafting and asking questions that elicit affirmative possibilities. The practice of appreciative interviews, of focusing on questions that inspire storytelling about organizations at their best, evokes hopes and dreams for the future and generates life-giving possibilities. This is the heart of Appreciative Inquiry.

A Story of Inquiry as Intervention

Staff members of the Cathedral Foundation, from CEO to secretary, had lost enthusiasm for their work. As a social service organization dedicated to the care of the elderly, they provided services such as Meals on Wheels and elder day care. They decided to use Appreciative Inquiry for strategic planning. In the course of their Appreciative Inquiry strategic planning process, they changed the focus of their inquiry, and hence their organization, from How do we care for the elderly? to How do we create a positive experience of aging? By making this change, they cleared the way for significant diversification and the addition of new services with significant and far-reaching effects. Enthusiasm rekindled as they collectively committed to their new mission.

Principle #3: The Poetic Principle

We Can Choose What We Study

The Poetic Principle suggests that organizations are like open books—endless sources of learning, inspiration, and interpretation. Like great works of literature, poetry, or sacred texts, organizations are stories that can be told and retold, interpreted and reinterpreted, through any frame of reference or topic of inquiry. The choice of what to study is ours and ours alone. Thus, we can choose to study virtually any topic related to human organizing—customer dissatisfaction or customer delight, debilitating bureaucratic stress or inspiring democratic processes, cross-functional conflict or cooperation, employee frustration or joy at work.

Further, the topics we choose to study are fateful. They not only determine what we discover and learn—they actually create it. Questions about joy and enthusiasm at work evoke stories, images, and experiences of joy. Conversely, questions about stress lead to stories, images, and experiences of stress.

One of the strongest ways the topics we focus upon influence our world is through the metaphors we choose to describe human organizing. We say, for example, that organizations are like machines, natural ecosystems, families, battlegrounds, or networks. Each metaphor, as an analog for organizing, rapidly stimulates a vivid set of images and evokes a unique way of being. Parker Palmer, a Quaker activist and teacher, proposes that metaphors take us from language to life, and our use of metaphors goes beyond naming experience to become our experience:

> Metaphors do much more than describe reality as we know it. Animated by the imagination, one of the most vital powers we possess, our metaphors often become reality, transmuting themselves from language into the living of our lives.[22]

Thus, metaphors prescribe culture. According to noted psychologist Rollo May, "They show people how to learn, organize, create, and change."[23] They create the world in which we ultimately choose to live.

The Poetic Principle in Practice

Organizational life is expressed as a narrative, a grand story, coauthored by its various stakeholders. Each person or stakeholder group brings a different story, a different piece of the interpretive puzzle. Like poets carefully choosing words to evoke sentiments and understandings, organizational stakeholders choose the language, topics, and metaphors to describe and make meaning of their organizations. Sometimes their words and metaphors will serve cooperation, customers, and competitive advantage. Sometimes they will stimulate conflict, dissatisfaction, and loss of business. In all cases, their choices reverberate throughout the organization through both stories and actions.

The practice of Appreciative Inquiry starts with the selection of Affirmative Topics. This places strategic significance on the choice of success-oriented and life-giving language and metaphors for organizing. Based on the notion that human systems move in the direction of what they study, topics are selected strategically to move the organization in the direction of the highest ideals and values of its stakeholders.

A Story of Fateful Topic Choice

In early 2002, organization development consultant Donna Stoneham agreed to help the University of California, Berkeley (UCB) and the city of Berkeley develop an ongoing collaborative relationship. Together with a twelve-person planning team composed of city and university representatives, she began what became a six-month process of creating partnership. At the initial retreat, a group of seventy-five people from the city and the university explored the topic of partnership. Through a combination of appreciative interviews, meaning making, and dreaming, the group determined points of effective partnership that already existed between the two organizations. One of the project leaders later reflected on this initial retreat:

By selecting the topic of partnership, we opened the door for a different kind of conversation—and a different kind of experience. To my surprise, we discovered that there were places where our similarities intersected. This helped us to begin seeing one another as allies rather than adversaries. It encouraged us to form powerful new relationships both within and between our organizations.

This meeting had a humanizing effect on both organizations and paved the way for further conversation among a larger community of stakeholders. Ongoing conversations about partnership succeeded in enhancing collaboration, as demonstrated by the following new joint initiatives that the group established:

- A law enforcement collaborative to promote crime prevention strategies and programs and to identify and share resources.
- "Town and gown" meetings to create regular opportunities for the UCB and city staffs to get together on an informal basis, to get to know one another, and to discuss common issues.
- An initiative to identify and evaluate joint housing and financing opportunities for all incomes and family types.
- A Southwest Berkeley Health Initiative to increase city and UCB participation in addressing health disparities in southwest Berkeley.
- An initiative to explore opportunities for joint procurement between the city and the campus.

Their topic choice was fateful. It encouraged previously unimagined levels of collaboration and partnership, which significantly enhanced the quality of life for both city and university stakeholders.

Principle #4: The Anticipatory Principle

Images Inspire Action

The Anticipatory Principle suggests that images of the future guide and inspire present-day actions and achievements. It says that organizations exist in part because people are drawn to and share images and projections of the future, which is full of inevitable and unpredictable surprises. Cybernetic scientists recognize this as uncertainty, complexity theorists describe it as chaos, Native Americans call it the Great Mystery. Simply put, the element of surprise and the presence of the unknown have always and will always exist. Given this element of surprise, all we can possibly know about the future comes from what we hope, dream, and imagine. In short, we create images of where we believe we're going—and then we organize to those images.

Dutch sociologist Frederik Polak suggests that images of the future influence action at all levels of social life:

> At every level of awareness, from the individual to the macro-societal, imagery is continuously generated about the "not-yet." Such imagery inspires our intentions, which then move us purposefully forward. Through their daily choices of action, individuals, families, enterprises, communities, and nations move toward what they imagine to be a desirable tomorrow.[24]

Thus success or failure hinges in part on the images we hold of the future. Fear-based images can incite widespread panic—as in the 1929 run on the American banking system. Conversely, clear, sustaining, and motivating images can mobilize powerful, positive, collective action—as in the 1960s American–Soviet space race. In writing about postmodern organizations, professor and theorist William Bergquist contends that "the continuation of any society depends in large part on the presence in the society of a sustaining and motivating image of its own collective future."[25]

What then do we mean by images of the future? How are they created? And where would an organization's collective image of its future be found? Images are sensory-rich descriptions of potential, elaborations of possibility, and explanations of the unknown. They are, according to author Linda Jones, "prophecies—spoken words that advance us and move us forward."[26] As such, they are more stories than pictures. While some images are portrayed visually, and are sometimes even referred to as visions, images are most often narrative accounts. They are the stories we tell ourselves about ourselves. Formed in conversation, they reside in day-to-day dialogue among individuals and groups of people.

The Anticipatory Principle in Practice

Organizational images of the future are created and exist in conversation among the many stakeholders of the organization. They reside in the inner dialogue—the informal communication—of the organization. Conversations around the watercooler, in break rooms, over coffee, and in cafeterias hold the key to an organization's collective images of the future and its potential for success.

The practice of Appreciative Inquiry ensures that an organization's inner dialogue is full of rich accounts of past successes and vivid images of future potential. Through inquiry into the positive core, dream activities, and the crafting of Provocative Propositions, it interrupts images of the status quo and stretches the organization's collective imagination. It provides opportunities for new images of the organization's future to be created and unfolded over time, like a flower growing toward the sunlight.

A Story of Image Inspiring Action

The founders of the United Religions Initiative had originally planned to call the global interfaith organization the United Religions. It was intended to parallel the United Nations in both scope and stature. This was indeed a bold vision—an image that attracted two hundred fifty people to a global summit to dialogue about the vision and values for such an organization. In the course of these early discussions, it became apparent that—while the image of United Religions did attract many people—it appeared to others to lack humility. And so the idea and image of a United Religions Initiative was born. The original plan was to hold the name *Initiative* throughout the first five years—while thousands of people worldwide were involved in crafting a charter and designing the organization. Then, in June 2002, when the charter was signed, the organization would become the United Religions.

Two interesting things happened along the way. First, even as people were crafting the charter and designing the organization, others began taking action to build bridges between people of different religions and faiths—and to foster interfaith peace building in their parts of the world. The image of an "initiative" inspired people to initiate action on behalf of an organization that had yet to be created. Second, as the deadline for signing the charter grew closer, spontaneous discussions emerged about the name of the organization going forward. The name United Religions Initiative carried with it the image of action: of always initiating and never growing stale. There was a consensus among founders around the world that the United Religions Initiative—rather than the United Religions—was the organization that was about to be born. And so it was.

Principle #5: The Positive Principle

Positive Questions Lead to Positive Change

The Positive Principle is not so abstract; it grows out of years of experience with Appreciative Inquiry. Simply stated, the Positive Principle says that positive questions lead to positive change. Based on their research into Appreciative Inquiry in team building, management professors Gervase Bushe and Graeme Coetzer elaborate:

> The more positive the questions we use to guide a team building or organization development initiative, the more long lasting and effective the change effort.[27]

Put most simply, momentum for change requires large amounts of positive affect and social bonding—hope, inspiration, and sheer joy in creating with one another. Thousands of interviews about passion for service or magnetic work environments have a different capacity to sustain positive action than a study about low morale or process inefficiencies.

Positive questions bring out the best in people, inspire positive action, and create possibilities for positive futures. But why do positive questions unleash enthusiasm and flourishes of positive change within human systems? They do so because they amplify the organization's positive core. They magnify the essence of the organization at its best—its remembered past, its enacted present, and its imagined future. Given opportunities to study, learn, and dream about the positive core, people and organizations feel hopeful, get excited, and naturally gravitate toward what works.

An organization's positive core, write David Cooperrider and Diana Whitney, is the wisdom, knowledge, successful strategies, positive attitudes and affect, best practices, skills, resources, and capabilities of the organization.[28] It is a source of life-giving potential, consisting of the organization's creative, life-affirming qualities, capabilities, and resources.

Some of the many ways an organization's positive core may be expressed include:

Business best practices	Positive emotions
Core competencies	Product strengths
Elevated thoughts	Relational resources
Embedded knowledge	Social capital
Financial assets	Strategic opportunities
Innovations, patents, and copyrights	Technical assets
	Values
Organizational achievements	Visions of possibility
Organizational wisdom	Vital traditions

Paradoxically, the positive core both exists in and of itself, and it unfolds and evolves as a result of an Appreciative Inquiry. Inquiry and attention both strengthen and augment the positive core. Writer Henry Miller observed, "The moment one gives close attention to anything, even a blade of grass, it becomes a mysterious, awesome, indescribably magnificent world in itself."

The Positive Principle in Practice

The more we inquire, the more we bring the positive core to life—ultimately shifting people's attention away from problems as the motivation for change toward unfolding gifts, capabilities, potentials, dreams, and visions. At the heart of the practice of Appreciative Inquiry is the quest to discover what gives life to an organization when it is at its best. In this sense the practice of Appreciative Inquiry is positive, or fully affirmative. Appreciative Inquiry is not a search for positive as opposed to negative, or good as opposed to bad. It is a search for what nourishes people for better performance and organizational excellence, what excites, energizes, and inspires employees, customers, suppliers, and the organization's community.

The practice of Appreciative Inquiry reflects the positive in numerous ways, most significantly through the discovery and mapping of the positive core. Affirmative topics are chosen, appreciative interviews conducted, and the data used to identify all that is good, successful, capable, and desirable about the organization.

A Story About Mapping the Positive Core

Jane Farthing, senior consultant for Cap Gemini Ernst & Young, was given the responsibility to help two large federal agencies merge their libraries. The project was significant and the time allotted scant by comparison. With only two days to bring together the staff of these two organizations, she considered how Appreciative Inquiry might best serve them. Ultimately she facilitated the two groups in conducting appreciative interviews with one another, and then together they mapped the positive core of their joint library system. People who had little interest in being part of a joint system were initially taken aback. Over the course of the two days, skepticism gave way to outright enthusiasm and delight as they recognized each other's capacities along with their integrated resources. At the end of the two-day session, they laminated their positive core map—a mosaic of all their strengths, resources, skills, assets, and capacities—and put it on display as a visual reminder of the best of who they are and all that they have jointly to offer their customers.

Principle #6: The Wholeness Principle

Wholeness Brings Out the Best

The Wholeness Principle posits that the experience of wholeness brings out the best in people, relationships, communities, and organizations. As quantum physicist David Bohm suggests, wholeness—the whole story, the whole system, and the whole person—is essential to a well-lived life:

> It is instructive to consider that the word "health" in English is based on an Anglo-Saxon word "hale" meaning "whole": that is, to be healthy is to be whole. . . . All of this indicates that man has sensed always that wholeness or integrity is an absolute necessity to make life worth living.[29]

The experience of wholeness is one of understanding the whole story. It comes about when people are able to hear, witness, and make sense of each other's differing views, perspectives, and interpretations of shared events. The spiritual teacher and author of *Kitchen Table Wisdom*, Rachel Naomi Remen, reminds us that different people have different stories about the same event:

> Stories are someone's experience of the events of their life; they are not the events themselves. Most of us experience the same event very differently.[30]

Thus, the whole story is never a singular story but is often a synthesis, a compilation of multiple stories, shared and woven together by the many people involved.

The Wholeness Principle leads participants to focus on higher ground rather than common ground. The experience of wholeness and healing emerges not in the discovery of commonalities but rather in understanding, accepting, and enjoying differences. The sense of understanding the whole story—with all its differences and distinctions—brings with it a kind of contentment that does not require agreement. Thus, it creates a context in which people can safely focus on issues of higher purpose and greater good for the whole. Former Soviet President Mikhail Gorbachev articulates the importance of transcending differences to serve a higher purpose:

> Ours is a time of acute problems and unprecedented opportunities. We shall be able to accomplish our historic task of developing our inheritance only if, irrespective of our political opinions, religious beliefs, or philosophies, we try to understand and help one another and act in concert for a better future.[31]

The Wholeness Principle in Practice

In a practical sense, wholeness means engaging the entire organization in the process of change by getting all stakeholders—or at a minimum, some microcosm of the organization—in the room at the same time. When the whole system is in the room, trust ensues and a can-do attitude prevails. As one workshop participant put it:

> Wholeness evokes trust. When everyone is there you don't have to feel suspicious about what the others will do—there are no others. It is collectively empowering. There is no one else who must approve your plan. You know that whatever you collectively decide can be done.

Involving the whole system also inspires uncommon action on behalf of the whole. In the experience of Benedictine University professor James Ludema:

> The unique perspective of each person, when combined with the perspectives of others, creates new possibilities for action: possibilities that previously lay dormant or undiscovered.[32]

The practice of Appreciative Inquiry brings a whole system together, and through appreciative interviews, it breaks down barriers and creates a setting for building respect, overcoming stereotypes, and renewing relationships. Large-group Appreciative Inquiry meetings of people in conflict—whether the conflicts are functional, cultural, generational, religious, political, or other—provide opportunities for healing. When people meet each other in whole-system dialogue, false assumptions fall away. They realize that others are not exactly as they imagined them to be, and respect grows for differences in background, practice, and vision.

A Story of Wholeness and Productivity

In a culture where negative comments and toxic behaviors received the lion's share of attention, John Deere Harvester Works wanted to achieve higher performance through flexible, self-directed teams. They achieved this by engaging two hundred fifty wage and salaried employees in a five-day Appreciative Inquiry Summit. During this time, employees broke through their cynical attitudes and moved beyond Solid, Stable, Still John Deere. With the whole system in the room, they were able to renew and establish highly productive collaborative relationships, significantly reduce product development cycle time, and create a shared sense of confidence about future performance.

Principle #7: The Enactment Principle

Acting "As If" Is Self-Fulfilling

The Enactment Principle suggests that transformation occurs by living in the present what we most desire in the future. Put more simply, positive change comes about as images and visions of a more desired future are enacted in the present. A well-known expression of this idea comes from Indian leader Mahatma Gandhi's assertion: "Be the change you want to see." As a social activist, Gandhi lived his belief that the only way to create a just, nonviolent world in the future is through just, nonviolent action in the present. His life was a living model, an enactment of his deepest beliefs and dreams for the future.

In the 1960s, civil rights leader Martin Luther King Jr. led the American people toward greater justice, equality, and respect for all. As he did so, he continually reasserted the belief that the only way to change the world is to live the difference:

As you press on for justice, be sure to move with dignity and discipline, using only the weapon of love. . . . Darkness can not drive out darkness; only light can do that. Hate can not drive out hate; only love can do that.[33]

From a spiritual perspective, the present is all there is. We are advised to *be here now*, to *be present*, and to *live in the moment*. Encouraging her dancers to be fully present as they performed, dancer and choreographer Martha Graham taught: "All that is important is this one moment in movement. Make the moment vital and worth living. Do not let it slip away unnoticed and unused."[34]

President Franklin D. Roosevelt understood the concept of living one's dreams today. Presiding over a nation deep in the throes of its worst-ever economic depression, FDR challenged the American people with a vision of possibility. In his inaugural address he urged the nation to courageously enact its desired future of work and justice for all, rather than simply waiting for the return of prosperity. He went on to affirm the future he would lead:

In this nation I see tens of millions of its citizens—a substantial part of its whole population—who at this very moment are denied the greater part of what the very lowest standards of today call the necessities of life.

It is not in despair that I paint you that picture. I paint it for you in hope—because the Nation, seeing and understanding the injustice in it, proposes to paint it out. We are determined to make every American citizen the subject of his country's interest and concern; and we will never regard any faithful law-abiding group within our borders as superfluous. The test of our progress is not whether we add more to the abundance of those who have much; it is whether we provide enough for those who have too little.[35]

Choosing to enact the future, FDR led the country in implementing radical New Deal policies that provided work for millions of unemployed Americans. In the process, he helped restore the self-respect and discipline that enabled the nation to move forward and beyond the immediate and seemingly insurmountable challenges of the time.

The Enactment Principle in Practice

The notion of enactment—of living one's dreams today—is a simple yet paradoxical practice. For decades, members of Alcoholics Anonymous have effected change by "acting as if" they are the people they want to be. They act as if they are courageous rather than indulging their fear; they act as if they are generous rather than submitting to selfishness.

Effective organizational change requires that the processes used for change be a living example or enactment of the desired future. In other words, the ends and means of a process for change must be congruent. To again paraphrase Gandhi, organizations must be the change they want to see.

The practice of Appreciative Inquiry creates numerous opportunities for organizations to enact their more desired cultures and leadership styles. For example, if organizations want people engaged in the business, they must act as if high participation and commitment are the norm—by inviting everyone to participate in appreciative interviews and by soliciting informal leadership for all aspects of the Appreciative Inquiry initiative. If they want people to speak up and hear one another, they must act as if all voices are equal—by creating forums for everyone to share interview stories and insights. If they want to level hierarchies, they must act as if rank and authority do not command decision making—by including people from all levels and all functions on their Appreciative Inquiry Advisory Team.

A Story About Acting As If

In late 2001, the city of Denver's Traffic Engineering and Traffic Operations groups were preparing to merge. They wanted a process that would dissolve boundaries between the two previously separate groups and create a new, high-functioning, fully integrated organization. They formed an Advisory Team, with equal representation from both parts of the organization, to plan and implement an AI Summit. From the beginning, advisors spent time getting acquainted, creating a shared purpose, and partnering across boundaries to achieve that purpose. Weeks before the summit, directors from other parts of the organization began asking what had happened. Looking in from the outside, it seemed that the new organization had already achieved its goal of unity! By acting as if they were one organization—in order to plan to become one organization—the desired integration occurred much faster and more easily than expected.

Principle #8: The Free-Choice Principle

Free Choice Liberates Power

The Free-Choice Principle posits that people and organizations thrive when people are free to choose the nature and extent of their contribution. It suggests that treating people as volunteers—with freedom to choose to contribute as they most desire—liberates both personal and organizational power.

What does it mean to treat people as volunteers? The words *volition* and *volunteer* are both rooted in the Latin word *velle,* which means "to wish" or "to choose." Thus, volunteers are people who choose to contribute based on their urge for fulfillment, desire to make a difference, or hope for a better world. To treat people as volunteers is to create a democratic work environment with processes for people to choose how and when to participate based on their strengths, interests, values, hopes, and dreams.

Free choice builds enthusiasm and commitment to the organization and fosters high performance. When people have free choice, organizations excel. Free choice is foundational to what management consultant Jane Seiling calls a Membership Organization. In her book of the same name, Seiling recommends that employees be considered members who choose to work in the organization—even if they must do so for economic reasons. She elaborates on the benefits of free choice:

In a Membership Organization, the members individually and collectively work beyond participation. There is a mindset of high personal responsibility, shared accountability, and member connectedness, making it possible for a more level working community to exist. The concept of membership stimulates enrollment in the organizational purpose, facilitates acceptance of a shared urgency for top performance, and expands opportunities for contribution and success for every individual and group within the workplace community.[36]

Organization development consultant Tom McGehee also emphasizes the benefits of free choice when he describes Creation Companies. According to McGehee, people in Creation Companies join teams and contribute as volunteers, yielding a number of long-term benefits to the organization:

Whenever possible, a Creation Company lets people work wherever they want and correct themselves. People usually choose to work for the best leaders and on the best opportunities. This has the advantage of identifying where the best ideas are, the best projects are, and the best leaders are. Think of it as an internal free market.[37]

Free choice for each person liberates power and high performance because it is an essential aspect of being human. According to psychologist Rollo May, making choices is central to human existence and identity:

A man or woman becomes fully human only by his or her choices and his or her commitment to them. People attain worth and dignity by the multitude of decisions they make from day to day.[38]

Human dignity and the dignity of work derive from choices. As Geoffrey Bellman, author of *Your Signature Path*, says, "Each moment of our lives, we are choosing what we want and don't want, will do and won't do, like and don't like."[39] When people are given opportunities to choose what they want to do, they can more freely respond to their intuitive calling and fulfill their full creative potential.

And indeed it is through the choices we make that we distinguish ourselves, contribute our gifts to the world, and leave our legacy. In the words of CEO Max DePree:

> Of what is hope composed? Certainly part of the answer is the ability to make choices. To be without choices is a great tragedy, a tragedy leading to hopelessness or cynicism. The ability to make choices leads to other consequences. What do we choose? How do we choose? Our choices after all set us apart and shape our legacy."[40]

The Free-Choice Principle teaches us to consistently create opportunities for choice, to give people options, and to encourage them to choose their work based on their intuitions, interests, strengths, and highest callings.

The Free-Choice Principle in Practice

The field of change management has evolved significantly in the twenty-five years we have been practicing. We have witnessed a shift from top-down processes to complete employee participation. We watched as organizations went from "let's take it slow and pilot the process" to "let's get everyone involved as quickly as possible." Both of these shifts expanded employee involvement—but not necessarily employee commitment. Mandating that everyone take part in a change initiative can often backfire. Without room for choice, people may feel pushed and resist, no matter how desirable the change.

The practice of Appreciative Inquiry is distinguished from other approaches to change by the amount of choice it offers people. In many cases people are granted complete freedom to choose if, how, and when they will engage in the process. People may choose to participate in the initial selection of Affirmative Topics or in interviews—and then drop out. Or conversely, they may choose to become engaged in a project that sings to them as action teams are formed—long after Discovery is complete. In short, people can and do choose to participate when they become curious, stimulated, or inspired by a task, activity, or dream for the future.

A Story About Customer Liberation

On the last day of a three-day AI Summit, a customer stood up in a self-organized session and invited people to brainstorm the next steps for one of her projects. The request, and her act of free choice, seemed to be outside the purpose of the summit; it seemed to have nothing to do with the summit sponsor's business. She had been invited to the summit as a customer stakeholder—to help the client system work on its organizational design. Sponsors were surprised by her proposal but decided to let it ride—supporting nearly a dozen members of the organization in joining her in an hour-long working session. Reflecting, the organization's leader said, "Her project had nothing to do with us—and yet, it had everything to do with us. We needed input on that project and never would have gotten it outside of this setting. Now our thumbprint is on what she does going forward, and our goodwill has been forever registered in her memory banks."

Conversations That Matter— The Eight Principles in Summary

Taken together, the Eight Principles of Appreciative Inquiry point to one simple message: Appreciative Inquiry is about conversations that matter. Our first impulse was to call this section "conversations that make a difference," but reflection led us to the current title. The phrase "conversations that matter" explicitly illustrates the power of Appreciative Inquiry to bring things to life—to literally make matter. It also implies that Appreciative Inquiry conversations are about what matters most to people. At their best, conversations—inquiry, dialogue, discussion, and debate—make real and tangible the highest potentials of an organization and its people.

The power of such conversations may be most evident through their absence, such as in traditional organizations where communication is a one-way street. Following an established chain of command, people at the top talk about and create the organization's future with one another, and then roll it out to those reporting to them—all the while hoping for a committed workforce that will follow through. They generate visions, values, and strategies—and then systematically tell and sell their plans to the members of the organization and its stakeholders.

In this system of communication, the majority of the organization's workforce, customers, and stakeholders are expected to swallow whole the information and ideas that have been conveyed. Those who are closest to the work and closest to the customers are excluded from the creative process, without a voice. In the end, these one-way conversations breed demoralized, uninformed, and uncommitted employees who produce low-quality products, miss targets, and treat customers the way they are treated by their supervisors.

In contrast, with the practice of Appreciative Inquiry, these conversations transform one-way, top-down communication into open, whole-system dialogue. AI dramatically shifts who talks to whom about what, involves genuine two-way inquiry and dialogue among improbable pairs of people—for example, senior managers and machine operators, customers and employees, functional departments and their merging counterparts—and focuses people's energies and efforts on what they value. In so doing, Appreciative Inquiry expands the realm of positive possibilities.

Throughout this book you will read stories about conversations that matter in businesses, governments, and not-for-profit organizations around the globe. You will see how these eight principles combine to form a highly improvisational practice of positive change—one that can move people and organizations from despair to possibility.

CHAPTER 4

Appreciative Inquiry in Action: From Origins to Current Practice

Since its inception in 1985, Appreciative Inquiry has spread around the world, gaining recognition as "today's most popular new approach to change." When David Cooperrider gave birth to Appreciative Inquiry, he did not know or intend to open the way for a bold new field of organizational change. Nevertheless, that is precisely what happened.

Over the past decades, Appreciative Inquiry has matured from a series of organizational experiments into a highly successful and sustainable philosophy and practice for positive change. As the stories in this chapter illustrate, many organizations around the world have embraced Appreciative Inquiry as their way of doing business. After using Appreciative Inquiry for four to five years, they have consistently achieved positive results in financial performance, customer satisfaction ratings, and employee engagement. Their successes with Appreciative Inquiry have added knowledge, innovative practices, and tools to the growing field.

This chapter begins with the birth of Appreciative Inquiry and describes the emergence of the field of positive psychology, which parallels the development of Appreciative Inquiry. Several case studies demonstrate the power of the Appreciative Inquiry process and the extraordinary results that were achieved.

Finally, this chapter introduces Hunter Douglas Window Fashions Division. You will learn about the company's inception, its rapid growth, and its need for culture transformation, all before it was introduced to Appreciative Inquiry.

The Origins of Appreciative Inquiry

Appreciative Inquiry was born at the Weatherhead School of Management, at Case Western Reserve University in Cleveland, Ohio. It came about through the collaboration of David Cooperrider, then a graduate student, and his faculty mentor, Suresh Srivastva. While consulting with the Cleveland Clinic, a world-class health-care facility, they began experimenting with a variation of traditional action research techniques—with surprising results.

Rather than conducting an inquiry into what was and what was not working in the organization, they focused on analyzing factors contributing to the organization's effectiveness. The results were profound.

The interviews seemed to encourage people to reinforce success stories about the organization at its participatory best. In other cases, the interviews encouraged people to make positive new meaning of their past experiences. The news of the inquiry spread quickly, infiltrating everyday conversations within the organization with discussions and debate about organizational strengths, high points, and effectiveness. The inquiry itself resulted in quantifiable increases in people's attention to and valuing of the behaviors they had set out to explore. As a result of their findings, Cooperrider, Barrett, and Srivastva concluded that

> The enlightenment effect of all inquiry is a brute fact. . . . By establishing perceptual cues and frames, by providing presumptions of logic, by transmitting subtle values, by creating new language, and by extending compelling images and constraints, perhaps in all these

ways, organizational theory becomes a constructive means whereby norms, beliefs, and cultural practices may be altered.[41]

The initial feedback report presented to the clinic created such a powerful positive stir that the clinic's board asked to have this approach applied to the entire group practice. The term *Appreciative Inquiry* was first used in a footnote in this feedback report to the Cleveland Clinic.

Cooperrider, Srivastva, and colleagues at Case Western Reserve University—early pioneers such as Ron Fry, Frank Barrett, Veronica Hopper, and John Carter—continued experimenting with affirmative practices for organizational change based on a series of positive assumptions about human organizing and change:

> Organizations can and do learn from their successes—their positive deviations—times when people, functions, and the organization as a whole have been at their very best. Those positive deviations are best identified when we purposefully ask questions about peak experiences or high points.
>
> Such questions determine what we find. They uncover examples, stories, and conversations that serve as grounded theories through which the organization can learn and organize toward its peak performance and highest potential.[42]

Cooperrider's 1985 dissertation offers the original conceptualization of the theory and practice of Appreciative Inquiry. Energized by new ideas about human organizing, action research, organization development, and change, Cooperrider and his colleagues began introducing Appreciative Inquiry as a theory and practice of organization change.

In the early 1990s, Appreciative Inquiry grew rapidly as a vehicle for the development of international nongovernmental organizations (NGOs). A multimillion-dollar grant from the U.S. Agency for International Development (USAID) enabled the creation of the Global Excellence in Management (GEM) Initiative at Case Western Reserve University. Led by Ada Jo Mann, the GEM Initiative brought together teams of people from international NGOs to learn

Appreciative Inquiry and to use it as the basis for their organizational development. To date, more than a hundred international NGOs have benefited from Appreciative Inquiry.

From the beginning, businesses in the United States, Canada, and Europe also began experimenting with Appreciative Inquiry. A large accounting firm used it for leadership transition, a major corporation used it for training to eliminate sexual harassment, and an auto repair company used it to boost customer satisfaction. With each successful experiment came greater understanding of the potential of Appreciative Inquiry and the creation of new practices.

Twelve years after the original work at the Cleveland Clinic, Cooperrider and his business partner, Diana Whitney, introduced Appreciative Inquiry to a group of two hundred fifty people at GTE. Tom White, then president of the telecommunications division, had just finished speaking. A young man raised his hand. "Do you know what you're doing?" he asked. "You're unleashing a positive revolution! You're giving us tools, and you're letting us run with them. This is a positive revolution that can't be stopped!" And indeed Appreciative Inquiry began a positive revolution at GTE that led to the American Society for Training and Development Excellence in Practice Award (Managing Change) in 1997.[43]

Since those early years of experimenting and the original conception of Appreciative Inquiry, hundreds of organizations and thousands of people around the world have awakened to the positive revolution through Appreciative Inquiry. It is now a well-recognized philosophy and methodology—an emerging field of organizational change.

The Emergence of Positive Psychology

While Appreciative Inquiry was taking hold as a viable approach to organizational change, the field of psychology was similarly redefining and rethinking its principles and practices. In 1998, Martin Seligman, president of the American Psychological Association, reviewed the history of the association's research. What he discovered was shocking, with broad implications. From 1970 to 2000, forty-five thousand studies were conducted on depression, psychosis, and other forms of mental illness. During the same time a mere three hundred studies were conducted on topics related to human joy, mental health, and well-being. Seligman had not expected to find such a focus on illness and pathology in psychological research. He concluded that the field of psychology had veered far from its original goals—to identify what is best in human beings, to heal the sick, and to help people live better, happier lives.

He began immediately to reframe the work of the psychological community away from what he described as "our half-baked approach to mental illness" that is single-mindedly fixated on the "repair of damage."[44] He proposed as an alternative a rigorous pursuit of "optimal human functioning and the building of a field focusing on human strength and virtue." He established a Positive Psychology Network whose mission was

> To discover and then apply psychological knowledge acquired in scientific research to cultivate strengths and virtues: courage, optimism, interpersonal skill, work ethic, hope, honesty and perseverance. In so doing, we will increase the ability of individuals and organizations to perform at the highest levels and help people to have the most fulfilling relationships possible.[45]

A mere decade later, the positive psychology movement held a prominent place in popular Western culture. It was the topic of many books, including the best-seller *Authentic Happiness,*[46] which garnered mainstream attention for this previously alternative field of study. The Positive Psychology Center at the University of Pennsylvania promoted research, training, education, and the dissemination of positive psychology.[47] Similarly, the Masters of Applied Positive Psychology[48] and Authentic Happiness Coaching programs[49]—which together had trained over one thousand professionals internationally—taught the theory, assessments, interventions, and exercises of positive psychology. Clearly, positive psychology is a growing force in the international psychology community. Why?

It seems that psychologists, like organization development consultants, have recognized that human systems move in the direction of what they study. To contribute constructively to human and societal well-being, we need to develop a vocabulary of joy, hope, and health. The accelerating shift toward positive psychology, along with Appreciative Inquiry, may well revolutionize the way we live, work, and organize our families, communities, and businesses.

The Power of Positive Deviancy

Appreciative Inquiry spread in the field of community development as a result of a project that profoundly impacted the lives of two million people. The project, reported in the *Harvard Business Review,* was part of an intensive effort by Save the Children to reduce childhood malnutrition in Vietnam's rural villages. Consultants who studied Appreciative Inquiry at Case Western Reserve University went into several villages in the Thanh Hoa province. They looked for people they described as "positive deviants"—people who, without the benefit of additional resources, had somehow found enough food to keep their children healthy. These villagers had found a way to create positive results. The consultants soon discovered that mothers in those families collected shellfish and greens from nearby rice paddies, and they fed their children three to four times daily rather than the customary twice a day. After discovering the villagers' root cause of success, the consultants launched a program—delivered by the villagers themselves—to demonstrate to their peers what they had discovered. Within two years, 80 percent of the children participating in the project were no longer malnourished.[50]

Subsequent iterations of the program were implemented in other villages and provinces with similar success. The authors describe the power of positive deviancy:

> What is important is identifying the relevant positive deviancy within each local community and then getting everyone to adopt that behavior. The community, in other words, cures itself.[51]

This initiative clearly demonstrates that purposeful Appreciative Inquiry into what works can have revolutionary and life-saving implications. When given information and tools to discover their strengths, people will adapt to and emulate what's best. When "positive deviants"—successful but uncommon patterns of inter-action—are discovered and shared, the life-giving knowledge of a community or organization expands.

Lifting Up a Global Organization

One of the earliest global experiments with Appreciative Inquiry began when William Swing, the Episcopal bishop of Northern Cali-fornia, received a call from the United Nations. It was the fall of 1993 and the United Nations was preparing a celebration to commemo-rate the fiftieth anniversary of its 1945 charter signing. Those orga-nizing the celebration hoped the commemoration would include an interfaith service at Grace Cathedral in San Francisco, the site of the original signing. Would Bishop Swing coordinate such a service?

Swing reflected on the call. "Though the vast majority of the world's conflicts have religious impetus," he thought, "the world's religious leaders have never gathered, as the UN leaders have for the past fifty years, to end conflicts and to work for peace. Why?"

He began talking to others, contemplating options, and visit-ing with his religious and spiritual counterparts around the world. At the fiftieth anniversary celebration, Bishop Swing articulated a highly provocative vision. He intended to create a kind of "United Nations of Religions," an organization that would bring world reli-gious and spiritual leaders together to end violence and work for peace.

Swing's ponderings did not stop there. Once he committed to the creation of a global organization, he began wondering how he would do it. Circumstances brought together David Cooper-rider and one of his graduate students, Gurudev Khalsa, with Bish-op Swing. Khalsa wanted to study the development of the United Religions. Swing agreed and invited a team of Appreciative Inquiry practitioners to join him and his small staff in creating the United Religions.

From 1995 through 2000, this team undertook one of the most complex organization development projects ever—to design and lift up an inclusive, grassroots, interfaith organization capable of local and global self-organized action. It came to be known as the United Religions Initiative (URI). Through a combination of global and regional AI Summits, a small organization design team, and regular Internet exchanges, the URI was envisioned, designed, and chartered.

For five dynamic years, the URI and the practice of Appreciative Inquiry grew side by side. Each step of the way, the team created processes and practices to do what had never been done before. To engage people from all religions and faith traditions from around the world, we refined the AI Summit methodology. To build bridges between people whose religions were at war, we carefully crafted appreciative interview questions. To balance vision with action right from the beginning, we learned to facilitate highly diverse groups of people with differing agendas.

Each year in the development of the URI offered a unique challenge:

- In June 1995 the first AI Summit was held in California. Fifty-five people from different religions as well as business, education, and community leaders attended. They responded to the summit's title, A Call to Action, by forging a shared vision of a global interfaith organization and outlining a plan to begin to realize that vision.

- In June 1996 two hundred people gathered on the Stanford University campus in California to discover the Vision, Values, and Action Agendas for the URI. Regional summits were held in Europe, Africa, and South America in the year that followed.

- In June 1997 the two hundred fifty people who attended the summit discussed the daunting task of writing a charter. They organized into twelve R&D groups to study topics related to the charter and offer proposals in time for the next year's summit. The R&D group that formed to study alternative organization designs introduced Dee Hock, former CEO of the Visa Corporation and founder of the Chaordic Alliance, to the URI. Hock and his team came on board and guided the work of the design team.

- In June 1998 approximately two hundred people gathered to review a draft Preamble, Purpose, and Principles put together by the design team. They committed to a project called 72 Hours of Peace to mark the turn of the century, which was ultimately carried out at dozens of locations around the world.

- In June 1999, with the charter signing just one year away, the meeting had a full agenda. More than two hundred people in attendance reviewed and provided input to the proposed organization design. They experimented with ways to initiate and organize Cooperation Circles, the most local unit of URI's organization. And they discussed the ideal characteristics of a Global Council member.

- In June 2000 over three hundred people assembled in Pittsburgh for the United Religions Initiative charter signing and celebration. Participants self-organized to realize the purpose of the URI: *"to promote enduring, daily interfaith cooperation, to end religiously motivated violence, and to create cultures of peace, justice, and healing for Earth and all living beings."*

On its tenth anniversary, the URI comprised over four hundred Cooperation Circles in seventy-two countries, with more than twenty multiregion clusters. Including outreach for youth and children, environmental projects, economic development, peace building, and work on HIV/AIDS, URI activities engage well over one million people annually around the world. In addition, the organization now serves as an educational hub for people seeking information about both world religions and peace building, and it is an active supporter of the United Nations International Day of Peace.

Charles Gibbs, executive director of the United Religions Initiative, believes that in discovering Appreciative Inquiry:

> The URI found a process for creating an organization that reflected the values we felt the organization should embody. At the center of those values was a belief in the essential nature of interfaith cooperation that honors, indeed celebrates, diversity and yet constantly strives to discover common vision leading to shared action for a better world.[52]

In partnership with members of the URI around the world, we advanced the field of Appreciative Inquiry into interfaith cooperation and peace building. As a result, religious organizations, churches, synagogues, and interfaith groups worldwide are using Appreciative Inquiry for organization development.

The Capacity for Rapid Change

Over years of experience, Appreciative Inquiry has proven itself as a process for enhancing an organization's capacity for accelerated positive change. By bringing together all the stakeholders of an organization and using Appreciative Inquiry, shared visions can be crafted, decisions can be made, and actions can be committed to in a relatively short period of time. When the whole system engages in an inquiry into the positive core of the organization, changes never thought possible can be rapidly and easily mobilized.

Nowhere is this more clearly demonstrated than in the case of Nutrimental Foods in Curitiba, Brazil. When founder and CEO Rodrigo Loures first learned of Appreciative Inquiry, his company was undercapitalized and deeply challenged. Loures believed that a turnaround would depend on the organization's ability to focus on people development and its capacity to promote accelerated organizational learning.

With this as a motivation, he embarked upon a bold experiment with Appreciative Inquiry and hosted a whole-system AI Summit. He turned one of the company's warehouses into a giant meeting room by replacing food processing and packaging equipment with plastic chairs, flip charts, a stage, and microphones. He gathered all seven hundred employees and included dozens of customers and suppliers. They spent four days clarifying the organization's purpose and short-term operating strategies by going through the Appreciative Inquiry 4-D Cycle.

The meeting was an immediate success. It gave people a chance to talk over what they believed needed to be done to turn the company around. It generated energy and enthusiasm for the future of the business. Within six months, the company realized a 400 percent increase in profitability and a notable increase in employee satisfaction.

Loures and his leadership team at Nutrimental decided to repeat what worked: they initiated whole-system AI Summits as annual events. They continued to invite all employees, each year including more customers, suppliers, and interested outside parties. And each year they took on topics of greater organizational significance, such as organizational purpose, strategy, structure, governance, and strategic social responsibility. As the effort unfolded, the bottom-line results were staggering:

- A 66 percent increase in sales.
- A 422 percent increase in profitability.
- A 42 percent improvement in productivity.
- A 95 percent level of employee satisfaction.

In addition, significant savings were realized because of the speed with which major changes could now be implemented. In 2000, for example, the company undertook the conversion of its Enterprise Resource Planning (ERP) system. The average implementation time for an ERP conversion is one and a half to two years; Nutrimental converted its system in only six months. This unexpected benefit yielded bottom-line savings beyond those that had already been tracked.

Nutrimental was recently named one of the top one hundred

best companies to work for in Brazil. Loures believes that this and other accomplishments have flowed naturally from its culture of appreciation and from its relentless commitment to balance the triple bottom line: people, environment, and profits. Over its five-year journey, Nutrimental has demonstrated over and over that Appreciative Inquiry promotes the capacity for rapid change. It creates organizational agility—is a strategic advantage, if not a must, in today's chaotic business environment.

Optimal Financial Performance Through Employee Engagement

Some of the boldest experiments with Appreciative Inquiry have been by companies seeking to enhance financial performance. When Roadway Express executives found Appreciative Inquiry, they recognized it as a powerful approach to change through which they could implement their vision of employee engagement at every level. To test their hypothesis, they experimented with a summit-style implementation of Appreciative Inquiry at four of their large strategic locations. Akron 211 was one of these sites. The purpose of its initiative was *Winning with Employee-Driven Throughput: Delivering Unsurpassed Speed and Leveraging Employee Pride and Involvement.* During the summit, employees from every job classification and from all levels of the organization participated in appreciative interviews, mapped the positive core, and self-organized into opportunity groups in which they crafted aspiration statements. In the end, they formed eight topic teams to ensure the ongoing success of the summit's purpose.

In the months that followed, these topic teams organized themselves for success. They fashioned a steering committee consisting of one person from each topic team. The steering committee met monthly to review progress, evaluate proposals, coordinate resources, and monitor for duplication of efforts. They also instituted a process for drawing more employees into the effort through topic-specific minisummits. Within the first year they hoped to engage more than half of the employees in the facilities in interviews, summits, or topic teams.

Without question, Roadway achieved its original objective of enhancing employee engagement. But what were the business results? One topic team tracked its financial progress. By first educating employees in the actual cost of materials and then engaging them in imagining better ways of doing things, this team achieved a series of what they called "small wins" in the first five months of their initiative:

- Dunnage costs reduced 31.6 percent, for a total saving of $4,100.
- Cost of skids reduced 66 percent, for a saving of $7,600.
- Airbag costs reduced 53 percent, for a saving of $60,000.

However, one of this team's wins was financially spectacular. After participating in the summit, a driver and a mechanic went to work on eliminating driver delay time. While investigating the delays, the team discovered that a great number were caused by overloads. When drivers had to wait for excess weight to be removed, service was negatively affected, and ultimately less cargo could be shipped. As they examined the issue more closely, the team discovered that the overloads were related to the size of the fuel tanks on some of the fleet's tractors. When this model of tractor was fueled to capacity, it became much heavier than other tractors in the fleet, resulting in overloading.

Realizing that either gas or cargo had to go, the team fashioned an ordinary fuel stick into a customized fuel gauge. The stick was placed into the gas tank while fueling—and fueling would stop when the marked line was hit. The simple solution virtually eliminated overloads. More importantly, however, it created space for an additional 2800 pounds of freight to be loaded into the trailers. As a result, this terminal has been able to save approximately $10,000 per month.

Because this and other early implementations of Appreciative Inquiry were so successful, the company chose to spread the approach to five additional strategic locations in the year that followed. As this experience shows, Appreciative Inquiry provides opportunities for employees to discover and generate a myriad of innovative and profitable ideas and put them into action on behalf of the organization.

A New Breed of Loyalty

As Appreciative Inquiry has grown, so has its applicability to questions of employee satisfaction, retention, and loyalty. For example, it has often been used to stop the flow of employee turnover. Inquiry into the conditions and causes of employee retention has led many companies to become the employer of choice in their geographic area or industry. Lovelace Health Systems is a great example of a company that solved the problem of high turnover.

In early 2001, Lovelace Health Systems in Albuquerque found itself plagued with nurse turnover rates as high as the national averages, ranging from 18 percent to 30 percent per year. The result was a variety of operational challenges, including short staffing, unfilled vacancies, low morale among staff and providers, continuous hiring of new people, and significant disruption of teamwork. Kathleen Davis, vice president of hospital operations, committed to address this crisis using a fresh, positive approach that would be congruent with Lovelace's vision "to be the best place to get care and the best place to give care." When she learned about Appreciative Inquiry, she knew it was the way to go.

She had applied for and received a Robert Wood Johnson Fellowship, which required a leadership project as part of the curriculum. Having selected the issue of nurse retention as the focus for her project, she chose Appreciative Inquiry as her methodology. The purpose of her project was straightforward and provocative: *to discover why nurses choose to stay at Lovelace—and to gather this insight in such a way that the process in and of itself contributes positively and minimizes negativity.*

Within a hospital population of over three hundred nurses, forty nurses conducted one hundred appreciative interviews. After several months of inquiry, a minisummit was conducted to make meaning of the stories and move forward through the latter phases of the 4-D Cycle. At the end of the summit, action groups chose to develop programs for a Nurses Day Celebration, recruitment and retention, orientation, training, and ongoing communication—as well as story-based recognition systems.

Susan Wood, consultant to the project, described some of the immediate benefits:

> The Appreciative Inquiry training provided value beyond the project. It affected how people asked questions, evaluated things, and approached difficult situations and conversations. It transformed the hallway talk in palpable and positive ways.
>
> At the same time, camaraderie within nursing increased. The process unleashed nurses' capability and energy to realize their value within the system. It gave nurses a heightened responsibility for their own satisfaction.

In addition, the hospital tracked quantitative changes in nurses' satisfaction and loyalty. Within less than one year they had documented improvements on the nurse segment of the annual climate survey ranging from eleven to twenty-two points. Perceptions of employee communication had improved the most, and there was a thirteen-point increase in nurse retention. This was more than a 30 percent reduction in turnover in one year. In addition, within eighteen months, patient satisfaction with nursing care improved from the thirtieth to the fortieth percentile ranking on the Press Ganey patient satisfaction measure.

Appreciative Inquiry gave the nurses at Lovelace a chance to do what they do best—care for patients and families—only now they were caring for each other as well. It brought out their best, personally and collectively, and gave them confidence that they could depend on one another.

The project at Lovelace Health Systems is one of a growing

number of Appreciative Inquiry initiatives in health-care facilities. Family practice clinics, major medical centers, assisted-living centers, and university hospitals have all used Appreciative Inquiry with equal success.

Appreciative Inquiry: A Field Is Born

Beginning in the 1990s, Appreciative Inquiry gained a following, in part because of its affirmative stance, in part because it got results. In the fall of 2001, just weeks after September 11, a group of twenty-two Appreciative Inquiry innovators, including ourselves, hosted the First International Appreciative Inquiry Conference. Five hundred people gathered from nine countries to share stories of their work with Appreciative Inquiry and to hear the new ideas and work of Appreciative Inquiry thought leaders David Cooperrider, Diana Whitney, Jane Watkins, Jim Ludema, Barbara Sloan, Frank Barrett, Marge Schiller, Bernard Mohr, and Ada Jo Mann. Two years later, a second international conference attracted a still larger group.

By the time of the third conference, Appreciative Inquiry had become what Robert Quinn described as a "positive revolution in the field of organization development and change management."[53] AI's radically affirmative approach—its focus on identifying and cultivating strengths—is now a widely recognized and valued approach to human and organizational change, as shown in the parallel development in such fields as positive psychology, positive leadership, and positive organizational scholarship.

In recent years, organization development literature has begun reflecting that *something new* is unfolding. For example, in their article titled "Revisioning Organization Development," Gervase Bushe and Robert Marshak suggest that "a different kind of OD practice has emerged, . . . based on different philosophical notions than those in foundational OD theory and practice."[54] They describe Appreciative Inquiry as having "most clearly articulated [this new] stance," which they further describe as Dialogic OD.

A variety of Fortune 500 companies, Big Five consulting firms, and religious denominations—even the United Nations—have used Appreciative Inquiry to institute change and drive results. AI is being studied in graduate programs and workshops around the world in multiple languages. Consultants and organizations now specialize in various applications, from large-scale organizational change to leadership development, evaluation, coaching, and even parenting. Indeed, the existence of this Second Edition of our best-selling book is a testimony to the many ways in which Appreciative Inquiry has come of age.

Collaborative from its inception, the field of Appreciative Inquiry continues to grow through an open exchange of ideas among practitioners and scholars, supported through venues such as the Appreciative Inquiry Commons: "a worldwide portal devoted to the fullest sharing of academic resources and practical tools on Appreciative Inquiry and the rapidly growing *discipline of positive change*."[55] Within the field, great value is placed on the interdependent development of theory and practice: good theory enables practical experiments, which in turn generate new ideas about human organizing and change. Cases such as the ones in this chapter are shared regularly as sources of learning and development.

Introducing Hunter Douglas Window Fashions Division

And now we introduce Hunter Douglas Window Fashions Division (Hunter Douglas)—a story we will weave into the rest of this book. Beginning in 1997, Hunter Douglas went through three separate iterations of the AI 4-D Cycle, designed to address three separate Change Agendas.

The first initiative, dubbed *Focus 2000,* centered on culture transformation; the second focused on strategic planning; the third, *Focus on Excellence,* concentrated on the development of customer-friendly business processes and business process improvement. In all three initiatives, participants went through all phases of the AI 4-D Cycle.

We have chosen to illustrate the concepts in this book with the Hunter

Douglas case for a variety of reasons. First, it tells the story of a Whole-System 4-D Dialogue that involved not only employees but also customers, suppliers, and community members. Next, it demonstrates AI's effect on people and organizations—how inquiry leads to innovation. Further, it shows how the same basic tools and processes can be adapted to a variety of Change Agendas. Finally, it demonstrates the unfolding, improvisational nature of Appreciative Inquiry. In short, the Hunter Douglas case illustrates the best of what Appreciative Inquiry can be.

But let's begin at the beginning and discover what led Hunter Douglas to Appreciative Inquiry in the first place.

The Beginning

In the early 1970s, on a wintry night in a big drafty Victorian house in Massachusetts, a young man was shivering in bed. It was the middle of the energy crisis. Thermostats were turned down in homes and offices across America. Motorists were gnashing their teeth at gasoline shortages. Everyone was asking questions about how to conserve energy.

Wendell Colson, a young inventor, contemplated what could be done to cover his windows—to keep the warm air in and the cold air out. As he pondered his dilemma, he noticed that a double curtain on one of the windows had come together in a series of folds that trapped air between them: a honeycomb-like configuration created a thermal insulating effect. He grabbed onto this accidental observation and the next day started playing with it. Soon he had a product that resulted in the transformation of both a company and an industry.

Eventually, Colson and his product found their way to the president of a small entrepreneurial company outside of Denver. He and the president, Dick Steele, eventually formed Thermal Technology Corporation. Soon they began manufacturing the Thermocell—a pleated window shade in the shape of a honeycomb, designed as a functional, energy-saving window covering.

Recognizing that they didn't have the resources to realize the product's full potential, the owners approached several window covering manufacturers about a possible purchase of the product. Eventually they reached Hunter Douglas—the New Jersey-based company that had pioneered the first aluminum venetian blinds in the 1940s and 1950s. Hunter Douglas saw the unique shade and quickly recognized its potential—not just as a functional energy efficient product but also as an exciting new decorative window fashion.

The Birth of the Window Fashions Division

In 1985, Hunter Douglas International purchased the twenty-seven-person Thermal Technology Corporation and established Hunter Douglas Window Fashions Division.

The division immediately began to manufacture and market Duette® shades—a unique variation of the Thermocell-like honeycomb shade, soon made with soft, durable fabric in a selection of colors. The highly functional and energy efficient shade was also successfully promoted as fashion for the home—a stylish and aesthetically appealing window covering targeted for the upscale consumer. From a marketing perspective, this was a revolutionary step for an industry that had previously marketed its products based almost exclusively on functionality.

Two years later the division had over a hundred people but continued to operate like a small "mom-and-pop" shop. Manufacturing machines were still made of wood and were burned when they became obsolete. Budgets were still calculated by hand on green ledger forms. Professional leadership was still a work in progress. Everyone knew everyone else—and somehow things got done.

Eventually, Hunter Douglas North America brought in Marvin Hopkins, a marketing genius from Lenox China, to become the new general manager. And things began to change—a lot. First came the neckties. As one person recalls, "This was back in the days when our idea of dressing up was to wear jeans without holes and T-shirts with sleeves." As the story is told, inventor Wendell Colson placed an article from *Scientific American* on Hopkins's desk describing how neckties reduced the blood supply to the brain—but to no avail.

Then came the classical music on the receptionist's hold button, the beginning of a comprehensive marketing network, and the initial establishment of the company's "push/pull" marketing strategy. Bit by bit, the Window Fashions Division began to establish its image as a high-end, even upscale organization—and a company to watch.

As the division worked to invent itself, Duette® took off like a rocket. The product achieved unprecedented success and renewed consumer interest in window coverings—an industry that hadn't seen a significant new product introduction in decades. Retail sales soared to an estimated three hundred million dollars by 1988, driving the company to increasing levels of complexity and sophistication.

Several years later, the division introduced a second unique proprietary product with early and explosive sales. Featuring soft fabric vanes suspended between sheer facing, it looked like a sheer curtain, rolled up like a shade, and had rotating vanes for light control. Like its predecessor, Silhouette® window shadings garnered top national design awards and became the fastest-growing window fashion in North America. Within two years of Silhouette's release, profits from the two products made Window Fashions the leading revenue-producing division in the entire Hunter Douglas organization.

The Unintended Consequences of Success

New products and blossoming market interest invited increasing sophistication from the organization and its leadership—and imitation by other parts of the organization. Two of the division's presidents were promoted in a single year, and Rick Pellett, former chief financial officer, assumed the position of general manager.

Pellett inherited an organization that had grown to nearly seven hundred people, three separate product lines, four separate buildings, and plans to launch another new product within the next two years. Through rapid and successful growth, the organization had changed—and not entirely for the better. It had outgrown the speed, intimacy, and sense of community that had originally facilitated its success.

In an effort to regain some of their original community spirit, Pellett and his new leadership team elected to split the division into separate business units. But instead of building a greater sense of community, the change created bigger silos—bigger chasms over which already inadequate communication had to reach. Leaders lost touch with the day-to-day aspects of the business, while production employees lost touch with everything outside their immediate functional or operational areas.

In addition to bigger challenges in the area of communication, the new business unit also called upon the services of every single one of the division's experienced leaders—and many of its inexperienced ones. People who just two years before had been serving as front-line supervisors were now running business units. Behaviors that had initially made people successful—a "can-do" attitude and the capacity to get things done— were interfering with the division's capacity to develop powerful midlevel leadership.

The new structure further obscured people's already fuzzy sense of purpose, direction, and community. The workforce showed decreasing levels of motivation and initiative, resulting in decreasing levels of productivity. Turnover increased at a time when the need for new recruits was at an all-time high. From top to bottom, people were frustrated, in over their heads, and confused about the organization's overall mission, vision, and direction. And to top it all off, the results of the annual employee opinion survey showed downward trends in employees' experience of Hunter Douglas.

In the hallways, cafeterias, and break rooms, people wistfully recalled the good old days. Who are we becoming? and Where are we heading? were more than abstract questions for employees and leaders who were overwhelmed, saddened, and confused by what was happening. The leaders eventually did the right thing. They began looking for ways to recapture what had been lost and to build an organization for the future from the best of the past.

This is the end of the introduction to the Hunter Douglas story, which continues in Chapter 5.

Getting Started with Appreciative Inquiry

A lot must happen in an organization before an Appreciative Inquiry 4-D Cycle process can begin. These preliminary activities are what we call Getting Started. Some organizations like to start quickly and plan as they go; others want a detailed route map, predetermined ways to measure results, and clear leadership roles and responsibilities in place before beginning. All organizations, however, face common decisions, and this chapter offers guidelines for this preliminary process.

In this chapter you will discover the essential decisions for Getting Started and will find step-by-step suggestions for creating an Advisory Team, for determining the scope of an AI project, for developing an Inquiry Strategy, and for beginning to engage large numbers of people in a long-term AI process. Finally, you will read more about Hunter Douglas and how they began their Appreciative Inquiry process.

Key Decisions in Getting Started

One decision takes precedence over all others in Getting Started: the decision to proceed with Appreciative Inquiry. Once an organization makes this decision, all others follow. Beyond the decision to proceed, organizations make a variety of big-picture decisions that focus the initiative and scope of the project, creating a strategy for the overall effort, thus establishing the parameters of the overall process. Some important considerations in Getting Started with Appreciative Inquiry include:

- *Is Appreciative Inquiry appropriate for us?* Are we ready for a fully affirmative approach to change? Are we truly open to learning?

- *What is our Change Agenda?* What are we trying to create? Are we shifting culture, merging two organizations, creating a strategic vision and direction, or improving business processes?

- *Who will serve on our Advisory Team?* Who needs to be involved from formal and informal leadership? Who can commit resources? Who has influence? Who is excited to participate? How do we represent the whole system on the team?

- *What training does our Advisory Team need?* Is the experience of an appreciative interview enough or do they need more?

- *What Form of Engagement will we use?* Given our Change Agenda, our sense of urgency, resources, business, and culture, what is the best form of Appreciative Inquiry for us?

- *What will our Inquiry Strategy be?* When will our inquiry take place? Who will champion which parts of the engagement? What process will we use to conduct interviews? Through what process will we dream, design, and deliver ongoing changes to the system?

- *How and when will we introduce the process to the organization?* How can we best launch the initiative? What will people want and need to know? What is the best way to build interest, excitement, and initial momentum?

Deciding to Proceed with Appreciative Inquiry

Considerations about whether to proceed with Appreciative Inquiry begin when people first hear about or experience the philosophy and practice. They may read an article, attend a briefing, or simply see Appreciative Inquiry's effects on another organization, department, or colleague. Appreciative Inquiry stimulates curiosity because its results are unquestionably positive and the approach is so unique. When people hear about it, they often want to learn more about what it is and how it might work for them. In our experience, the primary vehicle in deciding to proceed with Appreciative Inquiry is a sound introduction.

Introducing Appreciative Inquiry

Introductory sessions may last a few hours or several days. They may involve a group of executives or a diverse group from all areas of the organization. Whoever the audience is, the introduction needs to accomplish two goals: to provide an understanding of the philosophy and practice of Appreciative Inquiry and to help decision makers explore ways Appreciative Inquiry might benefit their organization. We offer the following tips for introducing Appreciative Inquiry:

- *Involve the whole system.* Involve as diverse a group as possible in both the introductory session and any decision to use Appreciative Inquiry. At the very least, include both traditional leaders and informal opinion leaders. At best, involve a microcosm of the organization, including people from a variety of functions, levels, tenures, socioethnic communities, and interest groups. By engaging the whole system in the introductory session, you give the organization an experience of the power of full-voice participation. At the same time, you drive positive anticipation into the organizational grapevine and begin the long-term process of transforming the organization's inner dialogue from cynicism to hope.

• *Facilitate an interview experience.* The introduction may be loosely designed around the 4-D model, but always, *always* include an appreciative interview, however brief. Mini-interviews give people a taste of the power—the affect—and what one executive described as the intimacy of the Appreciative Inquiry process. A tried-and-true approach is to ask people to partner with someone they don't know well and then answer the question, What was a peak experience or high point in your professional, organizational, or personal life?

Experiencing the mini-interview creates both a conscious and unconscious desire to re-create peak experiences—moving in the direction of what works. It tangibly demonstrates the capacity of AI to build relationships among diverse stakeholder groups. The four mini-interview core questions can be found in Figure 8, in Chapter 6.

We are firmly committed to this mini-interview experience, even when circumstances require us to modify the format. For example, when leaders in the Accenture organization took part in their four-hour introduction, two of the ten participants were teleconferenced in to the presentation. We showed PowerPoint slides on the company's network and on the screen in the conference room. When it came time for interviews, we arranged breakout office space, and four people interviewed four others by phone. Feedback from the virtual interviews was extraordinarily positive, leading to continued exploration of how AI could be used to design the "workplace of the future" in the Chicago office.

• *Introduce principles and the 4-D Cycle.* As you introduce AI principles and the 4-D Cycle, find ways to bring your descriptions to life with stories. Acquaint yourself with stories about other organizations that have successfully used Appreciative Inquiry in ways that are similar to those being considered by participants. The stories may come in the form of straight narrative, articles, videos, or even guest presenters. Even in business and corporate settings, be bold! Share accounts of

Appreciative Inquiry in social-profit and nongovernment organizations (NGOs) as well as in businesses.

Stories bring AI principles and practices to life and help people experience the shift from trying to solve problems from the past to anticipating and focusing on the future. They help people to see and understand how Appreciative Inquiry differs from their previous experiences of organizational change. Stories inspire new conversations, giving people the refreshing experience of talking about successes, best practices, and dreams for the future as a foundation for planning. In short, they encourage people to want to learn more.

• *Focus on applications.* Allow time for participants to examine alternative approaches for Appreciative Inquiry. Engage people in real-time conversations about whether they think Appreciative Inquiry makes sense, and why. Ask them to reflect on and discuss how to use it in their organization, department, or community.

As they consider how to move forward, encourage people to use Appreciative Inquiry to do what already needs doing rather than creating some sort of parallel "program du jour." Green Mountain Coffee Roasters, for example, considered a variety of applications during their AI introduction—everything from strategic planning to pure culture change. In the end, they arrived at an application that enhanced both efforts while also creating immediate effects in the area of business process improvement.

Facilitating the Decision to Proceed

Wherever possible, end even the briefest introductory presentation with some sort of go/no-go decision-making conversation. Once decision makers experience the Appreciative Inquiry process, imagine a variety of approaches, and consider applications within the organization, they are ready to consider important questions about what's next: *Are we ready for a fully affirmative approach to change? Are we open to the personal and organizational learning and change that will surely accompany inquiry?* The answer may be yes, no, or maybe. Participants may determine to go forward on a limited basis or to gather more information.

If you are working with people who want to gather more information before deciding to proceed, share relevant contact information and materials that can help them connect with and explore other organizations' successful implementations. If you are working with people who are ready to take the leap of faith, help them clarify their next steps, self-organize to get going, and schedule a Getting Started planning meeting.

Getting Started, Step by Step

Depending on the size and scope of the project involved, Getting Started activities may be completed in days, weeks, or months—in this era of rapid change, the activities should not take longer. Table 6 summarizes the five steps that broadly take place during this phase. The first two Getting Started activities focus on getting an Advisory Team in place and trained to lead the initiative. Once the Advisory Team is formed, the ball is in their court.

Create an Advisory Team

As soon as you get to yes on an AI initiative, establish an Advisory Team of eight to twelve people. Ideally, this group will be drawn from a variety of functions, levels, and disciplines that collectively represent the entire organization. Their multiple backgrounds will promote depth and breadth of thinking. Their multiple skills will promote creativity and diversity in delivery of the process. Their multiple perspectives will allow them to design an initiative that engages the most people possible in meaningful and inspiring ways.

Regardless of their backgrounds, Advisory Team members share several intangible qualifications. Ideally, they are informal

Table 6. Getting Started, Step by Step
1. Create an Advisory Team.
2. Train the Advisory Team.
3. Determine the scope of the project.
4. Draft the Inquiry Strategy.
5. Build organization-wide awareness.

leaders—people who command the respect of those participating in the inquiry, even without an associated title. Their life philosophies and personalities are consistent with Appreciative Inquiry, even if they have not been formally trained in the practice. They are interested in and committed to the project's purpose and outcomes. They want to participate. And finally, they are vested, through the organization's formal leadership, with authority to implement both the inquiry and the changes that emerge.

The role of an Advisory Team is to lead the organization into a calculated leap into the unknown—to engage people in ways that stimulate their curiosity and imagination and increase their willingness to experiment. Together, Advisory Team members make detailed decisions about who to involve in the initiative, in what ways, and to what end.

Although the Advisory Teams' day-to-day responsibilities vary among the initiatives, their overall purpose and function is constant. In general, they design, launch, and maintain organizational momentum for the initiative—and where necessary, adjust or shift course as the engagement progresses. They do so by ensuring that the project receives full, timely support throughout its life. This involves making several start-up decisions and backing up those decisions through a variety of ongoing supportive activities.

The role of the Advisory Team includes the following:

- *Determining the scope of the project.* The Advisory Team's first task is to clarify the intended Change Agenda—often referred to as the Purpose and Outcomes. Next, they select an overall approach to AI, or Form of Engagement. Finally, they design an Inquiry Strategy that will achieve the overall goals. This last activity involves answering a series of additional questions described in depth later in this chapter.

- *Building awareness and support.* Early in their tenure, Advisory Teams determine how to build organizational awareness and support for the initiative. This involves introducing the process in enough detail for people to understand and support it.

  Some Advisory Teams build support by establishing a brand identity or name for the initiative—for instance, The Power of Two, Simply Better, and Focus 2000. Others simply introduce the process through letters to all employees, videos in cafeterias, small-group gatherings, or large kickoff meetings.

- *Keeping communication flowing.* Particularly when engagements take place over an extended period, Advisory Teams foster timely and authentic communication throughout the effort. This communication provides continuity, accelerates learning within the organization as a whole, and maintains momentum between large-scale activities and events.

  Once an initiative has been launched, Advisory Team members serve as spokespersons—sharing information, listening to people's feedback, and promoting the process. In addition, they ensure a continuous flow of compelling, personal, story-based communication—delivered through videos, newsletters, banners, posters, and buttons, along with formal presentations in department and plant meetings. In some cases advisors will designate a subgroup to perform these activities.

- *Keeping the process integrated.* Depending on the complexity of the initiative, multiple groups of people may act simultaneously on a variety of tasks and activities. When this is the case, Advisory Teams also serve as project integrators by: keeping informed of the activities and resource requirements of various groups; ensuring that each group is building upon, rather than pulling against, the work of other groups; and promoting

Figure 6.   Tips for Appreciative Inquiry Coaching

Create opportunities for equal voice. Ensure equal air time for all—especially those whose voices are not often heard. Be a model of respect and good listening.
Focus on the affirmative. Consciously solicit, draw out, build on, and reinforce stories of what works. Help people achieve at least a two-to-one ratio of positive to negative talk.
Help people speak from the inside out. Share the hopes, dreams, and passions that are rooted in your personal experience, and encourage others to do the same.
Give away the power. Check your tendency to be the expert. Regardless of how people might treat you, stay in the back seat. Use questions to help people find their wisdom. Express confidence in their abilities to make decisions.
Be sure they succeed. Catch people doing things right and publicly recognize them for it. Help people make commitments that they intend and are able to keep. Connect them to resources, including people whose expertise can support what they are trying to accomplish.

alignment among the activities of the groups and the overall purpose of the inquiry.

• *Coaching for success.* One important responsibility of the Advisory Team is to provide ongoing coaching to ensure the success of the Appreciative Inquiry effort. We suggest that Advisory Teams discuss what it means to be a coach for an Appreciative Inquiry process. Often we provide tips such as those in Figure 6.

Train the Advisory Team

To fulfill their role, members of an Advisory Team need to understand Appreciative Inquiry. Three to four days of training in Appreciative Inquiry philosophy and practice can accomplish this. Participation in a training program also serves as a team builder. It can help team members get to know one another, establish positive, trusting relationships, and share their hopes and dreams for the organization. This in turn equips them to lead the organization on its journey of positive change.

We suggest that whenever possible, you give your Advisory Team the opportunity to attend an offsite Appreciative Inquiry training. Although in-house training is both useful and cost-effective, offsite training of the Advisory Team is a significant predictor of success for long-term initiatives. It provides the following:

- Gives members of the team space and time away for bonding and learning.
- Grounds members in the philosophy and practice of AI and its various applications, both proven and cutting edge.
- Helps members see themselves as a team in service to their larger organizational system.
- Places members in the larger community of Appreciative Inquiry practitioners.
- Gives members time for planning first steps in their process.

If you choose to deliver the Advisory Team training in-house, try to replicate as many offsite conditions as possible. Establish ground rules that protect people from the day-to-day responsibilities and activities of their work. Tell stories of other organizations' successes and insights. Build in prework and field trips that connect people to what is happening in the larger world of Appreciative Inquiry. Bring outsiders into the training to tell their stories "testimonial" style.

Determine the Scope of the Project

The next important task in Getting Started is to clearly determine what you are inquiring into, and to what end. We described this earlier as clarifying the Change Agenda and selecting an overall Form of Engagement. Chapter 2, "A Menu of Approaches to Appreciative Inquiry," offers options for both.

Committing to a Change Agenda

At this point, the Advisory Team works with the organization's executive team to determine the overall Change Agenda. Considering all that is happening in the organization, they put a stake in the ground. Will this effort focus on people, as the Value-Inspired People process did at British Airways? Or will it focus on customers, as did Canadian Tire's project? Together, the two teams choose a Change Agenda with strategic importance for the organization.

The overall purpose of the effort must be clearly articulated as a starting point for transformation. Consider these examples of Change Agendas for which Appreciative Inquiry has been used:

- Culture transformation at GTE, described in Chapter 2.
- Cross-gender working relationships at Avon Mexico, described in Chapter 9.
- Merging state and county child welfare services in Nevada, described in Chapter 3.
- Nursing retention at Lovelace Health Systems, described in Chapter 4.

In our experience, any lack of clarity in a Change Agenda is magnified over time, creating an unnecessary sense of disorder and confusion for members of the organization. A clear Change Agenda integrates and aligns departments and functions, creating a sense of confidence among members of the organization.

We are often asked how to use Appreciative Inquiry in situations of conflict or controversy. The answer lies in finding a Change Agenda that both transcends the conflict or controversy and compels collaborative action.

During a recent Foundations of Appreciative Inquiry workshop, a consultant who was working with multiple, conflicting divisions of an organization asked, "What is the best way to establish communication and ultimately collaboration? Should we focus on the relationships among them or something else?" Divisions that had worked for years in silos were now being asked by the corporation to collaborate to enhance customer service. Once we heard this, a Change Agenda that would require everyone to work together toward a higher purpose was clear: Partnership for Outstanding Customer Service.

Barbara Child used a similar strategy when she was asked to work with a church in a metropolitan area that included five other nearby churches of the same denomination. Rather than focusing on one church as a silo, she invited all six into an Appreciative Inquiry process, whose Change Agenda was to "discover the future of Unitarian-Universalism in the Greater Indianapolis area." According to Child, the results were surprisingly positive for everyone involved, including herself. "Even after the first planning meeting, people started behaving differently and imagining new possibilities. Appreciative Inquiry created a cooperative spirit among our congregations. It filled us all with joy, pride, and a sense of shared purpose."

Choose your Change Agenda wisely. Involve diverse stakeholders in dialogue about the Change Agenda to ensure that the purpose of your Appreciative Inquiry process matters deeply to everyone and will engender commitment.

Choosing a Form of Engagement

Be bold—choose a Form of Engagement that models the organization you want to be. The bolder you are in your Form of Engagement, the bolder and more dramatic will be the results you experience. As you consider which Appreciative Inquiry Form of Engagement to embark upon, think about the following: How fast do you want to see results? How many people do you want to involve? How will you involve stakeholders?

If you truly want change, the Form of Engagement you select will go against the status quo of your organization. You have to decide how far to go in challenging the status quo right from the start. For example, as illustrated in Chapter 4, closing down a manufacturing plant and bringing all seven hundred employees together for an AI Summit was a bold move for Nutrimental Foods, but this bold move paid off with immediate and significant increases in sales, profitability, productivity, and employee satisfaction.

Draft the Inquiry Strategy

The best inquiry strategy is the one that achieves the Change Agenda over time in ways that are congruent with an organization's culture and resources. The task of determining an Inquiry Strategy can be quite complex, because it is developed in response to multiple questions—to which there are no right or wrong answers—and it continues to unfold throughout the life of the initiative.

Still, a few macro-level choices about an Inquiry Strategy must be made during the Getting Started phase or the process will never get off the ground. Advisory Teams must find their own answers to each of these questions. By doing so, they will begin to frame a process that will engage the right people in the right ways, gain momentum over time, and focus organizational attention on sharing and learning about best practices and possibilities.

When Will the Inquiry Take Place? Will you benefit more from interrupting or maintaining "business as usual"? Are you looking for longer-term, more emergent change—or a quick and dramatic shift in the way things are done?

Generally, when more interviews are scheduled and more people are involved, a longer time frame is required. Whole-system inquiries, involving hundreds of one-to-one interviews, often take place over two to four months. You may schedule these inquiries during slow times in your business cycle or compress them by completing the inquiry as part of an AI Summit.

Longer Appreciative Inquiry processes and longer AI Summits have advantages. Longer inquiries can run parallel to other activities and programs over time. They invite spontaneous grassroots innovations, improvements, and advancements. AI Summits, by comparison, require less time overall but have higher costs and require greater levels of short-term involvement. They can jump-start systemwide shifts, forging unlikely opportunities for inspiration, partnership, and action.

In both settings, people learn about themselves, one another, and new ways of doing business. They then take the best of what they have learned and adapt it to their work situation. Without specific effort, both appreciative interviews and summits prime the pump for organizational innovation and improvement.

Who Will Champion Which Parts of the Engagement?   Is this a leadership-driven initiative—or is it more grassroots? To what extent will you rely on volunteers versus recruits? Who needs to be involved for the effort to be successful? It is frequently counterproductive to force participation in an AI-based initiative, so it behooves you to find creative ways to inspire and engage volunteers from throughout the system. In general, seek both leadership and grassroots championship and support. To do so calls for careful planning and recruiting, particularly in the early phases of an initiative.

What Process Will We Use to Conduct Interviews?   Who needs to hear what, along with whom? How will we keep our business going while people engage in these conversations? How will we prevent interviewer burnout? Are there other opportunities for dialogue beyond a one-on-one, face-to-face conversation? In response to these questions, Advisory Teams need to consider a variety of options. Some of the most common are listed in Table 7.

- *One-on-one interviews.* This is the most common inquiry approach. The one-on-one appreciative interview is a face-to-face dialogue of thirty to ninety minutes. In some cases, such as an AI Summit, it is a mutual process in which two people take turns interviewing each other. In other situations a designated interviewer may conduct as many as ten or twenty interviews.

  One-on-one interviews are generally conducted by members of the organization. In most cases volunteers are solicited from all departments, functions, and levels to be interviewers. They are provided with an Interview Guide and are trained to conduct appreciative interviews. They interview other members of the organization, customers, vendors, and other relevant people. For further information on how to mass-mobilize one-on-one interviews, see Chapter 2, "A Menu of Approaches to Appreciative Inquiry."

Table 7. Four Approaches to Interviewing
1. One-on-one interviews.
2. Group interviews.
3. Cross-organization interviews.
4. Electronic interviews.

- *Group interviews.* In some instances, the appropriate group interview process may be similar to a focus group. Group interviews allow all group members to hear one another's ideas, get to know one another, and discover their group's positive core and best practices. Appreciative Inquiry focus groups can be conducted with customers, within departments and functions, or with mixed groups of stakeholders. The more people who are involved, the fewer questions will be needed—and the longer will be the time needed for the process.

  A particularly useful approach to group interviews is the organizational topic of the week. Throughout a particular week, all teams, departments, and divisions in the organization begin their regular meetings with the same interview questions related to the topic of the week. This process of group inquiry takes discovery and learning to the shop floor and integrates Appreciative Inquiry into the way business is conducted.

- *Cross-organization interviews.* Some of the most exciting approaches to Appreciative Inquiry come when one organization interviews another. This occurs in benchmarking, partnership and alliance building, and merger integration. We have also used this process with great success in overcoming communication barriers between business units within the same organization.

  In cross-organization inquiry, a team of interviewers from one organization interviews a group of people from another organization—and then the roles are switched. In some cases, people will interview their counterparts in the other company; in others, they will interview people from other functions to broaden their understanding of the whole business. After the conversations, interview teams prepare feedback reports and presentations, telling their interviewees what they learned. Reports detail the positive core, exemplary practices, and core competencies they discovered. They offer up interviewees' dreams for their organization's future. The reports may even contain more personal messages from the interviewers, describing what they learned and why they are proud to be partners with the organization they interviewed.

Cross-organization inquiries accelerate people's learning about business as a whole, lift people's thinking out of their particular areas of expertise, and help them think more strategically. They build the foundation for positive partnerships, alliances, and mergers.

- *Electronic interviews.* Once members of an organization become familiar with Appreciative Inquiry, it becomes possible for them to respond to online inquiries. Anyone in an organization can initiate an inquiry, open to all employees, and quickly receive ideas for approaching a business situation at hand.

In some cases, advisors will design Inquiry Strategies that combine two or more approaches. For example, they may mass-mobilize inquiry within the organization while also conducting external benchmarking or customer and supplier interviews.

How Will We Dream, Design, and Deliver Ongoing Changes? Will we move toward an AI Summit, or will we have smaller gatherings over a longer period of time? How will we involve as many people as possible in cocreating our future? How will we keep those people connected to the original data—and to the positive core that has become apparent? What will be the "shelf life" for Innovation Teams, Action Groups, and other self-organized teams dedicated to implementing ongoing changes?

As inquiries progress, you must find ways to maintain the organization's wholeness by sharing the personal and immediate connections to the compelling stories, images, hopes, and dreams that emerge during one-on-one interviews with everyone in the organization. Because these goals are most easily achieved through summits, you may choose to implement the final phases of the 4-D Cycle in this fashion.

Long-term strategies for the last three phases of the cycle are subject to the same time and resource constraints as the interviews. You may find that a large, whole-system gathering is simply not possible. You may choose instead to design smaller-scale processes such as Innovation Teams that maintain continuity with earlier activities, build momentum, stimulate creative thinking, and unleash a profusion of self-organized innovations.

Appreciative Inquiry is a nonlinear approach to change, and thus it is never finished, even upon the completion of a full 4-D Cycle. So how will you maintain momentum for change over time? Continue to grow the pool of engaged stakeholders by inviting more and more people to participate in implementing inquiry-related innovations. Communicate and celebrate groups' accomplishments before they disband. Demonstrate an ongoing commitment to wholeness in areas such as training, business process improvement, and strategic and business planning. Systematically re-create systems, structures, and leadership practices to create an environment in which everything supports, rather than impedes, improvisation and self-organizing.

Perhaps most important, you can help the people in your organization commit to living the principles of Appreciative Inquiry and positive change. In particular, you can use inquiry, storytelling, and narrative analysis to make decisions—and to consider, introduce, and recognize organization changes. Tell and retell the stories behind systemic changes that have since become a way of life.

Build Organization-Wide Awareness

The Getting Started phase ends when the entire organization becomes aware of and committed to the initiative. Depending on the size and scope of the project, you may choose to achieve this awareness through letters to stakeholders, videos, small-group gatherings, or some other small-scale communication tool. On the other hand, you may choose to begin your initiative with a series of kickoff meetings—high-energy, highly engaging introductions for all organizational members that invite people's curiosity, commitment, and participation. If this is more your style, consider the following guidelines:

- *Match medium and message.* Design the meeting as an enactment of the desired future state. For example, kickoff meetings for an initiative to build cross-functional communication should involve a cross-functional mix of participants.

- *Describe the purpose of the initiative.* Use a language and a format that make sense to everyone.

- *Describe the engagement step by step.* If at all possible, find ways for everyone to experience it.

- *Include people in conversations about impact and first steps.* Help them see themselves as part of the long-term initiative.

- *Invite participation.* Help people see places where they might contribute in the meeting and in the long-term initiative, and provide ways for them to volunteer for activities that call to them.

An effective kickoff meeting will do more than simply inform people of an overall effort. It will strategically leverage an organization's strengths in areas such as marketing, customer service, or innovation. It will engage employees as if they were valued customers. It will inspire participation, and provide opportunities to solicit volunteers for various aspects of the inquiry—thereby creating a broader base of participants from the beginning. In short, it will accelerate an inquiry and build momentum for the longer-term aspects of the engagement.

Getting Started at Hunter Douglas

Hunter Douglas had begun the transformation to a new information technology infrastructure when it met Appreciative Inquiry. After learning about and experiencing this new positive approach to change, Hunter Douglas's leadership decided to give it a try. What follows is the story of how they made that decision.

First Steps Toward Transformation

In their efforts to regain what they lost in their growth, Hunter Douglas's leadership initiated a traditional organization development intervention in the spring of 1996. They hired a consultant to conduct interviews with the general manager, his direct reports, and their direct reports. The purpose of the interviews was to identify root causes of communication breakdowns, decreases in productivity and employee satisfaction, and increases in turnover. They formed a subgroup called the Rapid Action Team, whose job was to analyze interview and employee survey data and recommend a plan to the larger leadership team for correcting negative trends.

While the Rapid Action Team was engaged in its root cause analysis, the general manager, Rick Pellett, was also serving on a team responsible for guiding the conversion of the company's information technology to SAP. This team had been struggling for months to create a vision for the future of information technology throughout the North American organization. So they went away for a two-and-a-half-day retreat to bond as a group and develop their strategy for moving forward. Their consultant, Amanda Trosten-Bloom, chose to facilitate with an AI-based process.

Later, Pellett described his profound experience at that retreat:

> People engaged so much more than they ever had before. They came to life. They began drawing from a wellspring of intuitive business sense that we'd never really seen before. They began talking about and sharing their passions: their visions for what they could become in the future—for what they could contribute to the company and the world.

I'd always been a pretty self-sufficient leader. I was smart, and I knew it. Some of my best decisions had been made fairly independently. But what this team came up with, through these interviews and conversations, was head and shoulders above anything any of us could have imagined independently. The process got people powerfully and positively engaged in resolving a real, immediate company issue. It jump-started an initiative that, until that time, had brought us only anxiety and heartache.

On Friday, Pellett finished his work with the SAP team. On Monday, he joined one of the regularly scheduled Rapid Action Team meetings. Mike Burns, vice president of human resources, looks back on that infamous Monday morning meeting:

It didn't take long to figure out that something had happened to Rick at that SAP meeting. Here we were, stuck on some repetitive, annoying problem, and Rick said, "I've got an idea." First he asked a question. Then he asked us what we were trying to create—how things would be if this problem we were working on didn't exist.

Clearly, the man had been transformed! He wasn't the same person I'd known for eight years. Even our consultant noticed something was different. I thought, "That's it. Whatever they did, it worked. I need to learn more."

Mike and the consultant, Linda Sorrento, weren't the only ones to become curious. "What happened to Rick?" became the question, followed in short order by "What did you just do, Rick? Why?"

Pellett shared some of the principles behind what he'd just done. They asked for more. He suggested that the group learn more about Appreciative Inquiry philosophy and practice, and they quickly agreed.

It's Never Too Late for Appreciative Inquiry

So two weeks later, Amanda did a two-hour presentation for the subgroup. At the end of that presentation, the Rapid Action Team determined that Appreciative Inquiry was the way to address the issues they had spent months identifying. Over the following weeks, they reframed their problem statements as goals for the change initiative. In the end, they presented their analysis to the larger leadership team. The proposed solution was a whole-system Appreciative Inquiry.

This was no small leap. The larger leadership team had no relationship with the approach. They were deeply invested in the problem-solving methodologies that had worked so effectively in the past. They needed a compelling experience of the effect that Appreciative Inquiry could have on the organization to get on board with such a seemingly radical approach.

So they set aside a day. In that one day they asked the consultants to give them enough of a feel for AI to allow them to see if and where it might apply. The agenda for that day is outlined in Exhibit 1.

Exhibit 1.   Agenda for the Leadership Introduction
Meeting Objective: Provide a basic introduction to the philosophy and practice of Appreciative Inquiry, together with an exploration of possible applications.
• Opening and Welcome
• Background on Appreciative Inquiry
• Paired Interviews (The Four Core Questions)
• Topic Selection
• Crafting and Piloting of Questions
• Interim Summary of Learnings
• Field Trip to Production Facilities
• Debrief of the Experience
• Revisiting of Common Themes
• Application Conversation
• Go/No-Go Decision

Deciding to Proceed

The consultants used the first few hours of the session to describe Appreciative Inquiry philosophy and practice and to share stories of its successes. They provided participants with a grounded experience of Appreciative Inquiry—first through interviews with one another, then through a surprise field trip to the production facility. During this field trip, leaders did a second round of appreciative interviews—this time with production workers.

When they returned to the meeting, they shared their experiences and impressions. Leaders who had been with the company for years were visibly touched as they described their interviews with the people who assembled shades and ran machines. Clearly, participants had discovered a great deal through this field trip about themselves, the organization, and Appreciative Inquiry.

In thirty minutes, participants in the introduction discovered that people who worked on the floor of the production facilities shared many of the same hopes and dreams for the company as they did. Instead of being incapable of envisioning a meaningful future for the company, workers were able to enrich leadership's picture of what the organization could become.

They discovered that they could reach out across the artificial boundaries that had sprung up between the managers and the "hourlies"—as production staff had been known in the past. This was, for example, the first time in eleven years that the head of marketing communication had set foot in one of the production facilities.

They discovered that they could make a human connection with people with whom they previously had no relationship. A head of operations shared the pride he had felt when a printer from another business unit talked about the help she had received from fellow workers when her husband had gone through open-heart surgery the year before.

They discovered that floor personnel's peak experiences—just like their own—had emerged as a result of making a difference in their workplace. For example, a maintenance technician had described his pride at being described as "Dr. Bob"—the person who knew how to fix anything.

They discovered the hopes and dreams that they themselves had articulated in their morning session were mirrored essentially word for word—

that, far from distracting from the content of the inquiry, the afternoon interviews had enriched their understanding and experience of the possibilities for the organization. The experience itself had the capacity to address a number of the issues that had been identified as needing attention: communication, respect, and alignment across business units and functions.

Finally, they experienced the Principle of Simultaneity in action. Within a day, the production facilities' grapevine filled with stories of the "suits" who had descended—and questions about what they were doing and why. Almost inadvertently, the Road Show, as it came to be known, had created great curiosity—a kind of anxious anticipation about the effort that was about to take place.

All of these discoveries would have merit for the organization, even if AI subsequently dropped out of the picture. But it didn't. Instead, at the end of the day, the consultants "called the question." Despite the momentum that had already been built with regard to the traditional organization development intervention, 100 percent of the leaders voted to change trains and follow the Appreciative Inquiry track. The purpose of the AI work would be

- To create a collective vision that could engage and excite the entire organization and its stakeholders.

- To reinstill the creativity, flexibility, intimacy, and sense of community that had contributed to the division's original success.

- To enhance the skills of existing leadership and build bench strength by identifying and training future leaders.

- To transcend the silos that had recently emerged between management and the general workforce, across business units, and between operations and support functions.

The Window Fashions Division leadership committed to using Appreciative Inquiry with their entire workforce. They conceptualized their version of an Appreciative Inquiry 4-D Dialogue. They called this program Focus 2000. The purpose of the Focus 2000 program was to "create a shared vision for the year 2000 and beyond."

Creating an Infrastructure

The Focus 2000 Advisory Team was formed and trained. On the heels of their off-site training in Taos, New Mexico, they determined the scope and planned the first phases of the initiative. Early on, they were determined to interview every Window Fashions Division employee in the inquiry, plus a representative sample of external stakeholders and a handful of best-in-class organizations. In addition, they committed to engaging a full 25 percent of the workforce in some active form of inquiry—topic selection, interviewing, meaning making, organization design, or ongoing communication.

The team decided that a microcosm of the organization should own each aspect of the process. To put flesh on this decision, they conceptualized multifunctional, multilevel subgroups for everything from communication to selection of participants in conferences and training programs. They committed that the teams would be composed of both technical experts and informal leaders—people who had either volunteered to participate or had been nominated by their peers.

To accomplish such extraordinary levels of participation, the Advisory Team recognized the need for a kickoff process that would get people's attention and magnetically draw them in. They opted for a series of "town meetings" for seventy-five to one hundred fifty people, providing all shifts and all employees with a cross-functional, cross-level introduction to Focus 2000—its purpose, objectives, and process. Exhibit 2 shows the agenda for the town meetings.

Different from the Start

From the beginning, the team made a clear decision not to treat this first town meeting as just another plant meeting. Instead of memos posted or communicated through supervisors, hand-addressed invitations were sent to every employee. Instead of wearing suits, middle- and upper-level managers wore Focus 2000 T-shirts and greeted people at the door. Chairs were rented for everyone and were placed in a large, protected, unfinished mezzanine—in the past, employees stood through plant meetings, which were held in the middle of production areas or cafeterias. Snacks were provided, the program opened with handshakes, and people were asked to

Exhibit 2.   Agenda for the Town Meetings
Meeting Objective: Preview plans to engage everyone in Hunter Douglas in making this organization the best workplace possible.
• Opening, Welcome, and Experiential Introductions
• Story-Based Explanation of "The Change That's Already Started"
• Videotaped Excerpts of Appreciative Interviews
• Guest Testimonials / Lessons Learned Using Appreciative Inquiry
• The Plan to Make This Happen at Hunter Douglas
• Questions and Answers
• Solicitation of Volunteers
• Next Steps
• Meeting Debrief

introduce themselves to someone they didn't know and reseat themselves next to strangers.

These details and other cues suggested that for once the company had decided to treat its employees as customers. The Advisory Team's attention to the details of the experience had a significant payoff: even the people who remained skeptical had to admit that this seemed different from anything they had experienced before.

A Picture Worth a Thousand Interviews

The formal meeting began with some introductory statements and a videotaped statement from Marv Hopkins, president of Hunter Douglas North America. The introduction was a stroke of brilliance. In three to four minutes he introduced the term Appreciative Inquiry, demonstrated support from the existing hierarchy, and made a case for its value within the Window Fashions Division.

Following a few key stories, participants were further introduced to Appreciative Inquiry by watching a video of Hunter Douglas employees who were responding to variations of the Four Core Questions presented in Exhibit 3. These highly abbreviated interviews had been videotaped weeks before on the production floor.

Exhibit 3.   The Hunter Douglas Variation on the Four Core Appreciative Inquiry Questions

- Tell me about your beginnings with Hunter Douglas. What were your most positive first impressions or excitements when you first came to work for the company?
- Tell me about a peak experience or high point in your time here at Hunter Douglas.
- Without being humble, what do you most value about yourself, your team, and Hunter Douglas as a whole?
- If you had a magic wand and could have three wishes granted to make Hunter Douglas the most alive, most rewarding, most fun workplace possible, what would those be?

These production interviews did more than create a bang-up explanation for an unfamiliar phrase. They also created a premeeting splash in the window fashions pond. People were intrigued, curious, and honored to be interviewed.

Real People—Real Stories

Since the Window Fashions Division employee averaged only a fifth-grade reading level, the town meeting message had to be delivered in a straightforward, engaging, entertaining fashion. The Advisory Team chose to do this by retaining real people to tell real stories about Appreciative Inquiry. In addition to telling the story of the Cleveland Clinic (see Chapter 4) and showing employee videos, they brought in outside speakers to tell about the effect of Appreciative Inquiry on them and their organizations.

One speaker was a midlevel professional with Nynex in Boston; the other, an automobile mechanic from ProCare in Youngstown, Ohio. Their five- to ten-minute testimonials, together with their participation in the question and answer session, held more credibility for the employees at Hunter Douglas than any kind of stand-up presentation by even the most powerful expert.

Looking Back

The last town meeting was completed nearly six months after the first whisper of Appreciative Inquiry hit the Hunter Douglas grapevine. Finally, the organization was ready to move forward with its inquiry into its positive core. As we reflect on the deliberate ways in which the organization decided to proceed and got started with the engagement, we are reminded of a number of important principles.

First, the meetings were designed by and for the company and were built on what the company already did well. Second, the division's leaders were persistent and patient in their efforts to bring everyone on board. Third, from the beginning, their design enacted the organization they were trying to become. Finally, from the beginning, they recruited and designed around volunteers.

Years later, town meetings were incorporated into the division's way of doing business. Semiannual or annual gatherings were used to communicate information, create shared understanding of the business, and build enthusiasm for new initiatives. Their remarkable staying power is a reflection of the wisdom of the original design.

This ends our description of Getting Started at Hunter Douglas. The Hunter Douglas story continues with Affirmative Topic Choice, in Chapter 6.

Affirmative Topic Choice

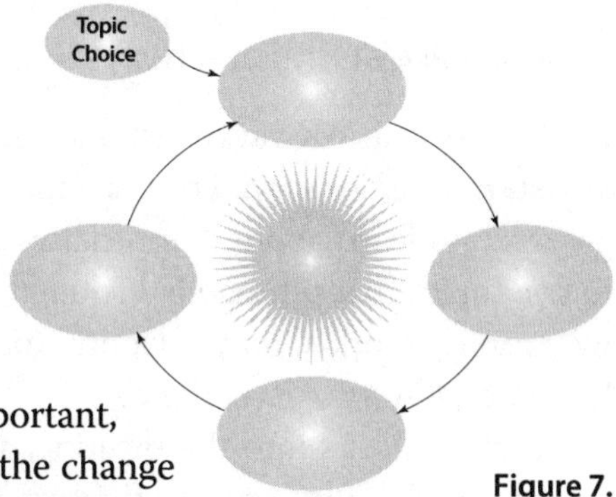

Topic
Choice

Affirmative Topic Choice
provides the focus for the
activities that follow in
the 4-D Cycle. Careful,
thoughtful, and inspired
topic choice is centrally important,
as it defines the direction of the change
process and lays the groundwork for sub-

Figure 7.

sequent interviews and organizational learning—processes that will
shape an organization or community. Affirmative Topics set the
stage for the entire 4-D process that follows.

This chapter explores the nature of topic choice, discusses the
various options for who will select Affirmative Topics, and walks
you step by step through the process for engaging your organization
in determining what it will study—and hence what it will become.
Numerous examples of transformational topics, from a wide variety of organizations, demonstrate how these organizations plan to
achieve their unique Change Agendas.

Transformational Topic Choice

Because human systems grow in the direction of what they study, the selection of topics casts the die on what an organization will become. When groups study high human ideals and achievements—cooperation, inspirational leadership, economic justice, or spirit at work—these conditions flourish. Organizations construct and enact worlds of their own making, which in turn act on them.

Affirmative Topics may focus on the enhancement of an organization's culture or its strategic relationships. They may explore issues of financial viability or human asset management. The most effective topics resonate with an organization's business and culture and are aligned with its Change Agenda. Table 8 shows the relationship between Change Agendas and Affirmative Topics.

Topic Choice at British Airways

In 1998, British Airways Customer Service NA selected topics for a systemwide inquiry. Forty people from twenty-two locations gathered to learn about Appreciative Inquiry and to identify three to five topics that ultimately included Happiness at Work, Harmony Among Work Groups, Continuous People Development, and Exceptional Arrival Experience.

Several hours into the meeting, as the group of forty selected Affirmative Topics, one participant raised a question about the applicability of Appreciative Inquiry: "I see how Appreciative Inquiry can make a big difference with people-related issues," she commented, "but can it be used for technical issues?" Sensing that this was more than a theoretical question—that she had a specific technical issue in mind—we asked her to share the technical issue she was hoping Appreciative Inquiry might help. She said succinctly, "Baggage." At that point, everyone in the room sighed a great sigh of relief. The issue they considered paramount to the well-being of their business was now part of the conversation.

Because we were relatively new to the airline industry, we asked the group to tell us some stories to illustrate the baggage issue. With

Table 8. Aligning Your Change Agenda and Affirmative Topics	
Exceptional customer service.	Going above and beyond.
	Service recovery.
	Delighting the customer.
	One-stop shopping.
Enhanced profitability.	Optimal margins.
	Discovering new business.
	Lightning-fast time to market.
	Customer retention.
Employee retention.	Magnetic work environment.
	Happiness at work.
	Creative job sharing.
	On-the-job learning.
Strategic advantage.	Being the best.
	Creative growth potentials.
	Culture as competitive advantage.
	Organizational learning.
Patient-centered health care.	The heart of collaboration.
	Healing conversations.
	Hearing the patient's story.
	Health: a family affair.

great energy, emphasis, and sometimes frustration, they explained that when customers and their baggage do not arrive on the same flight, it costs British Airways a great deal of time, money, and good-will. They shared stories of the wedding dress that didn't make it to the wedding and had to be replaced at the airline's expense; camping gear that didn't get to the Grand Canyon until the week's vacation was over; the daily disturbances of luggage not making the transfer from Heathrow to Gatwick in time for connecting flights.

We knew we were in the midst of people who care for their customers when one customer service agent said, "This is not how we like to do things at British Airways. It's not what our customers expect, and it doesn't make us proud of what we do or who we are. What can we do about it?"

We paraphrased their stories to demonstrate an understanding of their concerns for the issue. Then we repeated the Appreciative Inquiry principle that leads to powerful, strategic Affirmative Topics: "Given that organizations move in the direction of what they study, what is it that you want more of in British Airways? In this case, we know you do not want more lost or delayed baggage. But what do you want more of?"

The group's response came too quickly and unanimously to be anything other than the organization's habitual response to the situation. Several people almost simultaneously said, "Better service recovery." We paused to reflect upon the most helpful way to reply and then said, "Let's see if we have this right. It's OK to lose a customer's baggage as long as you recover it promptly?" The group got our point immediately and said, "No, no, it's not OK."

Again we asked, "So what do you want more of? What Affirmative Topic would move this organization in the direction you want?" Small groups talked for about twenty minutes and then shared ideas. Among the many innovative ideas was the topic Exceptional Arrival Experience. One group was emphatic that what they wanted more of was for all British Airways customers to have an exceptional arrival experience. When the whole group discussed this potential topic, there was a great deal of consensus. One person said how much more it would be like British Airways at its best if customer service agents were focused on providing exceptional arrival experiences rather than worrying about lost baggage.

In the end, the group of forty determined that one thing they really wanted more of was to hear stories of times when customers had an exceptional arrival experience. They wanted to uncover and transport from station to station all the best practices that would support British Airways' world-class service.

Key Decisions in Topic Choice

There are only two decisions to be made during Affirmative Topic Choice, but they are powerful:

- *Who will select the topics?* Executives? A core team? The entire organization?

- *What topics will we study?* What do we want more of in this organization?

The best answers to both questions will inevitably challenge your organization's status quo. To answer these questions, you must reflect upon the kind of human relationships you value, how you want people working together, and what you want more of in your organization. As the Principle of Enactment suggests, answers to these questions must be consistent with the organization you are trying to create.

Involving the Right People

At each step in an Appreciative Inquiry process, whole-system involvement is important. Ideally, topic selection is done by a micro-cosm of the whole system—a cross-level, cross-functional group of people from throughout the organization. Groups as small as twenty or as large as two hundred may engage in initial conversations and determination of topics, but involving more people from the start builds overall organizational commitment and momentum.

The topic selection group must be diverse, for variety brings out the richness of relationship, dialogue, and possibility. When a wide variety of people from throughout a system are included, the topics that emerge are often surprising and compelling. For example, during one health-care system's topic selection meeting it was a patient who proposed one of the most generative topics: Doctors and Patients Learning Together.

Diversity is essential because no one group or part of an organization can speak for the whole. Each group, level, or function has its unique perspective, interests, and ideals. Only when the whole system is present can topics inspire the whole organization to higher levels of well-being and achievement.

Let's return to the British Airways example. Conversations

about whom to invite to the two-day topic selection meeting were lively. The Advisory Team wanted the right mix of people to ensure that the process would fit the organization's culture and be owned by the entire organization. Ultimately forty people gathered to select topics and draft the inquiry strategy. The group included customer service agents from eighteen locations, union stewards, vice presidents, and directors and members of support organizations, including information technology, finance, human resource management, and corporate communication. As the meeting progressed, it was apparent that this group had the influence and resources to deliver whatever they collaboratively agreed upon. In essence, they became the greatest champions for the ongoing initiative.

Characteristics of Good Topics

Affirmative topics should focus on what members of an organization want to see grow and flourish in their organization. They should evoke conversations of the desired future. When we ask people what they want more of in their organization, the answers are often provocative. As conversations shift away from problems, obstacles, and barriers—and move toward the definition and description of people's highest ideals for their organization—energy and enthusiasm rise.

Good topics do more than simply identify an area of inquiry. They also suggest qualities of the topic that are most desired in a particular organization. Take the area of leadership as an example. We could conduct an inquiry into leadership in general, and we would indeed learn a lot. However, it would be more exciting and generative to focus on and study a particular kind of leadership—the kind you most desire. Over the years, our clients have chosen a diverse range of leadership topics: Inspirational Leadership, Democratic Leadership, Appreciative Leadership, Cross-Generational Leadership, Irresistible Leadership, Strategic Leadership, and Cooperative Leadership. Each leadership topic leads to the discovery of a different understanding and set of practices about leadership.

In keeping with the Poetic Principle, Affirmative Topics can focus on anything related to organizing at its best. They can have a technical focus as in Information That Serves, a relational focus such as Ultimate Teamwork, a financial direction such as Cooperative Cost Containment, or a social focus such as Legendary Learning Communities. They may be internally oriented as in Revolutionary Partnerships or externally oriented as in Magnetic Customer Connections.

Consider the following example: If your organization wants to enhance morale, what will you study—the causes of low morale or the causes of high morale and enthusiasm? Clearly, no amount of knowledge about low morale will sufficiently equip an organization to understand and create high morale. Imagine, on the other hand, an organization filled with inquiry and dialogue on the topic Whistle While You Work or Purposeful Work.

Whatever the focus, good affirmative topics share four characteristics:

- *Topics are positive.* They are stated in the affirmative.

- *Topics are desirable.* The organization wants to grow, develop, and enhance them.

- *Topics stimulate learning.* The organization is genuinely curious about them and wants to become more knowledgeable and proficient in them.

- *Topics stimulate conversations about desired futures.* They take the organization where it wants to go. They link to the organization's Change Agenda.

After completing the Affirmative Topic Choice phase, an organization will have between three and five compelling, inspirational topics that will serve as the focus for in-depth inquiry, learning, and transformation.

Measuring Affirmative Topics

Conversations in this phase of the Appreciative Inquiry process are explicitly about topic selection, but they also trigger a host of transformational dialogues about the way things are currently measured and reported in the organization. Many of our clients recognize during topic choice conversations that they are measuring, paying attention to, and analyzing precisely what they do not want in their organization. Light bulbs go off as they realize that no amount of research or knowledge about turnover will help them create a magnetic work environment where long-term, committed employment is the norm. Nor will an understanding of obstacles to profitability help employees develop business literacy and enhance margins. What are the alternatives? One client organization decided to study three topics: Retention, Magnetic Work Environments, and Employee Loyalty. A second organization designed a company-wide inquiry into the root cause of financial success, defined as optimal margins.

The recognition that organizations move in the direction of what they study stimulates an imperative to redesign customer- and employee-focused measurement systems throughout an organization. Over and over, customer service organizations trained in Appreciative Inquiry see the limitations of their customer surveys. They transform their surveys from inventories of problem and customer complaints to descriptions of what delights customers and keeps them coming back. Employee surveys and performance appraisal processes are often similarly revised to focus on affirmative topics.

Topic Choice, Step by Step

Topic selection can take from six hours to two days. Generally, the more people who are involved, the longer the process will take. Throughout this phase of the 4-D Cycle, every participant has an active role and an equal voice. Considerable dialogue and deliberation over particular words or phrases is not just semantic—it's essential. One fundamental assumption of Appreciative Inquiry is that words create worlds, so selection of a topic's wording has enormous impact on what is shared, what is learned, and how the organization grows into the future.

Table 9.   Affirmative Topic Choice Step by Step
1. Introduce Appreciative Inquiry.
2. Conduct mini-interviews.
3. Identify themes.
4. Share themes and stories.
5. Discuss criteria for Affirmative Topics.
6. Identify potential topics.
7. Share and discuss potential topics.
8. Cluster potential topics.
9. Select topic clusters.
10. Finalize topics.

The ten steps listed in Table 9 are the foundation for topic selection work. As we move from organization to organization, we adapt these steps to the situation at hand.

Introduce Appreciative Inquiry

We begin by providing a brief overview of Appreciative Inquiry to those who are selecting the Affirmative Topics. During this time we present the eight principles, give definitions of Appreciative Inquiry, explain the 4-D Cycle with a focus on the importance of topic selection, and share stories of Appreciative Inquiry from other organizations and communities.

Conduct Mini-Interviews

Participants then engage in mini-interviews, using four core questions (see Figure 8). Depending on the setting, these mini-interviews require thirty to forty-five minutes per person. This allows time for people to connect, share stories, and delve into their hopes and dreams for the organization. It also gives them an experience of the positive impact of appreciative questions—and the story-based raw material from which Affirmative Topics will be selected.

Figure 8.   Mini-Interview Core Questions

---

1. Tell me about a peak experience or high point in your professional life, a time when you felt most alive, most engaged, and really proud of yourself and your work.

---

2. Without being humble, what do you most value about

- Yourself and the way you do your work? What unique skills and gifts do you bring to this team and organization?

- Your work?

- Your team?

- Your organization and its larger contribution to society and the world?

---

3. What core factors give life to this organization when it is at its best?

---

4. If you had a magic wand and could have any three wishes granted to heighten the health and vitality of this organization, what would they be?

-

-

-

We ask people to conduct these mini-interviews with people who are different from themselves—different functions, levels, gender, age, tenure, ethnicity, and so on. This gives them a chance to form a genuine relationship with someone they wouldn't otherwise have known.

The conversations at the heart of these mini-interviews are often described as informative, enlightening, and inspiring. People remember times when they were at their best, then recognize that they share similar dreams for their organization. They become inspired to create the most vital and life-giving organization possible.

Identify Themes

Following mini-interviews, we ask people and their original partners to form groups of six or eight. On a round-robin basis, members of this small group should introduce their partners and share highlights from their interviews. As they do the introductions, they focus primarily on great stories and inspiring best practices and ideas that they heard.

As group members share stories within the group, common threads and themes begin to emerge. We support people in uncovering these common threads by demonstrating a process of narrative analysis to the whole group. Taking a single success story, we together uncover the root causes of success that are implicit within it. Small groups then continue to share stories and determine the factors that contributed to their high-point experiences.

Share Themes and Stories

After about an hour of storytelling and narrative analysis, small groups join others in a plenary session. Each small group shares one or two great stories with the whole group—stories that represent the essence of what the small group has been learning.

As they share their stories with the whole group, the small groups also communicate the themes that emerged over their previous hour of conversation. Often these themes are simply listed on flip chart pages; other times they are drawn or painted on a collective mural or communicated in some other creative fashion. However it transpires, individual groups' themes are listed and then compiled into a master list of themes. This master list becomes the raw material for the next activity.

Discuss Criteria for Affirmative Topics

While still in the plenary session, we discuss the significance of topic choice—emphasizing that human systems move in the direction of the things they study. We review the criteria for Affirmative Topics in much the same way we discussed it earlier in this chapter.

We share sample topics and discuss why they work. In addition, we present a series of problems that an organization might be interested in correcting and ask the group to consider Affirmative Topics that might indirectly resolve those problems by moving the organization toward what they really want. This leads to such comparisons as

- Turnover or retention?
- Customer dissatisfaction or customer satisfaction?
- Sexual harassment or positive cross-gender relationships?

Finally, we remind people that topic choice is a fateful decision and ask them to consider what they want more of in their organizations.

Identify Potential Topics

People return to small groups for this phase of the process. Each small group identifies three to five potential topics, which they extrapolated both from the stories and the master list of themes.

Share and Discuss Potential Topics

Again the groups return to a plenary session. Here they present their proposed topics to the whole group, posting them as they go. As they present, they explain the logic behind their choices. More important, they make the case for why they believe the topics are meaningful to the organization—both today and in the future.

After hearing all of the proposed topics, the entire group talks about the patterns and themes that emerged. Often the final topics organically emerge from this whole-group conversation.

Cluster Potential Topics

If the final topics are still unclear, however, either the whole group or a designated subgroup narrows the possibilities by clustering proposed topics into affinity groups. By gathering redundant topics or topics with similar meanings into groups, they reduce the overall number of topics. Even though the process of clustering takes place quickly, it involves everyone and includes dialogue and discussion.

It requires the identification of subtle similarities and differences between the various statements. Participants in this process are encouraged to hang on to the inspirational power of the original topics rather than form meaningless clusters of words.

Select Topic Clusters

Again, the process of clustering can result in a clear selection of the final three to five topics. But if it doesn't, the clusters must be further narrowed. We usually accomplish this by facilitating a vote.

We generally give each participant a total of three votes. We offer them the option of casting the three votes in any way they see fit—either all for one or spread out over one, two, or three different clusters. Votes are tallied so that the group can see its collective priorities. We then facilitate one last round of conversation, in which people can make their case for a particular cluster that might have been overlooked or can simply agree with the final tally. In the end, three to five clusters are selected.

Finalize Topics

After selecting the final topic clusters, participants self-organize into the topic group of their choice. When these new groups are formed, participants in the small groups review all the topics that were originally proposed and select a single topic name that best carries the spirit, essence, and intent of the original interviews and stories.

Affirmative Topic Choice at Hunter Douglas

From the beginning Hunter Douglas wanted to involve as many people from as many levels and functions in the organization as possible. As a result they gathered a group of one hundred volunteers to choose Affirmative Topics. On the following pages you will read how both the volunteers and the topics were selected.

Who Was Involved?

The Window Fashions Division Town Meetings ended the third week in May. Over the course of those meetings, more than a third of the workforce (three hundred out of eight hundred fifty) were nominated or volunteered to become part of a hundred-person Interview Guide Design Team. One employee described herself as "skeptical but willing to play"—a significant leap in light of her reputation as someone with an attitude. Another stood outside of the meeting room for the next two gatherings, lobbying people to nominate her to be on the Interview Guide Design Team. She was so enthusiastic about the process that she decided to stack the deck in favor of her involvement.

From an original group of three hundred volunteers, we selected a subgroup to identify and recruit an Interview Guide Design Team. This twenty-person subgroup consisted of both people who had self-nominated and people who had received many nominations from their peers. They then used the following criteria to identify approximately 10 percent of the total employee population to serve in the first phase of the 4-D Cycle:

- Identify a true representative sampling of the workforce, taking into account differences in business unit, function, shift, gender, race, and attitude.
- Build upon people's inherent interest and energy as much as possible by including both self-nominees and people who were frequently nominated at the town meetings.

Within two weeks, the final group of one hundred had been identified and notified of their participation in a three-day offsite meeting. Their job description was to generate topics for a Whole-System 4-D Dialogue, whose stated purpose was "To create a vision for the year 2000 and beyond, based on the best of who we've been." In addition, they were charged with crafting the foundational questions on which the internal and external interview guides would be based.

What Topics Were Chosen?

The topics were generated in response to the question, "What are the three to five topics that have the greatest potential to make Hunter Douglas the most effective, most energizing, and most fun organization it could possibly be?" They included People, Education, Quality of Work Life, Morale and Recognition, and Communication.

The topics tested the resolve of the division's leadership to follow the energy of the group. What about customers? What about products? What about innovation? What about the qualities that had made us great in the first place and that would ensure our success in the future?
The Advisory Team huddled on the side to be quickly refreshed on their commitment. "It's more important to follow their lead," said Pellett. "These may not be the topics that interest me most as general manager, but it's what matters to this group of employees. If we did our job right choosing the people who are here, we need to trust what they have to say. Let's go with these."

This ends our description of Affirmative Topic Choice at Hunter Douglas. The Hunter Douglas story continues with Discovery, in Chapter 7.

CHAPTER 7

Discovery: Appreciative Interviews and More

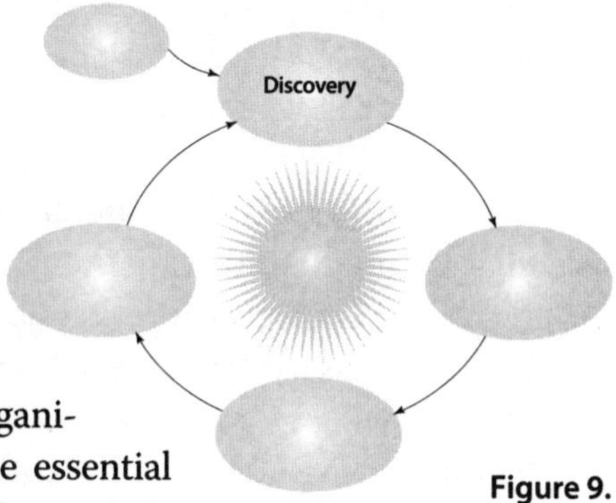

Figure 9.

People often ask us, What are the nonnegotiable aspects of Appreciative Inquiry? What differentiates Appreciative Inquiry from other approaches to organization change? What are the essential components of a successful Appreciative Inquiry process? Appreciative interviews are at the top of our list— an essential success factor for any Appreciative Inquiry process.

Appreciative interviews bring out the best in people and organizations: they provide opportunities for people to speak and be heard, ignite curiosity and the spirit of learning, and increase organizational knowledge and wisdom. They enhance the organization's positive core by bringing to the surface stories that illuminate the distinctive strengths and potentials. And they bring positive possibilities for the future to life.

This chapter shows you how to create appreciative interview

questions out of Affirmative Topics, how to create an Interview Guide, and how to train people to be appreciative interviewers. It gives a clear picture of what makes an appreciative interview effective. Finally, it offers a variety of ideas for using and making sense of appreciative interview data. In short, it is your guide to Discovery.

Key Decisions in Discovery

The Discovery phase revolves around appreciative interviews, which stimulate a variety of ideas for how to portray the organization at its best. Unfolding over days, weeks, or months, this phase involves writing questions and Interview Guides, conducting interviews, disseminating stories and best practices, and making sense of what has been learned.

Key decisions are often made as the Discovery phase progresses. Some of these decisions must be addressed before interviews can occur: Whom will we interview? In what time frame? Other decisions will not be relevant until the interview process begins and data flows: How will we communicate stories and best practices? For this reason, it is important that the Advisory Team or project decision-making team meet regularly to stay abreast of the interview process, making the necessary decisions to keep the process moving.

The following questions will generally surface during Discovery. As with all else in an Appreciative Inquiry process, each organization's answers will be different, resulting in their unique brand of Discovery.

- *Who will craft the questions and the Interview Guide(s)?* The whole group that selected topics? A core team? Consultants?
- *Whom will we interview?* Who are our stakeholders? Employees? Customers? Suppliers? Others? Which of these do we need to hear from?
- *Who will conduct interviews? How many interviews can each interviewer manage?*
- *What training will our interviewers need?*

Table 10. Discovery, Step by Step
1. Craft appreciative interview questions.
2. Develop an Interview Guide.
3. Create an interview plan.
4. Communicate the Inquiry Strategy.
5. Train interviewers.
6. Conduct appreciative interviews.
7. Disseminate stories and best practices.
8. Make meaning.
9. Map the positive core.

- *Who will make meaning of the data? By what process?* Will it be local groups or a core team? How will we keep people as close as possible to the original data?

- *How will we communicate stories and best practices?* Will we produce a written report? A video? A formal presentation?

Discovery, Step by Step

From beginning to end, Discovery involves nine broad activities. These activities may be thought of as what happens before, during, and after appreciative interviews. The interviews are the essence of Discovery, yet much more happens during the Discovery phase: preparation before the interviews, and afterward the process of making sense and use of the information collected. Table 10 lists the steps in the Discovery phase.

Craft Appreciative Inquiry Questions

The first step in Discovery is transforming the three to five chosen Affirmative Topics into positive questions. Who should be involved in writing questions? Most often the same group of people who identified the Affirmative Topics will write the interview questions. In some cases a large group will write a first draft of the questions and a smaller group or consultant will refine and finalize the questions and Interview Guide. As with all phases, the more people involved in the process, the more ownership and commitment there will be for the activities that follow—in this case, the actual interviews.

The Structure of Appreciative Interview Questions

Appreciative interview questions are written to uncover who and what an organization is when it is at its best. They are generally structured as follows:

- The title of the Affirmative Topic.
- A lead-in that introduces the topic.
- A set of subquestions, usually two to four, that explore different aspects of the topic.

This structure is illustrated in Figure 10 with a sample question from our book *Encyclopedia of Positive Questions.*[56]

Lead-ins introduce interviewees to the Affirmative Topic of the inquiry, playing a critical role in setting the tone for both questions and responses. Good lead-ins put people at ease with the topic and help them consider the topic from different angles. In some cases, the lead-in defines the topic so that people can begin to consider when they have been aware of it.

When writing appreciative interview questions, we think back to the old adage about the half-full or half-empty glass. We assume that the glass is half-full—that the topic or quality we are exploring already exists in the person, the organization, and the world. We see ourselves as detectives trying to uncover and understand where the topic exists, why it exists, and how it can exist to a greater extent.

Quality lead-ins plant that half-full assumption in the minds of interviewees. They describe the topic or quality at its best and show interviewees the benefit of the topic. Sometimes lead-ins paint pictures of the positive outcomes that are possible when the topic or quality is significantly present in an organization. They make people

Figure 10.   Sample Appreciative Interview Questions

Affirmative Topic	Community Service
Lead-in	When organizations are at their best, they offer a wide array of alternatives for community service. Programs such as educational outreach, speakers' bureaus, adopt-a-school, and financial contributions all demonstrate an organization's commitment to the community in which it does business. Both the organization and the community benefit. Employees who volunteer for community service become inspired and energized by helping dedicated social groups achieve their goals. Medical studies show that participation in community service increases people's sense of well-being and even their physical health: their immune systems are actually strengthened by volunteer service! Community service is a tremendous opportunity for employee renewal that also enhances community capacity.
Subquestions	1. Describe a time when you did some meaningful community service. What was the high point of this experience? What did it feel like? What was your contribution?
	2. What resources does your organization have that would benefit the community? How have your organization and the community cooperated meaningfully in the past?
	3. Dream into the future: your organization and your community have a wonderful mutual partnership. What does this look like? What three things might have been done to create this partnership?

want more of the topic, both within their organization and within themselves.

High-quality lead-ins are personal and affective, appealing to people's humanity, not just to their work-oriented selves. They resonate with the yearning for meaning that is so much a part of human experience. Because Appreciative Inquiry often involves inquiry into hard business topics such as finance, strategy, and quality, the lead-ins for these questions help people explore the topics from a human perspective. They help build bridges between the organization's needs and people's emotional needs for such things as a sense of pride, ownership, belonging, connection, and personal growth.

Great lead-ins set the stage for a whole-brain response to the questions that follow. They highlight the connection between good thinking and good feeling—a connection that must be internalized by the interviewee if he or she is to offer the fullest, most creative, most meaningful response possible.

Subquestions, which follow the lead-in in an appreciative interview question, may be focused on the past, present, or future. Often we include all three time frames when we write a question; sometimes we focus on only one or two. By inquiring into these different time frames, we help interviewees anchor the topic in their experience and their imagination. It can help if the subquestions follow a natural flow. Consider the following examples:

- *Backward questions* usually are first. They invite us to remember high-point experiences—times when we have experienced the Affirmative Topic to be most alive and most present, either within the organization or elsewhere. We probe deeply into the personal, environmental, and organizational conditions that contributed to the emergence and existence of the topic. Consider these backward questions related to the topic irresistible leadership:

  Reflecting back over your work life, recall a time when you were inspired by irresistible leadership. What was the situation? What made it irresistible? Who was involved? What did each person do to contribute to the strength of the situation?

- *Inward questions* generally follow backward questions. They refer back to the high-point experiences, asking us to find meaning in those peak experiences and to discover what can be learned about their root causes of success. For instance:

  What did you learn during that time that might be applied to this project? In what way did that situation influence your leadership style today?

- *Forward questions* typically come last. At their best, they elicit our hopes, dreams, and inspirations. They encourage us to imagine futures in which the Affirmative Topic is the best it can possibly be. For example:

> Imagine it is the year 2010 and your company has been awarded the Leadership Excellence Award. What is happening in the company that earned it the award?

• *Transition questions* are often embedded within the forward questions. They are retrospective reflections from the imagined future state—an opportunity for the interviewee to consider first steps and transitions from the current reality to the imagined future. For example:

> Looking back from 2010, consider what first steps you and your organization took that most contributed to success.

The Art of the Question

Crafting good appreciative questions is really more of an art than a science. Using the basic structure as a broad outline, good appreciative questions encourage imagination and play. For example, we might encourage people to describe their organization's positive core using metaphors or by painting a verbal picture of themselves at work. We might ask, "You are whistling while you work. Why?" Or we might ask them to describe their personal strengths through the eyes of their most admiring relative, customer, parent, or child.

People might be drawn to imagine the future through a "miracle" question: "You have fallen asleep for a very long time. Ten years have passed. As you awake, you discover that everything that you had ever hoped and dreamed for this organization has come true. What do you see?" Or they might describe an award they have received: "Five years from today, your organization is on the cover of *Forbes magazine*. Write the story." They might be given a magic wand or a magic lamp, together with the proverbial three wishes, "to heighten the health and vitality of their organization."

Whatever the approach, the best appreciative interview questions are clear, relatively simple, often subtle, and provocative.

The Key Components of Good Appreciative Interview Questions In good appreciative interviews, we are not just interested in data—we are interested in experience and relationships. Perhaps the most discernible characteristic of our best appreciative interview questions is that they invite people to tell stories and participate at that very human level.

Here are some responses from a group of interviewers we polled several years ago to determine what makes great questions:

- Great questions *help to forge personal connections between interviewers and interviewees.* They have a conversational quality, they value what is, and they spark the appreciative imagination. They convey unconditional positive regard.

- They *invite stories rather than abstract opinions or theories.* They are introduced by such phrases as "Tell me about" and "Describe for me."

- They *are personal and affective, almost intimate.* They touch people's hearts and souls. They ask people to describe something that they strongly identify with—to remember something or someone that really mattered to them.

- They *draw on people's life and work experiences.* They give people a chance to learn and create meaning from episodes and experiences that might otherwise have escaped their attention.

- They *invoke a kind of mental scan.* They force people to think about their powerfully positive experiences or insights, and then choose the best of the best.

- *Sometimes they are ambiguous.* They give people room to swim around, to answer in a variety of ways.

- They *walk people through an inner journey.* They ask people to interpret or deconstruct what worked or was meaningful about experiences and events they might have taken for granted.

- They *are uplifting.* They paint positive, attractive pictures. They inspire people to consider what's possible.

- They *give free rein to the imagination.* They take people far into the future and help them imagine infinite positive possibilities.

- They *suggest action.* They help people consider the immediate next steps that would begin to move them toward their dreams.

- They *have an emotional and logical flow to them.* As the Interview Guide moves from one question to the next, people are inspired to find deeper and deeper meaning—to become increasingly enlivened and inspired.

A number of books provide more information about crafting great questions for particular groups—for example, *Encyclopedia of Positive Questions,*[57] *Appreciative Team Building,*[58] and *Positive Family Dynamics.*[59]

Develop an Interview Guide

Appreciative inquiry questions—crafted around the organization's homegrown Affirmative Topics—are woven together to create an Interview Guide, also known as an interview protocol. The Interview Guide is the script for inquiry, providing background instructions for interviewers as well as appropriately sequenced questions directed to the person(s) being interviewed.

The Six Parts of the Interview Guide Interview Guides can be as short and simple as one page of questions or long and extensive, including an explanation of the process, the questions, and a summary sheet. The comprehensiveness of the Interview Guide depends on its use. If it is to be used by a small group of people who have themselves selected the topics and crafted the questions, then a short and simple version will do. A more comprehensive Interview Guide will be needed if it is to be used by hundreds or even thousands of people who are removed in time and distance from the crafting of the questions.

A comprehensive Interview Guide has six parts that appear in the following sequence:

1. *Introductory text.* It sets the stage for the interview and includes:
   - An overview of the inquiry process: what we are doing and why.
   - The significance of an appreciative interview—it focuses on what's best, not what's broken.
   - The need to share stories, details, and names so others can learn from best practices; therefore, there is no confidentiality unless interviewees request it.
   - How stories and information will be used.

2. *Stage-setting questions.* These build rapport and elicit information about the interviewee. Examples include:
   - Tell me about your beginnings with . . .
   - Describe a peak experience or high point with . . .
   - What do you value most about yourself? About your work? About your team? About your organization?

3. *Topic questions.* They are in-depth questions about the three to five Affirmative Topics you have selected:
   - Questions include lead-ins and subquestions.
   - Questions explore past, present, and future of topics.

4. *Concluding questions.* They wrap up the interview. For example:
   - What are the core factors that give life to . . .?
   - Looking toward the future, what are we being called to become?
   - If you could have any three wishes granted to heighten the health and vitality of this organization, what would they be?
   - Five years from today, your organization is receiving the Malcolm Baldridge Award for quality. Why? What specifi-

cally contributed to the organization receiving this extraordinary recognition?

5. *Summary sheets.* Used to collect interview data, these serve two purposes:
   - First, they are a repository for the best stories, quotes, and ideas.
   - Second, they are a reflection guide—a tool that the interviewer may use to begin making personal meaning out of the stories and reflections.

6. *Quick action sheets.* They collect items for immediate attention:
   - They provide a forum for identifying relatively simple and straightforward issues related to quality of life—broken water fountains, heaters in warehouses, and so on.
   - They are usually accompanied by a communication vehicle that permits immediate publication and celebration of "quick wins."

Create an Interview Plan

While the Interview Guide is being crafted, planning for the interviews begins. This involves addressing the next big round of questions related to how the inquiry will unfold: Who will be interviewed? By whom? In what manner? How will we engage as many different types of people as possible? Will we invite small groups to inquire into larger systems or will we provide vehicles through which whole systems can inquire into themselves? Will we have individuals interview their organizational counterparts or people with whom they have nothing in common? How will we bring external stakeholders—customers, suppliers, community members, industry partners—into the process? How will we gather information about and learn from unrelated best-in-class organizations? In general, how can we involve the broadest group possible, while working within our genuine limitations of time, availability, dollars, deadlines, and so on?

The best Appreciative Inquiries are full-voice and involve all of the organization's stakeholders throughout the inquiry. In other words, they engage anyone who has an interest in, an investment in, information about, and influence over the organization and its future. This certainly includes employees, customers, and suppliers. It might also include board members, stockholders, community members, special-interest groups, union leaders, regulators, industry partners, or even noncompeting best-in-class organizations. In particular, it should include people who are not normally in the foreground of organizational decision making: front-line employees, shop floor employees, minority employees, and so on.

The more diverse the interview population is, the better the results will be. A full spectrum of functions, levels, shifts, tenures, gender, and ethnic communities yields a much richer set of conversations than the highest functioning homogenous group. Multigenerational involvement, in particular, leads to extraordinary levels of engagement and learning. It heightens people's sense of passion and wonder while transmitting organizational wisdom. It fosters a sense of inclusion and belonging and ties people to both the past and the future—to history and positive possibility.

Can Appreciative Inquiry work in situations that are rife with conflict and competition? Proceed with caution—but most definitely proceed. We have brought together national unions and organizations in a "new partnership" using Appreciative Inquiry. We have supported merger and acquisition integration using Appreciative Inquiry. We have successfully launched new businesses using Appreciative Inquiry.

Appreciative interviews are acts of organizational intimacy. They give people forums for getting to know one another, being heard, drawing out another's best, and discovering common ground. They actively engage people in positive, productive working relationships—and in working together for the greater good.

Communicate the Inquiry Strategy

In the Getting Started phase, the Advisory Team develops an Inquiry Strategy and introduces the strategy through a variety of communications. These introductory communications have short shelf lives, however. They are intended to provide broad rather than deep information about the initiative. By now you have more to communicate. Your interview plan is ready to go public.

People will want to know what is happening. What are the topics? Who is being interviewed? When? By whom? How do I sign up? What will happen to the data? These and similar questions can only be addressed through ongoing, frequent, and sometimes repetitive communication. Letters from the organization's leadership or the Advisory Team, announcements in the company newsletter or on the intranet, presentations in department and plant meetings, videos, posters, town meetings—these can help maintain organization-wide interest and engagement.

Broad-based organizational support is a significant predictor of the success of an AI initiative. Communication at all stages of the process breeds high levels of involvement, commitment, and learning—which in turn translates into support. Without extensive communication, even Appreciative Inquiry can become something that "they" are doing. The desired culture—together with the positive communication practices the organization aspires to—must be enacted in the Appreciative Inquiry itself. Organizations can only create full-voice, knowledge-based, narrative-rich cultures through open, inclusive, and extensive interactive communication.

Train Interviewers

Most organizations choose to provide their interviewers with training in how to conduct an appreciative interview. Training may be as simple as conducting an interview and discussing what made it successful—or as programmatic as a two-day training in Appreciative Inquiry with a focus on interviewing.

We have experienced great success with three- to-four-hour interviewer training sessions. During this time, interviewers receive the following:

- Background information about the inquiry itself—what we are doing and to what end.
- Practice interviewing, using the Interview Guide.
- Guidelines regarding note taking, summary sheets, and quick action sheets, if any.
- Practice redirecting negative feedback.
- An interview schedule—who will interview whom by when.
- Instructions on how to invite others to join in the process, if appropriate.

Interviewer training not only prepares people to conduct appreciative interviews, but it also provides them with essential interpersonal skills—listening, summarizing ideas, sharing stories, and bringing out the best in people. As a result, beyond the Appreciative Inquiry process, interviewer training can be a significant developmental activity for people who do interviews, collect information, and depend on positive relationships to get their job done. Supervisors who do recruiting and hiring interviews, managers who do career development and performance management interviews, marketing and sales reps who conduct customer interviews, focus groups, and surveys—all of these people can benefit from appreciative interviewer training.

Conduct Appreciative Interviews

Appreciative interviews can be done in small-group settings, in focus groups, at staff meetings, and even over the phone or Internet. The one-on-one, face-to-face interview, however, seems to stimulate the most energy and enthusiasm among young and old, professional and front-line, cynical and inspired alike. This is evident in the following description of an appreciative interviewing session.

Davis Taylor, a former sales manager with the *San Jose Mercury News* national advertising team, shares his experience:

> It was delightful to see how intense some of the pairs were during the interviews. Then, in the afternoon, we were in three groups telling the stories we had heard and sharing highlights, and the room kept nearly boiling over with energy. This was right after lunch on a day that reached 103 degrees. You know how it can be after lunch in a typical workshop. But I guess we weren't typical.
>
> There were several surprises in the process, but perhaps the biggest one was "Joseph's" smile. Joseph is a member of the team who had not smiled at all in the last two or three months. He had been in a bad mood at best and severely depressed at worst. After the interviews, he started smiling. He seemed to be having a great time. Several others commented, saying things like, "I didn't know Joseph had that many teeth." I was prepared to have to deal with a lot of negative energy from him, and instead he turned out to be a source of joy. What is really cool about this is that Joseph was still smiling at work on Friday morning. In fact, I noticed that the energy carried over somehow for all of us. So, as you can tell, it's days later . . . and I'm still pumped.[60]

For many organizations, an important benefit of appreciative interviews is the way they enhance communication—by building bridges across cross-functional, cross-organization, cross-level, cross-shift, cross-gender, and cross-cultural barriers. This bridge building occurs in part because people are encouraged to "find someone to interview who is as different from yourself as possible." Appreciative interviews thus become great difference levelers, leading people to reflect that "deep down, we're not so different." At the same time, people come to appreciate some of the differences that emerge when people share their experiences, hopes, and dreams.

The Key Components of Good Appreciative Interviews   Several years ago we asked a group of interviewers for tips on conducting great appreciative interviews. Their responses included the following:

- *Prepare for the interview.* Be familiar with the questions, and have a good feel for the logic, the sequence, and the kind of summary information you will have to provide. Be familiar enough so you can avoid reading introductions and questions word for word, and so you can also hop back and forth in the Interview Guide or use alternative wordings when differences in language and education require it.

- *Prepare your partner.* When you schedule your interview, spend some time telling your partner what it will be like. Depending on the environment in which the inquiry is taking place, interviewees may wish to talk with their supervisor or manager before the interview. What's important is to help your partner arrive for the interview both curious and open to sharing.

- *Choose the right environment.* At the very least, it should be a neutral location—away from the work area, free of noise and stress. At best, it will be an expansive, comfortable space—a comfortable lounge, a restaurant, or a local park or picnic area.

- *Take time to build a connection before beginning the conversation.* If you're interviewing in a work setting and you normally wear a name badge, make sure people can see it! Share a little informal time listening to who this person is, letting him or her know a little bit about who you are, or simply telling the person about the interview process. Remember that this is your opportunity to get to know a really interesting person—not just an "interview."

- *Have a second copy of the Interview Guide available.* English may be someone's second language and thus more easily read than heard. In other cases, a person may be more visual than auditory. In either case, they might have an easier time answering complex questions if they can read the extra copy of the guide along with you.

- *Give people time to take things at their own pace.* Some

people warm up immediately; others take more time. If the interview begins to get really interesting just as it's finishing, ask if there is time to go back and think again about earlier questions. If your partner has difficulty answering a particular question, try saving it for last, when the person may feel more comfortable.

- *Show your partner that you are really listening and that you really care.* Keep your body relaxed and open, comfortably close, and gently facing them. Try to avoid being separated from them by a table. Make eye contact. Allow your facial expressions and verbal reinforcement to reflect your genuine interest. If you are curious and want some more information, by all means ask for it!

- *Go back over what you have learned to confirm its accuracy.* In particular, if you are handing in your notes to a central source or completing a summary sheet, consider having the interviewee read what you have written, with the option to modify or clarify anything to more fully express the essence of the responses.

- *Close by summarizing what most inspired you.* Because appreciative interviews are grounded in relationship, honor the relationship by sharing your experience. Tell people what you learned from them—how their stories have changed the way you see the organization and the world. Your partner has trusted you with his or her stories, hopes, and dreams. Honor that trust by returning it.

Disseminate Stories and Best Practices

Because Appreciative Inquiry focuses on what organizations do best, stories collected during an Appreciative Inquiry process provide a vehicle through which organization members can learn. Broad and wide dissemination of appreciative inquiry stories also recognizes work well done and sets a tone of being the best.

Stories and best practices can be disseminated in a variety of ways. Some ways that have worked well include the following:

- Print great stories and quotations in company newsletters.
- Display messages, quotes, and stories on posters and Web sites.
- Run continuous-loop videotapes in lunchrooms, cafeterias, and so on, to showcase great stories and interviews.
- Quote employees in marketing, recruiting, and orientation materials.
- Invite interviewers and interviewees to tell their stories at brown-bag lunch sessions.

When inquiries take place over a period of months, it is critical to provide interim opportunities for people to hear stories, make meaning of what they are hearing, and initiate innovative action in response to what they have learned. Without this interim dissemination of stories and best practices, organizations pass up one of the key benefits of whole-system appreciative inquiry—self-organized, inspired, emergent change.

Some clients meet this challenge by organizing mid-inquiry gatherings of interviewers. During these meetings people are invited to share stories, quotes, and best practices—and to pass messages along to the workforce as a whole. Ideally, these gatherings begin to transmit stories from individual interviewers to the larger community. At the same time, the gatherings build momentum for the inquiry as they demonstrate to interviewees that their input is being heard—that they can and do make a difference.

These storytelling sessions are even more effective when they are videotaped or otherwise transcribed and disseminated. Such transcriptions keep the organization as a whole as close as possible to the original interviews, transmitting stories, practices, and dreams in as raw and unedited a form as possible.

Make Meaning

Appreciative Inquiry meaning making is the time when interview data—stories, quotes, and inspirational highlights—are formally shared and made sense of in total. Meaning making provides opportunities for interviewers, interviewees, and the organization as a whole to actively engage in deeper levels of dialogue, learning, and exploration of their desired future. It enhances organizational wisdom and opens doors to short-term and long-term possibilities.

The process of arriving at shared meaning is what organizational theorist Karl Weick describes as "sensemaking." Meaning making, or sensemaking, is an ongoing, retrospective, social process. At its best, it is narrative based:

> What is necessary in sensemaking is a good story. A good story holds disparate elements together long enough to energize and guide action, plausibly enough to allow people to make retrospective sense of whatever happens, and engagingly enough that others will contribute their own inputs in the interest of sensemaking.[61]

Stories hold together cultures, communities, and organizations. They enable people to pass cultural conventions from generation to generation and serve as the vehicle through which cultural exceptions are made meaningful. Stories are at the heart of human identity—both personally and collectively. According to Jerome Brunner, "The negotiating and renegotiating of meanings by the mediation of narrative interpretation is one of the crowning achievements of human development."[62] It is certainly at the heart of human organizing at its best.

In general, Appreciative Inquiry meaning making has four characteristics:

1. *It takes place over time* rather than at some point in time designated as the conclusion of the inquiry. Mid-inquiry gatherings and interim dissemination of stories and lessons learned keep data fresh and locally meaningful over the course of extended inquiries. Such gatherings may be free standing

or they may be merged with previously scheduled meetings, as in the case of one client's inquiry for business process improvement.

2. *It focuses on participant experiences* rather than on consultant highlights. As much as possible, members of the organization, rather than outside experts, own the interview data. Even when we are dealing with hundreds of interviews, each of which includes two to three hours of data, we work hard to include the raw material of interviewees' peak experiences, insights, and inspirations. We also encourage the inclusion of interviewer reflections that have the most positive potential for the organization and its future—those aspects the interviewer found the most intriguing and inspiring.

3. *It revolves around qualitative, narrative analysis* rather than quantitative analysis. It focuses on stories and their generative potential. We begin by asking people to draw out and share the richest stories and quotes discovered during their interviews. After they have shared stories, we ask them to extract highlights and identify patterns and themes—to explore deeply all the factors that contribute to success in the stories they heard. In this way their stories are analyzed for the "root cause of organizational success." In short, we rely primarily on the narrative form to teach members of an organization about who they are and where they are going.

4. *It encourages attention to higher ground* rather than common ground. Although we do ask people to discover patterns and trends in the data, we also encourage them to seek out the lone, inspired voices—the individual stories, quotations, or comments that have the capacity to revolutionize the way they see themselves and their organization. Stories that depart from the situational norms are what Paul Grice calls "conversational implicatures."[63] They serve as triggers that set off meaning making. They are generative in their capacity to

make the exceptional seem plausible. They awaken the impetus and courage for transformation.

Lovelace Health Systems, introduced in Chapter 4, used a participant-guided process for meaning making during its AI Summit. Prior to the gathering, a three-person "story-collection team" reviewed summary sheets and determined which stories and quotes best brought the original topics to life. They sorted these stories and quotes by topic and recorded each on a color-coded index card.

At the summit, cards were distributed equally to the forty participants. People read their cards aloud, elaborating on them if they had originally heard or told the story. The stories and quotes were posted on a collective mural, and in some cases people drew pictures illustrating them. As a group, participants continued to tell more stories, posting and illustrating them, then explored in conversation what the stories were telling them about the original topics. The mural became the collective record of the interviews and their meaning—and the foundation for the Dream, Design, and Destiny phases. As consultant Susan Wood said, "It was one of the best meaning-making processes I've ever seen—and it was completely homegrown."

A useful tool for meaning making is a narrative analysis, a process that helps people extract themes and energizers from the stories that have been collected through appreciative interviews.

In small groups of six or eight, participants take turns sharing the most inspiring story they heard during the interviews. As stories are shared, group members listen and together find the meaning in them by naming the root causes of success embedded in the stories. Ideas can be recorded on a worksheet or flip chart page, as in the Excellence in Health Care example illustrated in Figure 11.

After all the stories have been heard and analyzed, the group identifies patterns, trends, and common themes. For example, in the case of Excellence in Health Care, we can see several common themes, including patient centered, compassion, and initiative beyond the job description. The narrative analysis process enables

Figure 11. Sample Narrative Analysis: Excellence in Health Care

Stories	Causes of Success
Susie's Surgery	Patient centered, family involvement, pain management, asked the child what she needed/wanted, compassion.
Helpful Housekeeper	Went beyond her role, took initiative, cared, patient centered, dared to do the right thing.
Patient's Last Request	Deep listening, outside-the-box actions, did what needed to be done—not just a job, patient first, just did it, acted on behalf of the patient and what was right.
(continues)	(continues)

groups to look across the stories collected from many interviews and identify common elements. It is a very useful tool for identifying the root causes of success—an organization's inventory of strengths, or the positive core.

Mapping the Positive Core

Appreciative Inquiry is based on the assumption that every person, group, organization, and community possesses a unique set of strengths, resources, skills, and assets. Taken together, we call this the positive core.[64]

The positive core—the essence of the organization at its best—can serve as the foundation for the future: the raw material for what might be. Even in the midst of significant transition, organizations that successfully manage positive change do so by preserving and building upon their positive core. Because the positive core is the essential goodness and capability that enables an organization or community to thrive in the process of positive change, it must be retained.

Thus, Appreciative Inquiry as a process for positive change begins with a discovery of the positive core and its portrayal in an illustration. To do this we ask people to

1. Read and share stories collected in the interview process.

2. Conduct a "root cause of organizational success" analysis to identify all the factors that lead to the organization's success—values, technical assets, leadership strengths, strategic advantages, human and financial resources, beneficial relationships and partnerships, best practices, processes, systems, and structures.

3. Portray all the success factors on one chart, picture, or illustration. This becomes the positive core map.

The best positive core maps are metaphors for the business of the organization. For example, at Roadway Express, a nationwide trucking company, the positive core map was represented as a huge truck drawn on the wall. Having each been given a piece of poster board with a box drawn on it, small groups were asked to "fill" their boxes with strengths and "load" them onto a picture of a truck. When they finished the task and stood back to see their work, what they saw was inspiring—a huge truck, filled with Roadway's strengths, capabilities, and strategic potential.

Other examples of creative positive core maps include a mosaic, a puzzle, a library of books, building blocks, and stepping stones—each one a different success factor. Exhibits 4 and 5 are examples of positive core maps. Whatever metaphor is used to map the positive core, it must facilitate the coming together of many diverse data points into one integrated visual representation that can then serve as an inspiration for Dream activities.

The best Appreciative Inquiry processes continually refer back to and incorporate the positive core into the latter phases of the 4-D process. During the Dream phase, people consider how to amplify the positive core. During the Design phase, they contemplate how to leverage it to enhance performance. During the Destiny phase, they reflect on its implications for future action. By knowing and consciously leveraging their positive core, organizations and communities strengthen their identities and enhance their capacities to sustain positive change.

Exhibits 4 and 5.   Sample Positive Core Maps

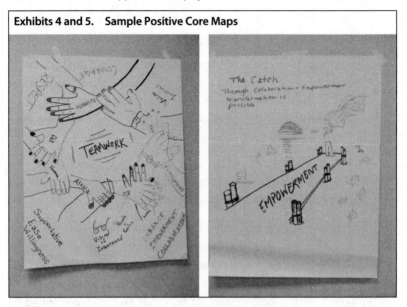

Discovery at Hunter Douglas

In the following pages, we continue the ongoing story of Focus 2000. In addition, we add details from the second iteration of the 4D Cycle, related to strategic planning. The details we've chosen illustrate how you can vary the process of Discovery to keep employees excited and engaged over time.

The Test of Commitment

At the end of the Interview Guide design meeting, interviewers organized into two teams. The first, dubbed the Seventh Generation, was organized to interview every employee who wanted to be interviewed. The second team, named the Outsiders, was designed to conduct one hundred external interviews with customers, suppliers, community members, and a small sampling of best-in-class organizations.

From the beginning, the Outsiders faced unique challenges that led them to reenact some of the company's core cultural issues. Decisions would be made in meetings—and then unmade outside the meeting as clusters of professional and managerial staff became privy to additional insights or information. Senior-level team members began to raise financial and professional concerns about the possibility of sending nonprofessional staff out for interviews with general managers and community leaders.

In response, nonprofessional staff began to feel disrespected and excluded—two of the core themes that had led the organization down the Appreciative Inquiry path. Line-level participants began complaining to their peers and filing grievances with the human resources function. Two or three people threatened to pull out of the process entirely, while others meekly and quietly complied with the trend to have interviews conducted only by members of the professional and managerial staff, who would be at the location anyway.

The team looked as if it were about to implode. Leadership became concerned about both the integrity of the Appreciative Inquiry process and the precedent that this team's success or failure would set for the future. Clearly, the group was in desperate need of some support—but in what form? Some sort of catharsis, using a traditional team-building approach, would reduce the pressure, but such an approach seemed contrary to the principles of the process. The Outsiders crisis became a test of commitment to the Appreciative Inquiry process.

The Advisory Team decided to address the group's issues in a six-hour team-building session founded on the principles of Appreciative Inquiry. The session was mandatory for every participant in the Outsiders. The general manager and the facilitating consultant personally delivered invitations on all three shifts. The meeting began with appreciative interviews and flowed through the following topics of discussion: peak experiences on the team, life-giving factors that contribute to the team at its best, hopes and dreams for the team's future, design of agreements for team self-management, and planning for the team's interview process.

The session worked. Issues were satisfactorily resolved, and decisions were made that allowed the team to effectively move forward.

The Outsiders' experience proved that even a single positive experience can help retrain and reeducate large groups of people. Had the Outsiders gone under, as it briefly seemed that they might, their failure would have been anecdotal proof that "nothing can ever change within the Window Fashions Division." Because the team succeeded—and in such a stellar way—they proved the opposite: that line employees and leaders could indeed work out differences and collaborate effectively to accomplish great things for the organization.

This initial conflict was the first of several episodes that threatened to derail the positive energy of the Focus 2000 effort. In fact, as safety and trust began to increase, more and more of the company's habitual patterns came up for inspection and repatterning. Hunter Douglas's leaders learned from this and subsequent episodes the importance of walking the talk—of believing in Appreciative Inquiry as a viable tool and using it, even in the most seemingly dysfunctional situations.

Wave After Wave of Interviews

By the end of the early June offsite meetings, the two interview teams had been mobilized. The Seventh Generation team was queued up to conduct the five hundred internal and external interviews over three months—approximately half of the Hunter Douglas workforce plus one hundred outside stakeholders.

Using Mass-Mobilized Inquiry as the model, the first wave of interviewers interviewed, recruited, and trained others, creating two hundred fifty interviewers to conduct the five hundred interviews in less than two months.

Having come through the "valley of death," the Outsiders also went to work. Production workers, professionals, and midlevel managers traveled around the country in teams of two to interview a variety of customers, suppliers, and community members. Together, these teams created priceless business relationships, gathered valuable information, and gained immeasurable wisdom.

Joan, a woman who worked in production, interviewed a customer who had made Hunter Douglas history through his incessant complaints and demands. During the interview, as "Ken Jacobs" would begin to complain about something that was wrong with the Hunter Douglas product or process, Joan would redirect him: "Now Mr. Jacobs, I know this is very important—but that's not really the purpose of our interview. Let me write that down and have someone else get back to you to talk about your problem." At the end of the interview, Jacobs gave her a big hug and a tour of his

production plant. Two months later, he was a frequent, positive, and insightful contributor at the division's first AI Summit. At the end of that gathering,
he shared with the group of summit participants:

> In my mind, the Window Fashions Division has been engaged in one
> of the most powerful, positive activities I've known in my experience
> with the company. This is what will keep this company great in the
> future.

John, another production employee, traveled to Omaha to interview
one of Hunter Douglas's biggest distributors. While there, he learned how
the company recruited and retained homeless people as employees by
providing them with advances on their first paychecks to both purchase
basic clothing and make deposits on living quarters. During his interview, the
distributor boasted of the results: a measurable reduction in turnover and
the satisfaction of helping people lift themselves out of desperate poverty.
A month or so after returning from his interview, John asked permission to
make a presentation to the president of Hunter Douglas North America. He
arrived at the meeting with a detailed proposal for piloting a similar program
in the Window Fashions Division as a way of simultaneously filling vacant
positions and providing a significant community service.

Benefits of Front-Line Employee Interviewers

Several interviewers came back from their experiences filled with appreciation for Hunter Douglas and its work environment. One man said:

> The employees at that other company [the one he'd interviewed]
> couldn't believe that they'd send a machine operator like me out to
> do this kind of interview! They said I must be working for the best
> company in the world, and I began to think that might be true.

Another woman reflected:

> I never knew how good we had it here, until I saw some of the work-
> ing conditions at those other plants and heard about their pay and
> benefits. The people here need to know what they have. They need
> to know what a good place this is to work.

Having personally seen alternatives and received feedback from their interviews, employees more fully recognized the excellence of the Hunter Douglas work environment and the level of responsibility they had been given through the Focus 2000 program.

As the interviews continued, managers and professionals throughout the Window Fashions Division began to feel that nonprofessional involvement in external interviews was one of the most important elements of the Focus 2000 process. Nine months later, Rick Pellett reported:

> This was the most significant and positive decision we made in the entire Focus 2000 process. I can't believe we almost didn't let them go. It was a "moment of truth," and thank goodness we made the right decision.

Stories Have Wings

As Discovery proceeded, interviewers were excited, energized, and ready to change the world "one interview at a time." Everyone else in the organization was more than curious about what had happened at the offsite meetings. People were dying to share and hear stories—but they had nowhere to share them! For it turned out that a big reason for the long-touted "black hole" in communication was circumstantial rather than malicious. Neither telephone, voice mail, e-mail, nor a personalized mailbox was available to anybody in a line-level position in the company. In other words, nearly two-thirds of the workforce was essentially unreachable through any form of direct personal communication.

This was a major challenge. The internal communications team—self-named the InTouchables—came up with a series of strategies that were quick, easy, inexpensive, and strikingly effective. They focused on two questions: How can we spread the word about what we're learning? How can we draw people into Focus 2000 and the good work that is already taking place? Together, these activities engaged the entire workforce and built enthusiasm and momentum for the larger process.

"Ask Me About Focus 2000"

At the first interviewer gathering, people shared their successes—along with their dismay at the general lack of awareness about Focus 2000. Despite the initial kickoff meetings, the workforce in general remained unaware of the details of how Focus 2000 was unfolding. As ideas were being discussed, someone blurted out, "I need people to be asking me questions! As soon as they ask me questions, I'll have space to tell them everything."

The room grew quiet as people thought. Then in the far back someone whispered something: "A button—we need to wear buttons that ask people to ask."

This conversation evolved into the "Ask Me About Focus 2000" buttons. People wore them on their work shirts, attached them to the walls of their cubicles, and pinned them to their baseball caps. The buttons invited people to inquire. And once people had inquired, participants told everything. They told about the interview topics and the interviews, about their hopes and dreams, and about the company that was emerging in their imaginations.

Traveling Posters

Beginning at the first meaning-making session, participants created hand-made posters and placed them in cafeterias and break rooms. The template for the posters was a dry-mounted white page with the Focus 2000 logo on the top. Below the logo were printed such sentence fragments as

- The most important thing I learned at the first Focus 2000 offsite was . . .
- The best thing about being a Focus 2000 interviewer is . . .
- The best thing about being interviewed for the Focus 2000 program is . . .
- The message that I want everyone at Hunter Douglas to hear about the Focus 2000 program is . . .

Blank index cards were distributed on which people completed the sentence fragments, one statement per card. They were asked to write legibly and, if they were willing, to sign their names. The unedited responses were glued onto the boards, and the resulting posters were circulated on a weekly basis to different parts of the campus.

General curiosity about these posters was tremendous. People clustered around them during their lunch hours and read their peers' comments. It was a personal, idiosyncratic way for each offsite participant to share his or her insights with everyone else in the organization.

What did we hear on the posters? Every card was different, but here are some highlights:

- "The most important thing I learned at the first Focus 2000 offsite was that my voice makes a difference."
- "The best thing about being a Focus 2000 interviewer is finding out that we're really the same, underneath our differences."
- "The best thing about being interviewed for the Focus 2000 program is remembering people and situations that have helped me become the person I am today."
- "The message that I want everyone at Hunter Douglas to hear about the Focus 2000 program is that we're the only ones that can bring our dreams to life."

All the News That's Fit to Print

The division's newsletter was great, but it was only printed quarterly. Clearly, given the scope and scale of what interviewers were discovering, they needed something different. So the InTouchables created a monthly newsletter called the Inquirer 2000. The full-color newsletter included photographs and stories about Focus 2000 events and activities, individual stories from people's appreciative interviews, and examples of how employees were applying Appreciative Inquiry in their work and home lives. Each issue also reinforced information that had been communicated through plant and department meetings and provided a calendar of upcoming events.

These newsletters were such a hit that we leveraged the approach when it came time to write the synthesis reports. Inquirer 2000 Special Editions were cast in a newspaper format and included late-breaking stories, photographs, funnies, crossword puzzles, and classified ads inviting people to participate in upcoming Focus 2000-related activities. Both visually stimulating and fun, the reports engaged people in the Focus 2000 experience and communicated the best stories, practices, and images of the future.

Back to the Movies

Video had worked in extraordinary ways during the town meeting, so the InTouchables decided to do more of what worked. Using televisions and VCRs that already existed on the campus, they produced and displayed video footage throughout the life of the inquiry.

Every few weeks a new video was released featuring highlights of off-site meetings and sharing stories and practices from people's appreciative interviews. Throughout the division, people moved chairs closer to television sets during lunch and break time. They saw their peers on screen and began to ask more questions. They became engaged.

The Many Faces of Inquiry

The first ten months of Appreciative Inquiry at Hunter Douglas were full to the brim of one-on-one interviews, followed by small-group reflections. But as we finished up with those first one thousand interviews and began looking for ways to incorporate Appreciative Inquiry into the business of the business, we got a surprise. "No! No more interviews!" became the cry of the desperate. People had adored the process and what it had brought to them—but they had simply burned out on the approach.

Once again, frustration led to inspiration. The consultants began designing new approaches to inquiry that forged relationships, unleashed the positive core, stimulated dreams, and encouraged the establishment of improbable partnerships. Prior to the 1998 strategic planning summit, for example, they had distributed a prework Interview Guide to all participants. The instructions offered a wide variety of options for inquiry:

- Between now and the Strategic Planning Summit, please purposefully and intentionally gather information from employees, customers, and suppliers. Using this Interview Guide, there are a number of ways in which you might choose to do this. Here are a few ideas that we've had. . . . Feel free to be creative and come up with some of your own and share them with one another.

- Dedicate ten minutes at the beginning of regularly scheduled team or plant meetings to discuss one question or topic at a time. Do this at each meeting until all the topics are covered.

- Conduct three or four interviews with a mix of people from within your business unit or department—preferably with those who won't otherwise have the opportunity to be involved in the strategic planning process this year.

- Informally ask for people's insights about the topics in the Interview Guide—in the lunchroom or wherever else you share casual conversations with people outside of your immediate work area.

- If your job regularly brings you in contact with customers or suppliers, do the same thing with them! Ask them a question every time you have them on the phone, interview them when you're on a site visit, or schedule a special lunch to hear their thoughts and insights.

- Host a focus group and invite members of your department along with people from two to three other departments you work with closely.

By encouraging people to vary their approaches to Discovery, they maintained the spirit of inquiry while consistently injecting new life into an ongoing process of organizational change.

Keeping the Momentum Going

Part of what made Focus 2000 so successful was Hunter Douglas's commitment to engaging larger and larger groups of stakeholders in various aspects of the inquiry. From the beginning, they were committed to involving a diverse representation of the organization and to building on people's passions. This meant that people would come and go throughout the life of the inquiry. They would volunteer, do a lot of good work, and then turn their attention back to their primary responsibilities.

At the same time, newcomers would be invited in for an appreciative interview, a meaning-making session, or some other activity—and would get hooked. In the end, some of the strongest proponents of Appreciative Inquiry were people who were never explicitly trained in the methodology but who joined midway through the process and saw the benefits.

As they cast this ever-widening net of involvement, the Advisory Team and leadership continued to attend closely to issues of continuity and transition. For example, when they trained new interviewers, they established a buddy system through which newcomers would be partnered with experienced interviewers who knew the spirit and intention of the original topics and questions and who had already refined their techniques. Similarly, when they invited people who had no previous experience with Focus 2000 or Appreciative Inquiry to large events, they built in transitional people and activities that ensured continuity in the entire process. By attending to issues of inclusion and transition, they maintained and built momentum. They provided a structure that supported people in following their bliss—in contributing to the organization according their energy and interests.

This ends our description of Discovery at Hunter Douglas. The Hunter Douglas story continues with Dream, in Chapter 8.

CHAPTER 8

Dream: Visions and Voices of the Future

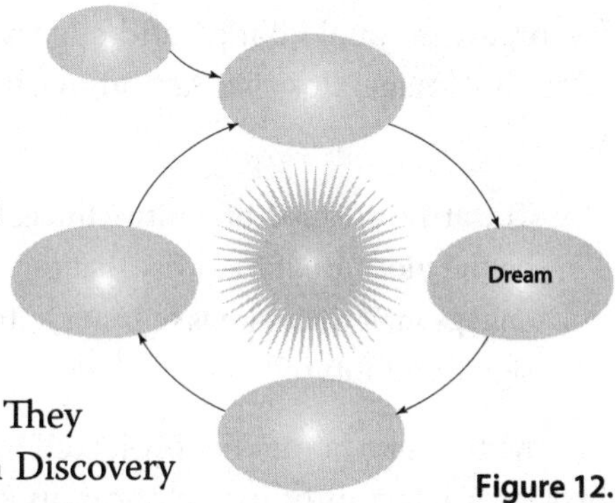

In the Appreciative Inquiry Dream phase, all members of the organization and its stakeholders engage in processes to envision the future of the organization. They discuss what they learned in Discovery and then go one step further—to imagine

Figure 12.

a more inspiring, positive, life-giving world and organization. In the process, they share rich personal dreams, describe and creatively enact collective dreams, and often write an organizational mission or purpose statement.

Appreciative Inquiry dreaming lifts up the best of what has been and invites people to imagine it even better. It amplifies the positive core of the organization and stimulates more valued and vital futures. In so doing it challenges the status quo and magnetically draws people toward the next phase of the 4-D process, in which they will design organizations through which they can bring their greatest hopes and dreams to life.

The Power of Images

As the Anticipatory Principle suggests, human systems are like plants. They organically and instinctively grow in the direction of their "light," which is their collective image of the future. For people, this "running stream of consciousness," as William James called it, serves as a collective image of personal possibility. Everyone has an inner dialogue or self-talk—a series of personal questions that together delineate the parameters of performance. The more positive our personal self-talk is, the more positive our personal potential will be.

Suppose that the same is true of organizations—that the images they hold about the future do indeed influence their performance, both now and in the future. If this is the case, then the cooperative capacity to generate positive images becomes a crucial resource for organizational change and success. In a hallmark article titled "Positive Image, Positive Action," David Cooperrider puts forth this thesis:

> The artful creation of positive imagery on a collective basis may well be the most prolific activity that individuals and organizations can engage in, if their aim is to bring to fruition a positive and humanly significant future.[65]

Much like a movie projected onto a screen, organizations project a horizon of expectation, imagination, and possibility that brings the future powerfully into the present as a mobilizing agent. The more powerful and compelling an organization's images of the future are, the more positive the outcome will be. For example, when Sir Colin Marshall took over the reins of British Airways, he inherited an airline in great disarray. Employees and customers alike were dissatisfied. Despite appearances, Marshall's eyes were fully open to the current reality when he declared, "We are the world's favorite airline." Whenever anyone told him it was not true, he said, "That may be so—but your job is to make it true." His image became a guiding light to the future, a challenge, and a worthy goal—one that many now would say has been attained.

Images as the Limit of Performance

Henry Ford put it simply when he said, "Whether you think you can, or you think you can't, you are right." Images, created in conversation and held in belief as real, are more than the seeds of positive performance. They are also the limits to performance.

Images that make a business successful often become its limiting factor and the target of transformation. About eight years ago, faced with the need to reduce the costs of health care in all aspects of delivery, the president of a national clinical laboratory business addressed his organization's sales force. He told them that the company could save significant dollars—thereby reducing the cost of service to doctors and customers—if doctors would agree to send their tests to regional labs rather than local labs. He outlined the proposed organizational change, saying that the biggest challenge was convincing the doctors that the images of effectiveness they believed in were no longer true.

Ironically, only four years earlier, many of the same sales reps had convinced the doctors those images would be good business! The clinical laboratory had established a network of local labs and had built its reputation and business on the image of local service. Now the business environment and technology had changed, and fewer regional labs could provide the same quality of service as a national network of local labs. Yet doctors still believed that they and their patients were best served by local labs. The sales force's job was not to sell clinical testing but to help doctors change their image of the ideal testing process. The image of the ideal that built the company into the biggest and most successful in the country was now its limiting factor.

Expanding the Context for Excellence

To create new images, organizations must see themselves in a larger context—they must first consider and then act upon questions of purpose and "calling." As Albert Einstein said, "You cannot solve a problem at the same level of abstraction at which it was created." This is certainly the case with organizational change. To effect change in the collective images held among stakeholders in such a way that new images are compelling and inspire action, you must expand the context for excellence. You must invite people to imagine beyond the boundaries of their daily work, role, or responsibility and to consider questions of purpose and calling.

Organizations that endure, that are able to successfully change and adapt over time, display what professors and consultants Jim Collins and Jerry Porras call "pragmatic idealism."[66] They cite Merck Pharmaceuticals' decision to give away a drug that cured a parasitic disease that ravaged the Third World. The relationship between this decision and the company's dream—to be "in the business of preserving and improving human life"[67]—illustrates the importance of a higher purpose, or broader context, for excellence. Merck had a compelling calling that led them to give the drug to the people who needed it—and they trusted that such a compelling act of goodwill would "somehow . . . pay off."

In the Appreciative Inquiry Dream phase, we help individuals and organizations see themselves in the largest possible context for excellence by asking questions such as: *What is your dream for a better world? In what ways might your organization serve that dream? What is your calling? What unique contribution can you make to your community? To the world?* These are more than abstract questions. They serve as a practical template for dreaming about the organization—a way of stimulating practical idealism.

Take Nutrimental Foods SA, for example. When they dreamed of their future, they did so in the context of their country, Brazil. They dreamed first of a safe, healthy, and prosperous life for their children and grandchildren. Then they discussed the way the food they processed, packaged, and distributed could positively influence the health and well-being of their country. As a result, they changed the purpose of their business to be in the business of healthy food, whereby they would contribute to a healthier lifestyle in their country.

For many stakeholders, Appreciative Inquiry dreaming is a first invitation to think big and to imagine bold possibilities for their organization. When asked to envision beyond the boundaries of their work, people find new meaning in their work. They come to see how what they do contributes to the whole; to a larger, more life-enhancing purpose for their organization and beyond.

Key Decisions in the Dream

The decisions to be addressed in the Dream phase relate to both the process and the content of the initiative. They include the following:

- *Whom should we involve?* How do we get all relevant voices in the room? How do we include the voices of those who are not physically present?

- *What experiential activity will we use to reveal our images of the future?* Will we simply write, or will we paint, draw, or enact our dreams? How will we stimulate creativity?

- *What will be the outcome of our dream?* Are compelling creative images sufficient? Do we need a strategic vision? A purpose statement?

Getting All the Voices in the Room

Because organizations' images of the future are created and maintained in community dialogue—in conversations among members and stakeholders of the community—they are a kind of public property. This public property is only enriched when larger and larger groups of people are invited to contribute to it. The larger and more diverse the communities involved in dreaming are, the more compelling the outcome will be. An assortment of perspectives, experiences, and thinking styles allows positive images of hope and potential to rise, like cream, to the surface. Everyone owns them. Everyone grabs hold of them and takes responsibility for their implementation. And as a result, everyone has a stake in enhancing the organization's potential for achievement and vitality.

In the Appreciative Inquiry Dream phase we include as many people as possible, including of course as many stakeholders as possible. One of the most common forums through which these large, diverse groups of people can dream in community is the AI Summit. During an AI Summit, hundreds or thousands of people can dream together. They can share personal hopes and dreams, and then, in small groups, they can create collective dreams for the whole organization. Group dreams can then be presented and woven together into one powerful dream for the whole. When the whole system is present for such activities, the results are dramatic. New visions lead to inspired actions that in turn strengthen employee engagement, customer loyalty, and financial performance.

But sometimes getting all the voices in the room can be challenging. When this is the case—when you can't get everyone together for an entire meeting—it's time to get creative. Ask yourself, If we can't get all the bodies in the room, how can we get all the voices in the room? In some cases we have invited customers, consumers, or clients to join meetings for two hours of inquiry and dialogue. On other occasions we have taken groups out to meet people: to conduct interviews or focus groups with community leaders, investment brokers, or school children, for example—all as a way to get other voices in the room as cocreators of images of the organization's future.

Consider, for example, the five-day Academic Leadership Institute at the University of California, Berkeley. It involved only forty-five people, all of whom held similar leadership positions in their respective institutions. Because the dreams they would articulate would make a difference to institutions of higher education throughout North America, they needed more than their own dreams. To bring other voices into the room, we asked participants to conduct interviews with students, faculty, staff, alumni, community members, and others prior to the meeting. When participants arrived, they were saturated with a variety of voices, stories, ideas, and points of view. We invited more voices to the room during the meeting by bringing in outside speakers on global trends within and beyond the field of higher education.

When it came time to dream, everyone was polyphonic—they easily reflected the ideas and ideals of the many others who were not present but who were integral to the future of higher education. As a result, the dreams they expressed were highly innovative, responsive, and fulfilling to the hopes and aspirations of the larger community.

Choosing the Right Creative, Fun Approach

During Affirmative Topic Choice and Discovery, participants engage largely in "talk and tell" activities. One-on-one interviews and small-group conversations are interspersed with experiential mapping of the positive core, but by and large, the process is focused on building knowledge, learning, and relationships through conversation.

Dream activities bring a radical shift in energy and approach. More important, they stimulate creativity. But also significant is the way in which they level the organizational playing field. Creative Dream activities are a forum in which people's often-unexpressed creative talents can be seen and valued by the whole. After they have dreamed and played together, people are virtually incapable of returning to stifling organizational roles and forms.

AI dreaming can involve anything from guided imagery and silent reflections to playful, dramatic skits: talk shows, commercials, songs, poems, and so on. People draw, paint, perform, and play the future they most prefer as if it already exists. Creative and fun dream activities take people into the realm of the unknown but imagined—they open doorways to "right-brain," intuitive ways of knowing.

When they are too small, dreams can limit success, so we extend the horizon of imagination as far as possible through boldly creative dream activities. At their best, these activities tap into the right hemisphere of the brain, which knows images but not language, music but not written reports, play but not work, present but not past or future. In short, these activities provide a whole-brained medium for expanding the organization's images of the future.

Creative, playful dreaming is not the norm in many organizations. Because of this, we periodically find ourselves faced with questions like these: Can't we just *talk* about what we want? Isn't all this play a distraction from the *real work*? Our answer is no, this is the real work—of having fun at work, of being creative, of bringing out the diverse strengths of people, and of generating images of a more desirable future.

In short, we strongly recommend using experiential approaches to dreaming in even the most conservative environments. Without this temporary shift in energy and approach to knowing, organizations seriously limit their capacities for creating new images and forward progress. If your organization would balk at the idea of dramatic skits, consider drawing or painting dreams. Consider poetry or an awards show. Consider making collages by cutting images from magazines. Or consider building a giant model out of cardboard boxes, egg cartons, and supplies from a hardware store. Whatever activity you use to reveal and uplift your organization's dream, make it creative and fun.

Determining the Right Take-Aways

Your Change Agenda will determine the outcome of your Dream phase. Outcomes can range from bold new images registered in the minds and hearts of those who participated, to videos of the dreams to be shown in cafeterias and break rooms, to documented strategic visions or purpose statements. Remember: the overarching goal of Appreciative Inquiry is to change the images told in the stories and inner dialogue of the organization. To do this you may or may not need a document. Great experiences have a way of creating their own life—together with stories that can spread like wildfire though the organization. So at a minimum, the best Dream take-away is a great story about a great experience.

In other cases Appreciative Inquiry dreaming calls for a concrete outcome: a written document. For example, the Dream phase may culminate in the creation of a purpose statement for the new business or a clearly defined strategic vision for an organization. It may result in a vision and values statement for a new alliance or a long-term vision for two merging organizations.

Piñon Management Company operates fifteen long-term-care facilities in Colorado and New Mexico. Seeking a process that would build enthusiasm and teamwork while creating the foundation for a solid strategic and business plan, they engaged in a two-day AI-based strategic planning retreat. After interviewing one another and mapping their positive core, participants engaged in a guided visualization that took them years into the future—imagining the world ten and twenty years out, when they themselves might be residents in an extended-care facility.

Based on what they saw, they created a mind map of the most positive macro trends that were emerging—the things that gave them the greatest hope for the future of their business. From this map, they identified half a dozen strategic business opportunities that were unfolding, based on those trends, over the coming ten years. These strategic business opportunities served as the foundation for the next phases of the 4-D Cycle, during which they affirmatively described how their organization would adapt to these opportunities and made concrete decisions through which their descriptions would unfold.

Dream, Step by Step

Dreaming often begins in the interview process, during which imaginative questions about the future awaken people's longings and stimulate recollection of forgotten hopes and dreams. Collective dream activities build on the energy of these interview questions, inviting people to further envision and enact their most innovative and desired future.

Dream activities generally take place in large gatherings, involving from fifty to two thousand people. From start to finish,

Table 11. Dream, Step by Step
1. Reflect on a focal question.
2. Engage in a Dream Dialogue.
3. Clarify the collective dream.
4. Creatively enact the dream.
5. Determine common themes and opportunities.
6. Create an opportunity map.
7. (Optional) Document the dream.

they take from an hour to half a day. Through the seven-part process shown in Table 11, Appreciative Inquiry dreaming leverages the best of people's interviews and stories and creates a rich context for Design.

Reflect on a Focal Question

Begin the Dream phase by asking participants to quietly consider a focal question. It may be the final dream question from the Interview Guide or it may be completely different, tailored to the particular event. For example:

> It is twenty years from today—just one generation from now. Your children have grown to adulthood. They have their own children— your grandchildren. The world that your children and grandchildren have inherited is a good world, a better world than the one you once knew.

> • What does it look like? How and where do people live? What do they do for work? How do they travel? How do they learn?

> • Imagine that you are sitting with your youngest grandchild, telling her the story of how this world came to be. What decisions and choices did you and others make in the early twenty-first century to pave the way for this brave new world they are enjoying? What seeds did you and others plant? How were the seeds fertilized? Harvested?

Give participants the focal question and provide them with individual time for reflection. They may conduct a short interview; review what they learned from prior interviews, meaning-making reports, or presentations; or journal quietly for a few minutes. Better yet, introduce the question through some sort of guided visualization—a slower, more hypnotic process through which they will enjoy a gut-level experience of the question at hand. Whatever the approach, create an imaginative, inspiring futuristic focus that will "prime the pump" for the rich, creative Dream Dialogue that is to come.

Engage in a Dream Dialogue

Following individual reflection, ask people to cluster in diverse groups of ideally no more than twelve people and engage in a Dream Dialogue. This is an open-ended conversation, scheduled for half an hour to an hour. Ask participants in the dialogue to share what they have learned from others as well as what they hoped and dreamed during their own reflections. Watch how the conversations stimulate more images. Watch how themes and patterns begin to emerge organically.

Clarify the Collective Dream

Now ask the group to focus on clarifying their collective images of the future. Stimulate their thinking with questions such as *What have you heard? What does it look like? How will you know when it's there?* Encourage people to articulate vivid details about the future state, including the role of their organization or industry.

Creatively Enact the Dream

Next give small groups about thirty minutes to develop a three- to five-minute creative enactment of their collective dream. The more playful the enactments are, the better. We like to offer a variety of ways in which the dream may be expressed—pictures, stories, skits, commercials, newspaper articles, songs, poems, and others are all "open game." We encourage people to use any supplies that are available to them in the room; and in some cases, we provide props such as musical instruments, art supplies, fabric, and clothing for costumes.

In general, we state only two ground rules for these enactments: everyone in each small group must be involved in creating and in presenting the enactment.

As an alternative to enactments, organizations may choose to draw pictures, make one big dream mural, or create items for a time capsule. For example, in 2002 the United Religions Initiative decided to support regional summits rather than hosting one global summit. North America was the first region to have a summit. During its planning, organizers became clear that they wanted some way to send messages from summit to summit. The idea emerged to create a traveling URI Dream Book. At the North America summit, each small group painted their dream on a page, then wrote down their hopes and signed the back of the page. Before the pages were compiled into a book, they hung as a clothesline art exhibition, showing participants' collective dreams for peace. The book was hand carried to Africa, along with blank pages on which their summit participants would paint their dreams. In the end, the URI Dream Book traveled to seven continents, carrying and stimulating dreams for peace on Earth.

Determine Common Themes and Opportunities

Following presentations of the dream enactments in the plenary, reconvene the small groups to discuss the common themes and opportunities they saw embedded in the dreams. Themes tend to be high-level, values-based visionary statements, such as "go green," "share leadership," or "service with a smile." Opportunities for innovations tend to be more specific, such as "create a community garden in the empty lot next to the cancer center," "design electronic window curtains," or "train greeters to meet customers at the front door." Both themes and opportunities are important, as they point the way to Design.

How the groups make meaning of their dreams will depend on the question(s) you ask them. Consider and choose among the following questions:

- What are the three most energizing themes you saw presented in the dream enactments?
- What are the three boldest opportunities for innovation that you saw presented in the dream enactments?
- Based on your dream enactments, what elements of your organization—processes, systems, leadership, purpose, strategy, relationships, and so on—offer the greatest opportunities for improvement?
- What new possibilities presented in your dream enactments best build on the strengths of your positive core?

As with everything about Appreciative Inquiry, the questions you ask as a facilitator will determine what the groups discuss and create as their future.

Create an Opportunity Map

After the small groups have time to discuss and make meaning from their dream enactments, return to full group. Ask each small group to share the common themes they have heard as well as the specific opportunities they have identified. As each group shares, record their ideas on an Opportunity Map—a mind map organized around the topic of the group's Appreciative Inquiry process. Exhibit 6 depicts an Opportunity Map on the Future of Health Care, showing the many themes and opportunities that were embedded in the dreams of members of a large regional health-care system.

Opportunity mapping is a great tool for recording a wide range of ideas in one place. It can then be used as a visual support for

Exhibit 6. Sample Opportunity Map

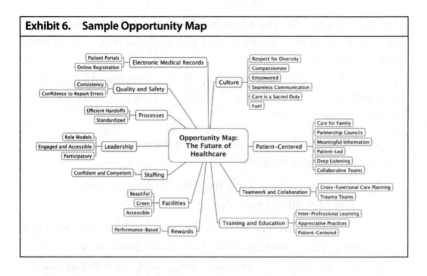

conversations about potential innovations and priorities, both important conversations in the transition from Dream to Design.

Document the Dream [optional]

Crafting a final dream or vision statement may be accomplished by a subgroup or it can be facilitated in a large group. If a subgroup creates the document, be certain they have adequate input from the entire organization. Drafts can be generated in a large group meeting and then reviewed and revised by a small group. The small group can host focus groups, Internet dialogues, or review meetings to collect input from the whole organization. Whenever a small group takes on the task of documenting a dream, be clear that they are working in the service of the whole, and that their job is to best reflect the highest collective dreams of the organization. In many ways, the people in these groups are "ghost writers" for the larger community.

Although it takes time to write a document in a large-group setting, the benefits can be worthwhile. Next we describe an innovative approach we used to facilitate a diverse group of seventy-five Hunter Douglas stakeholders in crafting a strategic vision statement.

Dream at Hunter Douglas

The AI Summit was first introduced to Hunter Douglas as the vehicle for dreaming during *Focus 2000*. Very quickly the organization's leaders recognized the AI Summit as a powerful process for engaging large groups of people in discovering, dreaming, and designing the future. From that time forward, a variety of gatherings—from annual meetings with customers to communication task forces—took on summit-like qualities.

The following sections describe the Dream processes in both the first and second AI Summits. The first continues the ongoing story of Hunter Douglas's *Focus 2000* initiative. The second offers unique insights into the application of Appreciative Inquiry Dreaming to Strategic Planning.

The First AI Summit at Hunter Douglas

The first AI Summit took place in the fall of 1997. One hundred people gathered for three days to Dream, Design, and Deliver on the promise of the Focus 2000 tag line: All Voices . . . All Opinions . . . All Ideas. Participants represented all positions, functions, and levels in the organization, as well as key external stakeholders: customers, suppliers, and community members.

After a morning of appreciative interviews, dialogue, and sharing about the findings from five hundred employee, customer, supplier, and community member interviews, it was time to dream. Since the purpose of Focus 2000 was "to create a vision for the next millennium," summit participants were asked to reflect on the organization's future excellence:

> Imagine it is five years from today. You are part of a benchmarking team that has come to study Hunter Douglas Window Fashions Division. What do you find? What is it about this organization that merits your attention? What makes it so great?

After a short time in personal reflection, groups were formed to share ideas and assemble those ideas into a collective dream. Each group was given forty-five minutes to discuss their dreams, then thirty minutes to prepare a creative enactment of their most powerfully positive dreams.

The dream dialogues were lively, and the dream enactments livelier.

In the dream enactments, pipe-cleaner-antennae-adorned aliens who visited Hunter Douglas reported to their high command about the organization's people and communication practices. A team of Window Fashions employees attended an Academy Awards–like ceremony that celebrated their exceptional collaboration and industry leadership. Another group offered up a particular product innovation.

Zany though the presentations were, they had serious implications for the future. For example, one group unveiled—to the opening music from 2001: A Space Odyssey[68]—"Virtuette: Programmable Window Coverings." These window coverings could be "anything you want: a sunrise or a sunset; a mountain view or an ocean view." Though outrageous and hysterically funny, the concept of some form of programmable window covering was far from absurd. Less than three years later, for example, participants in a strategic planning retreat discussed the possibility of creating "smart shades" that would automatically go up and down, based on the time of day and/or temperature.

Each of the twelve lighthearted presentations contained an essential message that was both powerful and provocative. The images that were portrayed were never forgotten—years later, people still talk about them. In many cases, these images and messages created an imperative for a new kind of organization that would only become apparent over time.

The Second AI Summit

The second wave of the Appreciative Inquiry 4-D Cycle at Hunter Douglas was focused on strategic planning. With this as a backdrop, the purpose of the second summit, in 1999, was "to develop a clear, compelling, and creative long-term vision for the Window Fashions Division, along with the 'path forward' for getting there."

Dream activities at this summit were different from those of the first summit in three ways. First, they were informed by prework—pages of company information (products and services, sales, technology, markets), articles about both strategic planning and shifts in strategic direction and vision, and appreciative interview stories collected in advance by participants. Second, the group's Dream activities focused on articulation of the division's core capabilities, strategic advantages, and strategic opportunities. And third, the take-away was more than a playfully enacted collective dream—it was a clear, compelling, and creative ten-year strategic vision.

On the afternoon of the first day, a midlevel professional—someone who in most organizations would have had little or no involvement in a strategic planning activity—articulated a business-changing "aha." He suddenly understood and communicated to others that the division's core capability had nothing to do with window fashions but rather with the technology with which those window fashions had been created. The room became silent as everyone realized that what he said was indeed true.

This shift in understanding had a radical effect on the way the organization began to see itself. As a result, the first-ever description of the future of the business posited changes in both industry and market scope. Rather than focusing exclusively on North American window fashions, it put forward the image of Hunter Douglas as a leader in the global interior design market. In short, it invited whole new possibilities for the future.

Writing the Dream—Together

In this same strategic planning summit, Hunter Douglas experimented with a new and daring culmination of the Dream phase. Rather than designating a subgroup to work offline crafting the division's ten-year strategic vision statement, consultants asked participants to write the statement together. But how could seventy-five people accomplish such a task in less than ninety minutes? To this day, the approach remains a model high-engagement process for documenting the Dream.

Participants had already been reflecting and dreaming in groups of eight. Having all formulated their version of the company's strategic vision, each small group designated one person as its representative to the whole. Thus, members of a new subgroup of ten seated themselves around a table in the middle of the large group, where they became like fish in a fishbowl: they could talk to one another, but other participants could only listen and take notes.

In addition to the ten chairs for designees, this central table contained a single empty chair. This was an open seat, available for anyone in the room, including facilitators, who felt they had something to contribute. The only ground rule was that these "drop-in" participants would empty their seats as soon as they felt they had made their contributions.

The people in the "fishbowl" were given the task of crafting a ten-year vision statement for the division that captured the best of what had been discussed and enacted within both the small groups and the whole. They could begin with conversation, but very shortly thereafter the writing would have to begin. The process would continue until everyone in the room could support both the concept and the language of what they had written.

After twenty minutes of conversation and initial drafting, the facilitators hit the pause button. They asked fishbowl participants to return to their original groups for conversation and coaching. Each group could then choose to send another designee into the fishbowl if they wished. Following ten minutes of conversation, the reconfigured fishbowl continued for another twenty minutes, followed by another check-in with the original groups. Throughout both twenty-minute segments, members of the larger group continued to move in and out of the fishbowl's empty chair on an ad hoc basis.

Two rounds and one hour later, the large group of participants was instructed: "When you fully support the statement that the central group has proposed, silently stand up and move to the right side of the room." For nearly twenty minutes, plenary participants sat, stood, sat, and stood. Tension rose as larger and larger clusters of people moved to the right—and then in some cases returned to their original seats. Those in the fishbowl received immediate, compelling feedback from the whole, to which they rapidly responded. Then suddenly everyone was standing and cheering and applauding the statement! The ten-year vision was crafted. A new image of the future was launched, and with it a new era for products, services, and employees.

The Benefits of Wholeness

During each iteration of the 4-D Cycle, Hunter Douglas engaged its whole system in Dream activities. This promoted an unplanned breadth of thinking and unleashed the organization's most positive potential. Leaders did not have to tell groups to dream of new products and processes as well as culture. Participants simply did so—in part because of the different kinds of people, experience, and information that were present in the groups. Wholeness produced a categorically different level of thinking and dreaming. Facilitators and leaders could trust the whole to consider things from multiple angles and to do what needed to be done.

In addition, this whole-system dreaming had an intensity and power that transcended the actual images it created. It unleashed energy and built relationships. In a sense, it gave people a positive experience of the future toward which they were heading—a future in which people knew and trusted one another, collaborated for the higher good, and nurtured one another's personal and organizational hopes and dreams. As one employee remarked:

> There are new employees at this summit that might otherwise have thought this was just another job, who are now thinking it will be a career, a place to stay forever. We'll never go back to the way it was before.

Similarly, an employee of another Hunter Douglas division commented on the Window Fashions Division's leadership, through Focus 2000 and the Appreciative Inquiry summit:

> We talk a lot at Hunter Douglas about reinventing ourselves. This process and this division are the epitome of reinventing the business that used to be. Boy, have we come a long way!

The overall effect is best summarized by one customer's comments on the last day of the gathering:

> I'm so grateful, as a customer, that I've been given the honor of feeling ownership in this process. Because of this, I can talk to our folks and tell them Hunter Douglas is doing beautiful, wonderful things. The next time one of my co-workers is upset about one of the products—maybe the glue—I can tell them that I've met the glue guy, and he really knows what he's doing, and he can work it out!

This ends our description of Dream at Hunter Douglas. The Hunter Douglas story continues with Design, in Chapter 9.

CHAPTER 9

Design: Giving Form to Values and Ideals

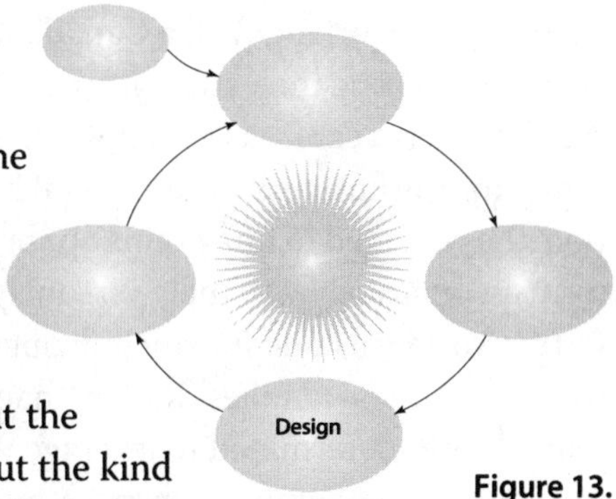

Design—the next phase in the
4-D Cycle—represents the
culmination of an extend-
ed process of expansion.
It engages large groups of
people in conversations about the
nature of organizing and about the kind
of organization that will enable the real-

Figure 13.

ization of their values and dreams. In short, it involves sorting, sift-
ing, and serious choices about what will be.

This chapter discusses the concept of design—of bringing
preferences to life through an organization's "social architecture."
It shows the relationship between a chosen Change Agenda and
an Appreciative Inquiry Design process. It provides step-by-step
instructions for implementing a variety of Design activities. And
finally, it illustrates these instructions with examples from a variety
of organizations—including, of course, Hunter Douglas.

Values-Based Design

We live in a designed world, a world created by human thought, word, and deed. Language is the human design tool, dialogue the process. Everything from fashions to automobiles to school curricula to health-care practices to industrial production processes to organizations and communities—everything is designed in conversation.

The purpose of organization design is to give form to the expression of human creativity and values and to enable the realization of human aspirations. Organization designs are expressions of values embodied in structures, systems, strategies, relationships, roles, policies, procedures, products, and services. As a result, organization design requires choice.

We experienced a vivid example of conscious, values-based design when working with a Canadian health-care company several years ago. During their strategic planning process, it became evident that long-term care was an emerging market and a strategic opportunity for the business. After several hours of dialogue and deliberation, they decided to forego this opportunity because nursing homes were incongruous with their personal values and dreams. Their preferred world was one in which people age with dignity at home, in the care of their families. Rather than entering the long-term-care market, they determined to leverage what they were anticipating in the way of demographic changes by creating a home-health-care business that continues to be highly profitable today.

All of us are both the designers of our world and the product of our own designs. Once implemented, the products, services, and organizations we design act on us and influence the possibilities of our lives—for better and for worse. Margaret Mead, in *Cultural Patterns and Technical Change,* told how the introduction of the fork—a design for eating—transformed the social patterns of culture in New Guinea.[69]

A somewhat more high-tech and contemporary example is the progression of information exchange we call mail. Within the past fifteen years, information exchange technology has evolved from written letters mailed via the postal service, to speedy express shipping via FedEx, to information sent via electronic fax machines, to e-mail exchanges via the Internet. As you have most likely experienced, with each progressive design for the exchange of information, the context of work life changed. New imperatives for action were introduced. Everything about work has sped up along with our capacity to exchange information.

People can be complacent in the face of what they perceive as fate, or they can influence their destiny by making choices and acting in ways that design their values into the fabric of the future. Recently, a small town in the Pacific Northwest used design as an opportunity to influence their destiny. Threatened with the construction of a four-lane superhighway that would bisect the town, they chose to be proactive rather than become victims. They gathered together and initiated a period of Discovery. They took time to consider everything that was best and most positive about their community. They determined what, in their minds, had to be maintained through whatever changes might take place. They conducted research about possibilities and alternatives, including benchmarking of other communities. Then they Dreamed and imagined what it would take to retain or even enhance their current sense of community despite the inevitably forthcoming hoards of cars, noise, and pollution. Finally, they hired construction engineers and landscape architects to help them Design their future.

The result was a very innovative solution that balanced the needs of the state to transport large volumes of traffic as directly as possible and the needs of the town to maintain a sense of tranquility and a connection to one another and the environment. Members of the community met with representatives from the state and negotiated the construction of a tunnel through which the highway would run underneath the town, from one end to the other, beginning and ending two miles outside the town limits. Above the superhighway tunnel, the town built parks and open spaces. The two-lane highway that had previously bisected the town disappeared. In its place they purposefully designed communal and pastoral spaces. What could have been a disaster became the impetus for strategic, positive change that makes this one of the most desirable residential communities in the state.

When people dare to dream of the life-giving and positive contributions they and their organization might make to the world, no existing organization design is suited to the realization of their dreams. Simply put, organizations designed to embody the values and achieve the dreams of prior generations are inadequate to the realization of twenty-first century values and aspirations. Hierarchies and bureaucracies are not suitable forms of organizing to achieve global democracy, natural capitalism, or peace among religions. Current organization designs are unequal to the task of manifesting today's postmodern dreams for social justice and environmental sustainability.

Appreciative Inquiry holds potential for organizations of the future. Through conscious conversations about organization design, it seeks to answer the question, What forms of organizing can bring out the best of people, liberate cooperation, and give form to our highest values and ideals?

Key Decisions in Design

There are three broad decisions to consider during the Design phase: the *what, who,* and *how* of Design. All three decisions must be made at the beginning of the Design phase, in ways that are congruent with your chosen Change Agenda. What you are designing comes first because it will influence both who needs to be involved and the most appropriate way to describe your ideal.

- *What are we designing?* A start-up organization? An organization culture? A partnership or alliance? A value chain? A series of work processes?

- *Who needs to be involved?* All stakeholders? A small design team?

- *How do we describe our ideal organization?* Provocative Propositions? Design Statements? Principles? Process maps?

Table 12.	Connecting Your Change Agenda and Design Target
Change Agenda	**Design Target**
"If you want to change . . . "	*"Then you might discuss and write . . . "*
Organization culture.	Propositions describing the ideal organization.
Union-management relationships.	Purpose and principles of union-management partnership.
Strategic planning.	Strategic vision and business strategies.
Business processes.	Work-process maps.
Customer service.	Principles of service excellence.
Organization structure.	Propositions describing the ideal structure.
Leadership development.	Principles of leadership.

What Are We Designing?

In each Appreciative Inquiry, the question of what is being designed is essential, strategic, and answered implicitly during the Getting Started phase—when you clarify and commit to your Change Agenda. The Change Agenda creates a target for Design. Table 12 provides a series of scenarios showing the relationship between a Change Agenda and a Design Target.

Congruence between your Change Agenda and Design Target is essential. The key is to design what you set out to change. For example, the U.S. Navy embarked upon a series of AI Summits to develop leadership at all levels in the organization. During the Design phase of these summits, participants discussed and crafted propositions describing the ideal organization—one that fosters and brings out the best of leadership at all levels.

The connection between your Change Agenda, Affirmative Topics, interview data, and Dreams is never more apparent than it is during Design. In each unique application of Appreciative Inquiry, the Change Agenda suggests relevant Affirmative Topics that in turn guide Discovery. The stories and data collected in Discovery combined with the hopes and dreams expressed in Dream provide the organizational knowledge upon which the Design is crafted. For example, when Avon Mexico committed to enhancing positive cross-gender working relationships, they needed to learn about the conditions under which such relationships would thrive before they could design them into their organization. What they discovered was that great cross-gender relationships were not created in training programs. Instead, they came about as women and men worked together on teams, sharing leadership and responsibilities. And so they crafted a new organization, in principle and in practice, in which all task forces and project teams are co-led by a woman and a man in partnership. As a result, cross-gender relationships now flourish, and the company has been recognized as one of the best places for women to work.

Who Needs to Be Involved?

Quite often, Design is both initiated and completed in an AI Summit. On occasion, however, Design Teams form to work on behalf of the whole—either drafting materials for subsequent review and embellishment, or finalizing drafts that were initially crafted in community. Such was the case with the design of the global interfaith organization known as the United Religions Initiative. At the end of the third annual global summit, members formed an inquiry group, charged with studying alternative organization designs. A year later, responding to a call to be stewards of the Purpose and Principles of the newly forming organization—always with input and feedback from the global community involved—the inquiry group emerged as the Design Team.

   As with other aspects of Appreciative Inquiry, involving all relevant and affected parties is essential to successful Design activities. It is especially important to include some people who have been involved in other aspects of the Appreciative Inquiry process. This includes members of the Advisory Team, interviewers and interviewees from all stakeholder groups, and meaning makers. In this way people can draw from their direct experience of the stories gathered throughout the Appreciative Inquiry process to determine and illustrate the characteristics of their ideal organization.

In the selection of people to be involved in Design, it is also beneficial to include:

- *People with diverse organizational affiliation.* Conversations about design possibilities are greatly enhanced by hearing stories about different organizations and different ways of doing things. For example, during the year of conversations about the design of the United Religions Initiative, stories were shared about a wide range of organizations, including the United Nations, the Catholic Church, the Brahma Kumaris, Alcoholics Anonymous, McDonald's, and the Mountain Forum. As Design participants told stories about various organizations at their best, creative potential for the design of the United Religions Initiative moved to higher and higher levels.

- *People of all ages, from youth to elders.* Generational diversity ensures creativity and consideration of long-term consequences. Elders carry the wisdom of experience, the freedom to express the most basic and simple elements of life, and a desire to leave a sustainable legacy. They are valued resources in designing the future. On the other hand, youth are the spirit of the future; after all, it is their future and their children's future that is being designed. Cross-generational conversations awaken innovative potentials for organization design as generations consider the situations, values, and modus operandi of their respective times.

- *Designers in diverse fields, such as the arts and architecture.* These are people whose life work revolves around design, creating the spaces, structures, and services that give meaning to life. They bring a variety of perspectives, experiences, and questions to the task of organization design. Whatever their field, designers understand the task of creating the world according to values, preferences, and aspirations.

- *Students of organization.* In every organization, at most universities, and in groups of consultants, there are people who are intrigued with organization design. They study forms of organizing, metaphors for organizing, and the relationships among organization design, productivity, social well-being, and environmental sustainability. To their conversations about organization design they add their knowledge of organizational alternatives and the capacity to think about macro social systems.

The number of people involved in Appreciative Inquiry Design varies from as few as twenty people who consistently engage others in review and revision until the final design is articulated to a group of one hundred to three hundred people in an AI Summit. Clearly, the more people involved, the more readily the new design will spring to life through action.

How Do We Describe Our Ideal Organization?

When asked to describe an organization, most people will take out a piece of paper and draw boxes with names in them to illustrate roles and reporting relationships—the things that they consider to be the organizational structure. When asked to describe how things get done in an organization, they will laugh, say, "Well now, that's another matter!"—then tell stories of accomplishments achieved through cooperation, working around the structure, and bending the rules. Through stories, our organizations live and our values become apparent. Through stories, we learn how to get things done. Ideal organizations live in stories—rich narrative accounts that are statements of beliefs and values in action.

And so the Appreciative Inquiry Design methodology involves people sharing stories of their organization at its best and then writing statements of their ideal organization. These statements are most often called Provocative Propositions but have also been called Design Statements, Possibility Propositions, and Design Principles. At different times we call them by different names, always ensuring that they are

- *Narrative statements,* proposing the ideal.

- *Provocative,* stretching beyond the norm into novel and more desired forms of interaction.
- *Stated in the affirmative,* using vivid positive imagery.
- *Statements of intention,* constituting the ideal.

Conceptually, Provocative Propositions build on the idea that words create worlds. The power of language to evoke realities has been recognized across cultures for generations. As an ancient Hawaiian proverb says, "There is power in the word—the countenance of life and the countenance of death."[70] Provocative Propositions serve organizations in the same way that affirmations serve individuals. They are a kind of organizational affirmation—a statement of the ideal desired in the future and stated in the present tense. At their best, they create an irresistible attraction in the direction of what is desired.

Provocative Propositions build bridges between the best of what is and the best of what might be. They are statements that stretch the realm of the status quo, challenge common routines, and suggest tangible actions, events, structures, practices, or relationships. Although they imply action, they do not prescribe a specific action or course of action. For example, a group of state government leaders wrote the following Provocative Proposition after interviewing citizens and hearing their dreams:

> The doors of government are open to all citizens of the state. We welcome citizen visits to our offices and provide easy access to information about programs and services, face-to-face as well as online and on the phone.

This highly provocative statement indeed implied action. At the time it was written, no one imagined the ways in which it would be realized. One of the most surprising and enlivening outcomes was an open house in the capitol building. The doors of government were literally opened. The public attended in record numbers, and the level of citizen awareness and involvement increased dramatically as a result.

Table 13. Design, Step by Step
1. Identify a meaningful social architecture.
2. Select relevant and strategic design elements.
3. Identify organizational design preferences.
4. Craft Provocative Propositions.

Design, Step by Step

As we have said repeatedly throughout the book, there is no single way to carry out any of the activities in Appreciative Inquiry, including Design. The four steps in Table 13 provide a broad framework for thinking about Design. The ultimate goal is a set of affirmative statements that describe the ideal organization. These steps can take place over one day at an AI Summit or over the course of years, as was the case with the design of the United Religions Initiative.

Identify Social Architecture: A Set of Organizational Design Elements

When we talk about organization design, we plan to address much more than mere organization structure. So the first step in Design is to identify the social architecture that we plan to transform. This social architecture is a model for organizing that implies a set of essential design elements.

What are design elements? We're all familiar with the design elements of a building—foundation, roof, walls, windows, doors, floors, and so on—all those aspects of a building that must be designed and constructed for the building to exist. Buildings include hundreds of design elements—some as large as floors, walls, and heating system; others as small as door knobs, hinges, and water faucets. In designing and constructing a building, each design element is carefully and consciously considered and selected based on owners' preferences.

Metaphorically, organizations too can be said to have design elements—those things that must be designed and operational for the organization to exist. An organization's social architecture might include any of the following as design elements: vision, purpose, strategy, structure, leadership, decision making, communication, systems, relationships, roles, knowledge management, policies, procedures, products, and services. Taken collectively, design elements serve as a social architecture.

There are many recognized and often-used organization design models, offering different sets of design elements that may be used as a framework for describing your ideal organization. For example:

- *The McKinsey 7-S Model* offers a set of seven design elements recognized as the social architecture for many modern corporations: subordinate goal, strategy, structure, systems, staff, style, and services.

- *David Korten's nine "system design elements for a postcorporate world"* offer provocative possibilities for use as an organization's social architecture. The nine elements are human-scale self-organization, village and neighborhood clusters, towns and regional centers, renewable energy self-reliance, closed-cycle materials use, regional environmental balance, mindful livelihoods, interregional electronic communication, and wild spaces.[71]

- *Dee Hock's chaordic model* affords a way of looking at the relevant design elements for twenty-first century organizing that balances chaos and order. A chaordic organization is any autocatalytic, self-governing, adaptive organization that exhibits the characteristics of both chaos and order. Based on a deep reverence for natural order, the organizational social architecture includes: purpose, principles, organization concept, people, and practices.[72]

- *Diana Whitney's social architecture for life-affirming organizations* describes nine elements: evolutionary purpose, harmonious wholeness, appreciative leadership, positive emotional climate, strong centers of meaning, just-in-time structures, liberation economics, engaged participation, and caring culture. Each of nine elements is an arena for innovation and transformation in organizations and communities. Taken together, these elements constitute an appreciative organization capable of bringing out the best of people and manifesting the enduring capacity for positive change.[73]

These organizational models and others like them may be used to guide Design activities. In many cases, however, participants in an Appreciative Inquiry process choose to create their own social architecture by identifying design elements relevant to their business and industry. For example, in their book *Appreciative Inquiry: Change at the Speed of Imagination,* Jane Watkins and Bernard Mohr offer a clear and easily applicable process for creating your own social architecture.[74]

Select Relevant and Strategic Design Elements

The second step in Design is the selection of those aspects of the social architecture that will be designed—that is, the relevant and strategic design elements.

Seldom do organizations choose to totally redesign themselves all at once. More often, they engage in an iterative process of organization redesign, in which transformation of one design element creates the need for change in another. For example, a new business strategy may create the need for new relationships with customers, which may in turn lead to the need for culture transformation, which may lead to the need for a new structure, a new information management system, a work-process redesign, and so on.

At this point in the Design process, look for any relevant design elements that might have surfaced during the inquiry process. This requires you to look at your existing organization through the bifocal lens of both the positive core and dreams for the future. The original Affirmative Topics and questions elicited descriptions of the organization at its best. Then, as stories were collected and dreams for the future shared, images of the ideal organization emerged.

These images of the ideal organization suggest relevant design elements. Consider the following examples of how design elements are embedded in and emerge from images of the ideal future:

- Participants in a health-care summit imagined "patient information portals": ways for patients and their families to freely review and even add to their records. The design element embedded in this image is their electronic medical records system.

- Members of a university curriculum redesign committee envisioned "highly interactive teaching processes taking place in classrooms designed to foster interaction." Two design elements embedded in their dreams are teaching methods and classroom design.

- A global information management company described how they would "leverage technology enablers to facilitate bidirectional communication" across the business. The design element embedded in this statement is communication.

The most relevant and strategic design elements are those that lead to the realization of your dreams. For example, consider office space as an organization design element. We have been in organizations where people espouse the value of open communication and equality among people, while housing their business in structures designed with opposite values in mind. The higher one's position is, the higher the floor of one's office, the larger the office space, the bigger one's desk, and the more costly the art on the walls. The incongruity between the espoused values and the embodied values is apparent.

In contrast, one of our clients held transparency as a core value and a pivotal element of its positive core. The members of this organization chose to design the walls in its corporate headquarters entirely in glass. The executive offices, which are often located far away from the everyday noise and activity, were moved to the center of the main floor of the building, where they could be viewed and visited by anyone with an inclination to do so.

Consider also the design elements of work flow and job design. Many organizations manage the ebb and flow of work by hiring and firing contract employees. In contrast, another client identified job security as an element of its positive core. With this as a touchstone, the company designed an organization that operated two otherwise unrelated businesses, both of which ebbed and flowed but on opposite business cycles. As one business tapered off for the year, the second picked up. People organically moved back and forth from business to business throughout the year. Their job design was to alternate jobs, performing those until the seasons changed again. In this way the company balanced the work-flow needs of the businesses with its members' employment needs.

Finally, consider authority and decision making—two of the more significant elements to address in organization design. In many companies we hear a variation on the theme "it's not my job," as employees express their inability to make a decision. By contrast, consider a company that wanted to restructure work processes to give greater authority to teams. After much deliberation over the pros and cons of manufacturing redesign or start-up, the company opened a new, innovative manufacturing facility and located it in a Mexican village that was characterized by intimate extended family relationships and a history of successful family-run businesses. Families were hired as work teams. Authority and decision making were vested at the team level. In this case, the positive core of the business and the village were compatible—and as a result, both thrived.

Identify Organizational Design Preferences

The third step in Design involves the identification of preferences or ideals related to each design element selected. A preference specifies the quality, nature, or kind of design element that is desired. In other words, which of all the possibilities do the people involved consider to be ideal? What do they prefer?

What Are Preferences? Let's return to the building metaphor. In designing a youth center, one community's preferences might include a cement foundation, a pitched roof, wooden doors, stained-glass windows, and walls painted pale blue; another community's preferences might include a dirt floor, a grass roof, open doorways and windows, and mud walls. Both communities would have buildings based on the same design elements—but expressing very different preferences. As a result, their ideal buildings will be very different.

Applying the social architecture metaphor to organizational design, we see that there is a wide range of possible preferences or ideals for any given organization design element. Take decision making as an example. Some people and organizations consider consensus decision making the ideal. They see great value in consideration of diverse perspectives. They ensure that everyone has an opportunity to express his or her views. They take whatever time is needed to arrive at full agreement.

Other people and organizations prefer quick decisions—even those made based on incomplete information and without full involvement. They establish clear lines of authority and articulate who can decide on what, under what circumstances. They value and reward those who take risks and act—even unilaterally. Both the consensus and quick-decision preferences have validity; both sets of design have integrity through the lens of the different preferences. But clearly, these very different preferences suggest very different images of an ideal organization.

Going Back to the Future Identifying organizational preferences is a process of going back to the future, so to speak. It is a time to refer to your inquiry data—to the stories that have been collected, the map of the positive core, and the organization's dreams for the future. Go back to see what the data has taught you about your organization at its best. Reflect on your dreams and discuss the kind of organization that would be alive with your best and highest aspirations. This is a great time to review your Opportunity Map, if you

Figure 14. Sample Design Worksheet

1. Our Chosen Design Elements	2. What We Learned in Our Discovery	3. What Our Dreams Suggest We Want	4. Our Provocative Proposition

have done one, as it will provide great insight into specific prefer-ences related to your chosen design elements.

Use your data to identify organizational preferences for each of the design elements selected. What did people say they most valued about leadership? The work they do? The organization at its best? Teamwork? The answers to these and other questions will give you a rich understanding of your organizational preferences. At this point simply list your preferences for each design element. Later you will turn this list into a Provocative Proposition.

We often use a Design Worksheet to help integrate what was learned in the Discovery and Dream phases of the Appreciative Inquiry process into the Design phase. As Figure 14 illustrates, this worksheet helps people document key findings and organize them in relation to their chosen design elements. Design elements are listed in the first column. Design preferences from Discovery are listed in the second column, and Design preferences from Dream are listed in the third column. In this way the data is organized and available for the next step in the process: writing Provocative Propositions.

Craft Provocative Propositions

The fourth and final step in Design is crafting Provocative Propositions. This entails turning everything you have listed as organizational preferences into affirmative statements. You may craft these statements in a large-group format or with a small design team. Either way, people must work on the design elements about which they care most.

Design activities are most successful when guided by the heart. We can all think about ideal organizations. It takes a great deal of courage, however, to truly say what we most desire. And it takes an equal amount of creativity to find innovative ways of designing our ideals into the fabric of our organizations.

In general, each Provocative Proposition addresses one or more pivotal organization design elements. It states, at some level of detail, how the preferences of the people involved will manifest in the organization. It describes the ideal organization—the one that lives the best of the past and at the same time enables the most hoped-for future.

To write Provocative Propositions, begin by reviewing the preferences you have listed for each design element. Then create a draft, get input from others in the organization, and finalize your work. In the end, your Provocative Propositions will be

- *Stated in the present tense.* They express future ideals as if they already exist.
- *Grounded in what works.* They are based upon best practice stories that surfaced through Discovery.
- *Provocative.* They stretch the organization beyond the familiar.
- *Desirable.* They take the organization where people want to go.

They will describe your ideal organization in ways that reflect the voices, ideas, and dreams of those who were interviewed and engaged in your Appreciative Inquiry process.

Figure 15 (following) shows three sample Provocative Propositions. Taken together, the provocative propositions written by, for, and about your organization serve as parameters for your future. Stated in the present tense, they plant the seeds of what you will become. They are inspirational intentions—the call to action that leads to Destiny.

Figure 15. Sample Provocative Propositions

Design Element: Communication

Communication with our citizens is the cornerstone of a responsive city government. We openly and honestly communicate with the residents of our city using equitable and participatory processes. We actively solicit input from citizens and guarantee a response. Systems within our organization are designed and redesigned with input from citizens.

Design Element: Information and Knowledge Management

Up-to-the-minute information is one of the vehicles through which we serve our customers and maintain our professional capacities. Everyone has access to the information needed to excel at their job. Our state-of-the-art knowledge management system allows each of us to create a personalized portfolio of information and to share best practices, to host online dialogues, and to keep ahead of the competition.

Design Element: Organization Structure

We are committed to self-determined work that is consistent with our overall mission and vision. Employees throughout our company contribute based on their unique knowledge, skills, and interests, even in areas beyond their immediate chain of command. Voluntary cross-functional contributions beyond the job descriptions are formally encouraged during promotion and award reviews.

Design at Hunter Douglas

The Design phase of Focus 2000 resulted in seven Design Statements that strengthened the organization's positive core and paved the way for future growth. By involving a variety of employees and outside stakeholders in the creation of these statements, Hunter Douglas leadership increased line employees' capacities to see beyond their immediate jobs. The following pages describe the short- and long-term effects of this provocative and energizing process.

Design at the First AI Summit

Focus 2000 Design activities began on the second day of the first AI Summit. After one and a half days of Discovery and Dream activities, small groups were charged with the task of drafting provocative Design Statements (Provocative Propositions). They were each to craft one statement describing a set of design preferences that had emerged in response to the question, Who are we when we're at our best? Teams worked for a couple of hours, reflected on their work overnight, and created final drafts first thing on the morning of the third day. Following a "gallery walk" during which every participant reviewed all the drafts and offered appreciative feedback, the Design Statements were finalized and presented to the entire group of one hundred.

Designing for the Whole Business

At this same summit, when it came time for participants to select their design elements, people's energy and attention shifted markedly. The original topics and questions that guided the inquiry had previously focused on people-related stories, hopes, and dreams. "What does all this mean to customers?" was the first provocative question, then "How about our new products? Our innovation? We wouldn't be who we are if it weren't for our capacity to innovate!" Senior-level leaders, executives from sister divisions, and external customers began poking and prodding the group as a whole, challenging people to think beyond people concerns and consider the whole business as they were designing the organization's social architecture.

What initially seemed like a disruptive line of questions became a significant and positive focus. The group that originally selected topics and wrote the interview questions had been heavily imbalanced in the direction of production-level staff. These employees, who had traditionally been "protected" from the majority of significant business decisions, were missing the knowledge, experience, and perspective necessary to design a sustainable and profitable business.

So with the whole system present, participants at the summit were collectively capable of thinking about and designing for the whole business. They chose to design around additional design elements, beyond the original five topics. Even the Design Statements that were constructed around the original five topics were eventually modified to incorporate customer- and product-related propositions. Thus, the final set of Design Statements described the ideal Hunter Douglas in the areas of creativity, leadership, people, education, communication, customers, and products.

Looking back, leaders realized that the presence of a variety of stakeholders at the summit helped people think beyond the immediate, personal, here-and-now aspects of their work, enabling them to consider new points of view. In effect, it cleared the way for them to act in service of the division's long-term viability.

Provoking New Ways of Working

One of the more intriguing aspects of Design at Hunter Douglas was the way in which seemingly inconsequential phrases in the Design Statements organically unfolded over time, subtly provoking new ways of thinking and working throughout the system. A good example of this was a single phrase in the Customer's Design Statement: "Customers eagerly do business with us because we are easy to do business with."

Over the months that followed the first summit, people throughout the organization began talking about that phrase. "We really aren't easy to do business with," people exclaimed. "We may want to be—but truth be known, our customers have a lot of red tape they need to go through to order products, they're besieged by a different piece of communication every day or two, our turnaround time is slow." Reading and reflecting upon their Design Statement, employees of the company began to imagine a world in which customers did business with Hunter Douglas not just because of the extraordinary products but also because of great customer service.

A year or so passed. The division completed its conversion to an enterprise-wide information system and in the process promoted a clearer and cleaner process for customers. At the same time, small groups of people self-organized to work on customer communication and basic quality related to key business processes. And then the parent organization determined to adopt a Total Quality approach throughout its North America operation.

Rick Pellett and members of the Window Fashions Division leadership searched their souls about the Total Quality mandate. How could they introduce an approach that was so anchored in problem solving, having seen such dramatic and positive results from Appreciative Inquiry? Over weeks of discussion, the answer emerged. Certain aspects of the Total Quality approach would be useful to them as they worked to become "easier to do business with." They would pick up on the portions of that approach that made sense and merge them with Appreciative Inquiry.

The result was a new program: Focus on Excellence. Introduced in early 2000, Focus on Excellence drew together three years of Appreciative Inquiry with process improvement, cutting production costs greatly—and perhaps most importantly, making the Window Fashions Division a significantly more customer-focused, customer-friendly organization. In this and other ways, the spirit of the original inquiry—together with the language of the Design Statements—began to infiltrate the way business was done, provoking new ways of working that over time became part of the organization's ongoing character.

This ends our description of Design at Hunter Douglas. The Hunter Douglas story continues with Destiny, in Chapter 10.

CHAPTER 10

Destiny: Inspired Action and Improvisation

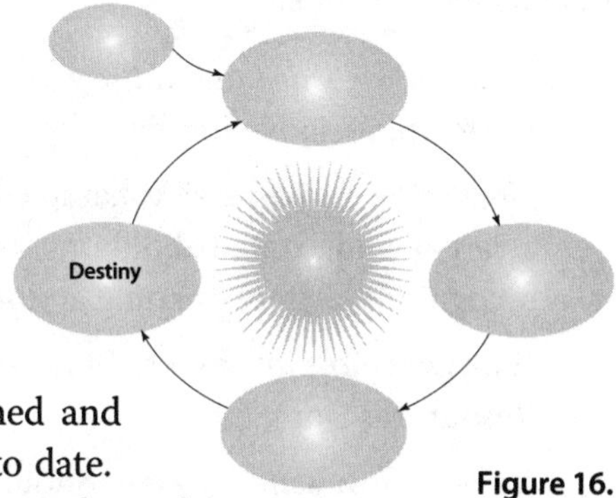

Destiny—the final phase of the Appreciative Inquiry 4-D Cycle—is three-dimensional. The first dimension is recognition and celebration of what has been learned and transformed in the process to date. This dimension supports the unplanned, improvisational changes that have already sprouted throughout the organization. The second dimension is the initiation of cross-functional, cross-level projects and Innovation Teams (one of the more common forms of an AI Learning Team) that together launch a wide range of goal-driven, action-oriented changes. And the third dimension is the systemic application of Appreciative Inquiry to programs, processes, and systems throughout the entire organization, enhancing the organization's capacity for ongoing positive change.

By now there is enormous energy and learning in the organization. The inner dialogue is buzzing with stories about interviews that

Figure 16.

changed people's personal and professional lives—that illuminated best practices and saved time, money, and customer relationships. People are talking about all the different ways Appreciative Inquiry has worked its way into the fabric of the organization. Success is in the air.

In this chapter, you will learn how to capitalize on the success of the earlier phases of the process and support self-organized implementation of your dreams and designs. In addition, you will see how Hunter Douglas's initial Appreciative Inquiry process transformed itself into ongoing cycles of inquiry and innovation.

Key Decisions in Destiny

The Destiny phase involves unleashing self-organized innovation, through which the future will be made real. Decisions to be made in this phase include:

- *How will we learn about the gains we've already made?* Surveys? Appreciative Inquiry? Open storytelling sessions?
- *How will we celebrate?* What needs to happen to keep people aware of and excited about ongoing innovations? How might recognition inspire ongoing action?
- *What are our parameters for self-organized action?* Time? Resources? Domains?
- *How shall we self-organize?* Should we engage existing work groups or form separate AI Learning Teams?
- *How will we support success?* What resources, support, and expertise do people need? Who are the best people to provide what's needed?

Destiny, Step by Step

Very little about Appreciative Inquiry is linear. As a result, whenever we provide a step-by-step description, we offer it as a broad framework rather than a single path or progression. Nowhere is this more the case than in the Destiny phase.

Table 14. Destiny, Step by Step
1. Review, communicate, and celebrate accomplishments.
2. Generate a list of potential actions.
3. Self-organize for inspired action projects.
4. Support the success of self-organized projects.
5. Begin systemic application of Appreciative Inquiry.

In particular, the first and last steps in Destiny—communication and celebration of accomplishments and systemic application of AI—can occur throughout an Appreciative Inquiry process. For example, as we described in Chapter 6, "Affirmative Topic Choice," organizations often initiate changes in many of their systems and processes even as they launch an organization-wide inquiry.

This being said, let's explore each step in more detail. Even when they have taken place throughout the process, each of the steps listed in Table 14 is revisited during the Destiny phase, often during the concluding activity of an AI Summit.

Celebrate Along the Way

At graduation ceremonies around the world, graduates hear the message, "Today is your commencement, a new beginning." Commencement is a new beginning at the end of an extended period of study, learning, and development. It is a time to benefit from what one has learned—to put new ideas into practice and to realize the fulfillment of one's development. So it is with Destiny.

An important step in Destiny involves identifying, communicating, and celebrating positive changes, innovations, and results of the Appreciative Inquiry process. In many cases, communication of a change is as important as the change itself. All too often, after months or years of a substantial change effort, companies' inner dialogues are full of the message, "All that time and money and nothing changed around here." A great deal may have changed, but no one knows about it. The art of Appreciative Inquiry includes regular, creative, and fun communication that lifts up stories of success and highlights what has been learned about the organization at its best.

Destiny is a time for people to reflect on what has changed since the process began, to share high points in the process, and to recognize and honor those people whose volunteer efforts made a difference. Remember, words create worlds. Asking people to respond to "Tell me about all the positive changes that have occurred around here since we began the Appreciative Inquiry" will definitely prompt a litany of successes and good reasons to celebrate.

Generate Ideas for Action

In the Design phase you created a set of Provocative Propositions or some other description of your ideal organization. Now, in Destiny, consider all the creative ways your ideals might be actualized. Either in an AI Summit or a series of small-group meetings, ask stakeholders "What are all the ideas you have for tangible actions, programs, or processes to bring the design into being?" Ask people to address this question for each of their Provocative Propositions. Encourage them to reflect upon their interviews and recall best practices and exemplary organizations as sources of inspiration.

The best ideas are both tangible and exciting. They stimulate a sense of confidence that the ideal is possible, yet they are enough of a stretch to inspire people to act. For example, during a summit on child welfare, a young man—who had been a foster child himself and had made too many visits to the courtroom—offered an idea that lit up the room with determination to make it happen. The Provocative Proposition was about the user-friendliness of the system for children. He suggested that the juvenile court be physically redesigned: that round tables replace long ones, that the judge come down from the stand and sit at the table with the child and his or her advocates, and that there be a special waiting room for children so they could feel at ease.

Self-Organize for Action

The idea of trusting that inquiry and dialogue will lead to emergent, positive change is anathema to many action-oriented, results-focused leaders. Even in the midst of clear and apparent unfolding transformation, we are often asked, "When are we going to create action plans, set priorities, and decide what to change?" Recognizing that all good things in life result from a combination of forethought (planning) and opportunism (improvisation), we often suggest forming Innovation Teams during the Destiny phase of Appreciative Inquiry.

As we described in Chapter 2, "A Menu of Approaches to Appreciative Inquiry," Innovation Teams are groups of people who volunteer to conduct a project that moves the organization toward its newly articulated Dream and Design. They are self-organized because members volunteer based on personal interest and enthusiasm. Together, Innovation Team participants select projects about which they are passionate—that they have a heartfelt desire to see realized.

The scope and size of selected projects varies. In some cases teams take on projects that are people oriented. In others, teams initiate projects with direct business impact. Innovation Team projects have included:

- A cross-functional team process for selling and account management.

- A process for appreciative issues resolution—in lieu of traditional conflict resolution.

- A new employee orientation based on Appreciative Inquiry.

- An employee inquiry into the potential relocation of corporate headquarters.

- A cross-training program named Me and My Shadow.

- A workshop on business literacy.

No matter what project they select, Innovation Teams can benefit by getting off to a good start. We have found that providing a planning framework—in the form of either a worksheet or a flip-chart-sized template—helps get team members on the same page and frees their minds for creative conversations. When creating a planning framework, we consider the organization's culture and planning needs. In particular, we use a language and graphic style that will appeal to members of the Innovation Teams, including as many of the following categories or prompts as teams have time to meaningfully agree on in their first meeting:

- The project name or description.
- The team's purpose or vision for the project.
- A list of group members, including a "team lead."
- A project overview—what, when, where, how, and so on.
- Short-, mid-, and long-term actions, help needed, and due dates.

We used this kind of planning framework when facilitating a summit for IHS, a global information and insight company that describes itself as "The Source for Critical Information and Insight." In this gathering, each Innovation Team worked with a flip-chart-sized reproduction of the template shown in Exhibit 7. The template focused teams' discussions and presentations, provided space to record decisions, gave team leads something concrete to help organize future activities, and standardized teams' notes — which facilitated transcription once the summit was complete. Planning frameworks channel conversations, helping Innovation Teams make the most of what may be limited time. But how can we help these same teams collaborate and learn from one another in a way that's efficient yet meaningful? A good way to balance time for thorough planning *within teams* with the need for rapid, real-time input and discussion *across teams* is with a process we call a gallery walk. Here is the process step by step:

Exhibit 7.   IHS Planning Template

Project Name/Description

Purpose/Vision	Group Members *(circle designated "lead")*

Project Overview *(what, when, where, how, etc.)*

Short-term Action Plan (2 months)		
Action	*Help Needed*	*Due Date*

Mid-term Action Plan (2–12 months)		
Action	*Help Needed*	*Due Date*

Long-term Action Plan (>1 year)		
Action	*Help Needed*	*Due Date*

1. Innovation Teams meet and work on their own projects for up to two hours.

2. Teams prepare for the gallery walk by choosing one presenter to stay with their work and present it to members of other

Innovation Teams and by determining which other Innovation Teams their members will visit. Ideally, someone from each group will visit every other group.

3. Everyone participates in round 1 of the gallery walk. Each round is brief—fifteen to twenty minutes at most. During that time, presenters read their plan to each small group of visitors, sharing primary discussion and decision points and answering questions. Visitors then write feedback and comments on color-coded index cards in response to such prompts as

- "Concepts I love . . ." (white)
- "Ideas to strengthen the plan . . ." (yellow)
- "Potential redundancies with other initiatives . . ." (green)
- "Available resources . . ." (blue)

4. Step 3 is repeated through three or four rounds.

5. When all rounds are complete, people return to their original Innovation Teams to share what they learned from their visits, review and discuss the feedback they have received, and make quick notes about how their plan will change based on what they have heard.

We used such a process during a regional transformation symposium for a five-hospital health-care system. In less than three hours, self-organized Innovation Teams drafted detailed plans related to nine different opportunities for transformation. Everyone then visited three different teams, hearing plans and providing structured feedback. Finally, members returned to their home teams to integrate their findings into "next-step" recommendations. Upon completion of the symposium, the recommendations were integrated into a final transformation plan and proposal for funding.

Years into our work with Appreciative Inquiry, we are still intrigued by the frequency with which newly formed Innovation Teams begin their creative process with inquiry. Having experienced the benefits of Appreciative Inquiry for relationship building, learning, and generating bold potential, teams often launch inquiries into their project domain. For example, a team dedicated to creating a company-wide values recognition program began its work with interviews asking for high-point experiences of recognition and reward. Another focused on designing an exceptional arrival experience for customers began by interviewing colleagues about exceptional arrival practices, customer wishes, and images of an exceptional arrival experience.

Establish a Supporting Infrastructure

If they are to be sustained, inspired action and improvisation must be enthusiastically nurtured, which involves integration, communication, coaching, resources, and recognition from throughout the organization. The organization must therefore establish a supporting infrastructure—ideally one that is integrated with the organization's existing structure and way of doing business.

The IHS Information Technology Department was particularly good at creating a supportive infrastructure. Members of their Advisory Team were asked to coordinate, integrate, and communicate the activities of the four Innovation Teams that formed at their global summit. The Advisory Team did this by both leveraging existing systems and processes and creating new ones as required:

- *Technology-assisted collaboration.* When summit participants returned to disbursed locations, Advisory Team members encouraged Innovation Teams to use a centralized SharePoint on the company's intraweb as a venue for storing, exchanging, and editing information. In addition, the team modeled the proactive use of the company's existing teleconferencing, videoconferencing, and WebEx technologies to foster positive virtual collaboration and relationship-based decision making.

- *Cross-team communication.* From their inception, Innovation Teams independently chose to meet monthly to share progress, exchange ideas, and integrate their efforts. In addition, however, the Advisory Team allocated time during its biweekly phone conferences for Innovation Team updates and discussions, thereby promoting regular cross-team communication.

- *Leadership backing.* To increase leadership commitment to the Innovation Teams and their goals, Advisory Team members immediately updated those who did not participate in the local, regional, and global processes that had led to the formation of the "Final Four" teams. In addition, executive leadership added Innovation Team reports to their monthly operations reviews, thereby ensuring the availability of resources and backing that would ensure the teams' success.

- *Engagement of the whole.* Regional implementation summits were launched shortly after the global summit. Prominent on the agenda were Innovation Team presentations and feedback, including invitations for volunteers who wished to become involved. Finally, the larger IT team received quarterly updates on the Innovation Teams' progress and successes via their previously scheduled all-hands meetings.

- *Rewards and recognition.* Team champions added personal objectives to their performance plans, reflecting the Innovation Teams' achievement of their goals. Similarly, the annual evaluations of team leads and members reflected their contributions to the organization's progress, as shown by implementation of the collectively identified initiatives.

This supporting infrastructure made perfect sense in the context of IHS's culture and goals, but other organizations might choose to approach the job in radically different ways. Whatever the approach, organizations that consciously and deliberately nurture inspired action and improvisation—through some combination of integration, communication, coaching, resources, and recognition—are most likely to experience sustained, compelling, even expanding results from large-scale, long-term Appreciative Inquiry processes.

Expand Applications of Appreciative Inquiry

The systemic introduction of Appreciative Inquiry involves the ongoing continuous redesign of core processes, systems, and structures to make them consistent with the organization's positive core, dreams, and designs for the future. In many cases, this effort takes place through the unfolding actions of Innovation Teams. In others, it involves additional training and the application of Appreciative Inquiry to a wide range of organizational processes and systems, such as new hire orientation, leadership development, performance review, customer satisfaction surveys, employee opinion surveys, team building, supervisor training, and diversity.

For example, on the heels of its 265-person summit, the U.S. Navy established a Center for Positive Change at the Naval Postgraduate School. The center's purpose was to continue nurturing the projects initiated at the summit and—perhaps more important—to build momentum throughout the Navy for this new way of working. In its first six months of operation, the center provided internal consulting to a variety of sites, facilitated three additional summits, coordinated development of an internal Web site through which people could exchange stories of exceptional leadership and best practices, and trained several dozen officers in the Appreciative Inquiry approach to change.

Sustainability: The Enduring Capacity for Positive Change

Now that Appreciative Inquiry has matured to become a broadly recognized and respected approach to organizational and community change, the issue of sustainability has become prominent. Consultants, leaders, and academics who have applied Appreciative Inquiry to countless organizational challenges are asking searching questions about its long-term effects. How do the principles and practices of Appreciative Inquiry move from being tools to get a job done to becoming cultural norms? How do organizations maintain or even grow their deliberate focus on the appreciative, their bias toward inquiry, their stance of relational responsibility, and their self-organizing structures? We believe these questions are subsets of a larger, more important question: How do organizations and communities cultivate an enduring capacity for positive change?

By supporting several organizations that have developed this capacity over years, we have discovered four key strategies:

1. *Deepen the appreciative wisdom.* Appreciative Inquiry initiatives almost always include some sort of best practices exchange, along with the training and education of a few key players. But an enduring capacity for positive change calls for the education and training of many more people, the everyday dissemination and application of best practices, and an ongoing dialogue about strengths and positive images for the future. In this phase of their work, organizations cultivate new ways for people to receive comprehensive training in Appreciative Inquiry and other positive change practices, using unique approaches appropriate to their environment. At the same time, they expand inquiry, engagement, and knowledge by actively soliciting contributions from newcomers and people outside the system, by regularly reflecting on strengths, by actively soliciting new images of what's possible—and by *always* engaging as many stakeholders as possible.

2. *Institute appreciative practices and processes.* Most 4-D processes result in the conscious redesign of a few key elements of an organization's social architecture. But organizations with the enduring capacity for positive change employ appreciative practices and processes broadly and regularly, long after AI-based initiatives or projects are complete. They may begin or end meetings with appreciative check-ins and feedback. Perhaps they will incorporate 360-degree appreciative feedback into coaching and performance reviews, or align job assignments around people's strengths and interests. They might experiment with new ways to institutionalize storytelling, through rewards, recognition systems, or celebrations. They look for ways to introduce new hires to such practices,

perhaps having them interview top performers or become involved in peer mentoring activities. In short, they institute appreciative practices and processes wherever they can, offering people many varied ways to participate.

3. *Extend the reach of Appreciative Inquiry.* Organizations with a strong and enduring capacity for positive change are always on the lookout for new powerful ways to apply Appreciative Inquiry to "the business of the business." They may use Appreciative Inquiry processes to facilitate merger integration or to open and staff a new business unit. When they build a new facility, they might study what gives life to environments and design accordingly. Even in the face of downsizing or layoffs, they might use appreciative processes to engage stakeholders in the decisions that affect them to help envision what might be. Whatever the question or challenge, these organizations think first of how Appreciative Inquiry principles and practices might help them find answers.

4. *Cultivate appreciative leadership.*[75] Finally, organizations with an enduring capacity for positive change consciously cultivate appreciative leadership at all levels through a combination of coaching, training, and experience. Appreciative leadership is a relational process for bringing out the best of people, organizations, and communities—of turning individual and organizational potential into positive power. Organizations that cultivate appreciative leadership actively encourage leaders at all levels to practice *inquiry, illumination, inclusion,* and *inspiration.* They provide opportunities for those same people to discover and cultivate their unique leadership values and strengths, and to apply those qualities with *integrity* to create a world that works for all. Organizations thereby strengthen the fabric of their appreciative culture, achieve results, and make a positive and enduring contribution to society.

A major credit bureau demonstrated an enduring capacity for positive change when—on the heels of a major reduction in force—

it chose to design and staff a new shift structure using Appreciative Inquiry. The affected parties came together to conduct an inquiry, envision what might be, and collaboratively craft a Provocative Proposition reflecting their ideal shift structure.

Leaders then gave participants thirty days to design and submit concrete proposals for how they would implement the Provocative Proposition. Five groups presented proposals, each of which was "evaluated" using an appreciative approach. Former vice president of human resources Tenny Poole said, "People were skeptical that we could redesign such a controversial system using a 4-D process, but the result proved the skeptics wrong. Team members unanimously agreed to a new shift structure that achieved the organization's goal and was implemented without a hitch. We were reminded that positive change is possible even in the most difficult of circumstances."

Through the years, we have been fortunate to bear witness to several organizations and communities that adopted Appreciative Inquiry as an abiding philosophy and practice. Their strategies, which we have just described, teach us much. May we learn from their example and create a legacy of positive change for generations to come.

Destiny at Hunter Douglas

In the following section we return to the Hunter Douglas Focus 2000 Summit and share with you how the Design Statements evolved into Action Teams. We track Destiny at Hunter Douglas from the summit to action team to tangible results. This is the last segment of the Hunter Douglas case.

Initiating Action Groups

On the third afternoon of the first AI Summit, self-organized groups formed to take action on the Design Statements that had been written earlier. A single microphone was placed in the center of the room of one hundred people. The question was posed: Who has a passion for doing something to bring these Design Statements to life through action?

It was "open-mic" time. Anyone who had an idea took the microphone and made their case. Thirty-five ideas were generated. The group clustered overlapping ideas, and through multiple votes reduced the list to fourteen. Those who had originally proposed the fourteen actions were asked to convene a small group for discussion. Everyone else was invited to join any one of the fourteen groups to talk over what, if anything, they thought needed to happen, when, and how.

Nobody was assigned or coerced to participate in any group. In fact, people were given overt permission to "take a walk or go watch butterflies for an hour" if that was how they felt inspired to use the designated discussion time. Despite the options, all but a handful of summit participants moved into hour-long conversations about one or more of the following fourteen action areas: recognition, career paths, new-hire orientation, promoting the AI philosophy, cross-training, communication, mentorship, peer support group, eliminating mandatory overtime, balancing work and family, Hunter Douglas University, fostering creativity, customers, and leadership.

At the end of their one-hour conversations, all but one group agreed to continue meeting after the summit. Some even scheduled their next meeting.

The Supporting Infrastructure

A week after the summit, more than half of the Action Groups reconvened and began thinking about what they wanted to accomplish. But within days, it became clear to the division's leadership that some of the groups would need help if they were to succeed. The good news was that groups had been convened by people who were passionate to do something. The bad news was that only some of these people had the background, skills, or abilities to successfully facilitate such a team.

Because of this, a member of the human resources department took it upon herself to develop an infrastructure and training to support the Action Groups. At her suggestion, each group selected a facilitator. Usually, though not always, this was the original convener. Many recruited additional group members from around the organization. In this way, the spirit of Focus 2000 took hold beyond the first AI Summit.

Each convener/facilitator received four hours of training on facilitation, including guidelines for leading an Action Group. Here are the guidelines that were provided:

- Clarify what you want your Action Group to accomplish.

- Recruit two cochampions from the business leadership team to support you in your work. Be sure to recruit people who, because of their function, expertise, or interest, are uniquely qualified to provide meaningful support and insight to your group.

- Schedule Action Group meetings in advance through production supervisors to ensure coverage on the floor. Members of your group may work up to two hours per week on Action Group–related activities during regular work hours.

- Members of your group will also be paid overtime for voluntary Action Group work performed during off-shift hours.

- In the end, your Action Group will develop a detailed proposal to implement your chosen change. Each proposal, including timelines, costs, accountabilities, and so on, will be presented to the Advisory Team for resource allocation and support.

Action Group cochampions attended an hour-long training, where they learned the importance of guiding, supporting, and helping the teams to succeed in their chosen task.

Eventually, members of the Focus 2000 Advisory Team came to serve as integrators for the work of the Action Groups. They kept track of the activities of all of the groups and helped eliminate duplication. The Advisory Team as a whole also reviewed the Action Groups' proposals and authorized action related to their implementation.

Procrastination or Incubation?

Within a month of the summit, everything seemed to stop. For months thereafter, the Action Groups seemed to disappear. People in the organization began to ask, "What's going on with all that Focus 2000 stuff?" The Advisory Team began to get nervous. Eventually, people became so concerned that each member of the Advisory Team volunteered to serve as a point person to support one of the thirteen groups. By taking that position, they assumed the role of project integrators.

Sometimes the Advisory Team point person happened to be serving already on an Action Group, either as member or cochampion. In other cases, he or she was simply an interested third party whose job was to do the following:

- Keep up with what the group was doing.

- Keep the Advisory Team informed about where the group was heading.

- Keep the question of resources and support in front of division leadership as necessary.

Once Advisory Team members checked in, they discovered that eleven of the thirteen groups had actually taken off like gangbusters. Most groups had gone through an initial period of confusion, trying to determine their scope and authority, membership, and so forth. But despite the initial confusion, nearly all of the groups had narrowed their focus and begun moving. It seems that all of the groups had created a sort of "incubation period" for themselves. Within ten months, the following actions were proposed, endorsed by the Advisory Team, and initiated on behalf of the division:

- *New-hire orientation*. A twenty-one-module new-hire orientation was created and implemented by the group. A couple of years into the program, the group offered it to employees who were hired prior to its inception as a way of building a sense of unity across the company and educating people on the business as a whole.

- *Recognition*. The first-ever employee recognition dinner took place eight months after the first summit, honoring the "heroes and heroines" of the Focus 2000 effort. Each person who attended the dinner was there by peer nomination. Five people who received multiple peer nominations were given larger awards. Steps were immediately taken to institutionalize this event and link the award to the general business rather than strictly to the Focus 2000 effort.

- In addition, a values-based recognition program was initiated to allow peers to recognize and tell stories about peers for behaviors that exemplify the company values. As people attain the highest level of recognition, they are eligible for gifts as significant as paid sabbaticals.

- *Fun in the workplace.* This group essentially became a standing committee, initiating monthly all-company activities whose purpose was to have a good time and enhance morale. In the first year, their activities included theme days for dress, including Dress Your Supervisor Day, Tie-Dye Day, and Clashing Day, as well as a Blast from the Past celebration, to which people brought photographs or mementos of themselves at a younger age.

- *Mentorship.* Two formal mentorship programs were initiated: mini-mentorships were designed for people interested in exploring particular career tracks, and full mentorships were designed for people who wanted up to half-time training in a field outside their area of training and expertise.

- *Promoting the AI philosophy and experience.* A monthly, invitation-only informal gathering called a fiesta was initiated for introducing the principles of AI to the hard-to-reach members of the workforce. This group included all the people who, because of language or cultural barriers or a natural skepticism, were unable or unwilling to participate fully in the Focus 2000 process.

- *Voluntary overtime and flexible scheduling.* At the time of the first summit, the number one frustration was mandatory overtime for the workforce. Just eight months after this summit, mandatory overtime was virtually eliminated through a combination of collaborative efforts across business units and improved planning. A year after that, one of the business units instituted a new shift schedule that allowed people to work four days on and three days off. Three years later, people in white-collar jobs had flextime and telecommuting options, and production employees were experimenting with flexible scheduling and job-sharing.

- *Hunter Douglas University.* Within six months of the first summit, steps were taken toward the formation of a Hunter Douglas Virtual University

—a central source for professional and personal development for HD employees, customers, and other stakeholders. Two years later, the division broke ground on a corporate learning center. Thus, in 1999 Hunter Douglas University was officially opened, complete with a computer laboratory, lending library, career resource center, multiple conference rooms, and a ballroom-sized dividable classroom wired for audiovisual equipment and capable of seating up to one hundred fifty people. This classroom has allowed the company to build upon what has now become a core practice of periodically hosting very large cross-functional, cross-level summit-style conferences that facilitate learning, relationships, and connection to the company's larger mission and vision.

- *Career paths.* Two years after the Focus 2000 inquiry, a half-time career-planning person was hired to provide one-on-one career counseling, resume writing assistance, and general career-related training and development. She headed the new career resource center that was established with Hunter Douglas University. The center accumulated current job descriptions and organization charts for every position in the company. Two and a half years later, computer kiosks containing basic career information plus links to the existing tuition reimbursement program became available in every building.

- *Creating a shared vision.* Over and over in the interviews, people's original wishes included a desire for greater clarity of vision within the company—a clearer, more compelling sense of "where we're going" that would allow people to allocate time and resources in a more methodical fashion. One year after the original Focus 2000 protocols were designed, the company hosted its first strategic planning summit. A cross-section of one hundred employees—all of whom conducted interviews prior to attending—articulated a bold new strategic vision for the company.

Emergent Changes

The success of the Action Groups was clear and compelling. But perhaps the most striking change that took place during the Focus 2000 initiative simply emerged as we methodically proceeded through the 4-D Cycle. Weeks into the initiative, the organization began to change in powerful, surprising, and organic ways.

Take Germaine Piper, a third-shift fabricator whose interviews with Lao refugees inspired her to take uncommon action. Said Piper, on the heels of her third interview:

> I'm overwhelmed by these people's heroism! They left their jobs, their homes, and their families. They lived in and escaped from refugee camps. They traveled to this country under inhuman conditions, and finally arrived in the U.S. And for what? Just to take whatever jobs they could get, because they didn't speak English?
>
> This just isn't right! I've decided to teach them English on my lunch hour. I've decided that if I can teach them English, I might learn some of their language too.

Within a day, Germaine had phoned the company's vice president of human resources and offered to teach English classes. Within months, she ended up coordinating courses that were brought onto the campus from a local community college. Ironically, the human resources department had been trying for years to get an English as a second language (ESL) program off the ground, with no success. Within weeks, the burst of energy generated by Germaine's interviews had managed to overcome the system's natural inertia.

A mere nine months into the initiative, the Advisory Team asked the organization, "What are the most important, most positive changes that you've witnessed or experienced as a result of the Focus 2000 program?" Interestingly, the answers to this question pointed to similarly powerful, emergent changes. Though 75 percent of the employees who were polled had been only tangentially involved in the Focus 2000 program, most described Hunter Douglas as a kinder, gentler, more open place to work than it had been prior to the introduction of Focus 2000. In response to the same question, leaders reported even more profound shifts:

- *Enhanced production and productivity.* Production and productivity had both improved, particularly in the departments or teams that had most fully embraced the AI philosophy and practice. Operations improvement suggestions were up more than 100 percent throughout the division. This in turn had a big impact on both quality and internal customer service.

- *Reduced turnover.* Turnover was the lowest it had been for six years, despite almost nonexistent unemployment in the local job market.

- *Process innovation.* In the process of conducting a routine cross-business unit interview, one of the division's printer operators had discovered the existence of a dual-fold printing machine that doubled the sister business unit's printer capacities. He imported the idea to his business unit and prototyped a similar machine that ended up saving that business unit $220,000 in new equipment.

Two years after the first AI Summit, Hunter Douglas leaders were asked to recap some of the accomplishments in the first two years of their whole-system inquiry. The general manager, Rick Pellett—now president of the Window Fashions Division—reflected on a few of the more striking changes he had noticed:

> Relationships between this and other divisions of the company really grew over the past couple of years—largely as a result of changes that were initiated as part of the Focus 2000 effort. Cross-divisional collaboration that was initiated at this location during Focus 2000 has resulted in an integrated, streamlined customer communication process. Under the division's leadership, the larger organization is starting to build relationships between quality and our customer service functions throughout North America, again using the tools that were learned through the division's work with AI.

At the same time Mike Burns, then vice president of human resources, commented:

> Perhaps the most telling change in our division is demonstrated by people's increased involvement in personal and professional development activities—both on and off the job. This includes such things as formal coursework, training programs, mentoring and career development activities, and peer support groups. For example, our Dale Carnegie enrollment soared within six months of our having started the intervention. First one and then several other "Toastmasters"

chapters formed and "graduated." Both programs were largely filled with employees from the hourly and nonprofessional ranks, particularly from the production areas of the company.

In short, AI began to change the company long before the company delivered its well-conceived, planned innovations.

AI As a Way of Life

After two years of service, the Focus 2000 Advisory Team voluntarily disbanded. In their closing meeting, members of the team reflected upon some of the many ways Appreciative Inquiry had been used and benefited the company.

First, when Hunter Douglas North America undertook the challenges of ISO 9001 registration and conversion to SAP, Appreciative Inquiry made life easier. According to Pellett, "These changes—which transformed the way we do business by raising the bar on standards for supplying quality products and services—were infinitely more doable because of Appreciative Inquiry."

Second, in the summer of 1998, the division instituted the ongoing whole-system strategic planning process that was initiated with the second AI Summit (see Chapter 8, "Dream: Visions and Voices of the Future"). The process eventually came to include annual, whole-system, business-unit, Appreciative Inquiry–based tactical planning sessions.

Third, the company implemented its Focus on Excellence program, which institutionalized Appreciative Inquiry Action Groups as business process improvement teams. In the first year of their existence, Focus on Excellence teams (formerly Action Groups) saved the division over three and a half million dollars.

Fourth, the newly founded communications group conducted an inquiry to create an oral history of the Window Fashions Division. Building on "in the beginning" stories that surfaced through the original Focus 2000 interviews, they had employees interview a variety of employees with less than three years of service to gather stories about the division at its best. These stories were ultimately videotaped, edited, and used as the foundation for new-hire orientations, brown-bag lunches, plant and department meetings, employee newsletters, and so on.

Five years after AI was first introduced into Hunter Douglas, there were probably only a few employees who would know how to describe Appreciative Inquiry if asked. It was no longer a "program." Instead, it had simply become a way of thinking and working that accomplished extraordinary results in a very short time. This was true even though—or perhaps because—Appreciative Inquiry slipped into the background and became second nature to the organization and its employees. Instead of doing AI, Hunter Douglas was simply being AI —they developed core competencies that facilitated whole-system positive change.

Today, ten years after the first AI initiative, Hunter Douglas Window Fashions Division remains the largest, most profitable division in Hunter Douglas worldwide—and the leading window coverings innovator and manufacturer in the world. Now, however, the division manufactures five different products (up from four, when Appreciative Inquiry was first introduced) and has increased revenues by 31 percent with only a 4.5 percent increase in headcount over the past ten years. It continues to reap the benefits of the positive culture, strategic gains, and efficiencies imagined and implemented in the early years of its work with AI.

In the 1998 Appreciative Inquiry strategic planning summit, employees' vision was to leverage the company's proprietary technology in a new market: interior design. They established a five-year goal, which they achieved in 2003 when they developed and launched TechStyle Acoustical Ceilings. Also in keeping with their plan, they maintained the focus on their positive core by spinning off the new business and continuing to do what they do best: window coverings. The new business, Hunter Douglas Specialty Products, currently manufactures and distributes innovative acoustic ceilings for the commercial market from a new Hunter Douglas campus in Thornton, Colorado.

During the same five-year period, 1998 to 2003, Hunter Douglas Window Fashions Division experienced significant gains in sales, profitability, and efficiency:

- Sales up 30.1 percent.
- Profitability up 37.1 percent.

- Employee turnover down 52.2 percent.
- Returned goods down 55 percent.
- On-time delivery, fabric: 97 percent.
- On-time delivery, shades: 95 percent.

In October 2009, a special twentieth anniversary edition of the division newsletter was distributed to employees, customers, and community partners. Stories and photographs highlighting the company's history included a section called "Remembering Focus 2000," in which Jim Anthony—a senior development engineer and early contributor to Hunter Douglas's culture transformation work—shared the following reflections:

> Appreciative Inquiry influenced how Hunter Douglas grew by showing how the answers we get are determined by the questions we ask. When we asked, "What are we doing well that we can improve?" we set a vision for our future as a "world-class" organization, and set the tone for our continued success. Many of today's most cherished programs—the scholarship and contributions committees, Hunter Douglas University, ISO, and recycling, to name a few—had their roots in Focus 2000 and Appreciative Inquiry. When organizational momentum moves and continues in a positive direction, great things can happen.[76]

As Anthony's comments suggest, Appreciative Inquiry permanently and positively transformed Hunter Douglas's culture. Indeed, the "Hunter Douglas Way" is to regularly engage mixed groups of people to study what has worked in the past, imagine what might happen, and create from there—to encourage people to do both what they do well and what they love. Appreciative Inquiry is an enduring force behind this culture—a philosophy and practice that is imprinted on the hearts and minds even of Window Fashions Division employees who were hired long after the early years of Appreciative Inquiry–based transformation and training. Appreciative Inquiry has enabled Hunter Douglas to build upon its positive core and maintain its leadership through a decade of industry changes. Indeed, Hunter Douglas Window Fashions was named among Colorado's best employers for three years in a row. As we write this Second Edition, we are grateful for the opportunities we've had to work with the people of HDWFD, and we hope that the company will continue to learn and benefit from Appreciative Inquiry for many years to come.

CHAPTER 11

Appreciative Inquiry: A Process for Community Planning

Over the past decade, many types of communities have used Appreciative Inquiry to create new kinds of conversations, leading to positive and powerful outcomes. Using Appreciative Inquiry, cities, states, counties, and national communities, religious communities, health-care communities, and professional communities of practice have articulated long-term directions, created visions for their future, built bridges across diverse populations, and forged innovative plans, policies, and programs for a sustainable future.

These initiatives have proven Appreciative Inquiry's efficacy as a process uniquely suited to community planning. They have also expanded our sense of what it means to truly engage the whole system in a process of transformation. In situation after situation, Appreciative Inquiry has helped community leaders address three questions that are essential to successful participatory planning in community settings:

1. How do we build leadership alignment and engage large numbers of people who live and work in the many varied subcultures and groups that constitute the community?

2. How do we ensure that everyone in the community has the opportunity to be involved and to be heard, so that the resulting plan is truly the community's plan?

3. How can our planning set the stage for inspired action and noteworthy results while building and strengthening relationships and the sense of community wholeness?

In this chapter, we focus on Appreciative Inquiry as a process for community planning by showcasing three community Appreciative Inquiry initiatives: the city of Longmont, Colorado; the Sisters of the Good Shepherd, Province of Mid-North America; and the Boulder County (Colorado) Office of Aging. We end the chapter with ten tips for using Appreciative Inquiry as a process for community planning.

Three Communities and Their Appreciative Inquiry Stories

The leadership of all three communities had the same high-level goal in mind, though they spoke of it in their own language. They wished to articulate a clear path forward for their community's future by gathering input and ideas from a broad range of constituents, in a way that would enliven their members and build and strengthen relationships. With this in mind, they chose Appreciative Inquiry as their large-scale, whole-system approach to planning.

Each of the communities engaged hundreds of people in a variation of the Appreciative Inquiry 4-D Cycle that was customized to their needs, context, and community. They all benefited from Appreciative Inquiry's unconditionally positive, life-affirming approach to community planning and development.

In the following sections we present the highlights and specific aspects of each case that make it unique and meaningful. In each case we identify a central Appreciative Inquiry lesson and tell that story, describing the community's Change Agenda (what they hoped to accomplish), their Inquiry Strategy (how they used AI), and the key outcomes they achieved.

Focus on Longmont: Share Your Vision, Create Our Legacy

The first case involves Longmont, Colorado, a city of about eighty thousand, located north of the Denver metropolitan area in a region characterized by rapid population growth and intense retail competition. Theirs is an Appreciative Inquiry story of Discovery—of varied and comprehensive ways of engaging a large, diverse population in inquiry that ultimately led to a plan with community commitment and momentum for action, all in a relatively compressed period of time.

Shortly after the turn of the century, Longmont's leaders recognized a distant but significant challenge: by the year 2020, the remaining areas planned for residential development would be built out within the city's planned boundaries.

The city council and staff chose to be proactive. Because they believed that Longmont should remain both separate and distinct from the urban sprawl, they initiated the Focus on Longmont project. Designed to involve the community in deciding what its future should look like and how it should be funded, the project's stated purpose was "to develop community-supported strategic policies that, if followed, will assure Longmont's future as a vibrant, freestanding community."

Like many municipalities, Longmont had a large, highly diverse constituent base and a complex leadership structure. They chose Appreciative Inquiry to reach out to the many diverse subcultures that make up the city. "As in most communities, the same people traditionally showed up over and over for city council meetings, community celebrations, and public forums," said consultant Barbara Lewis. "We wanted to enlarge the pool of interested, engaged citizens, and build relationships that would enhance acceptance for implementation of the plan."

Interviews Broad and Deep

The project's leaders chose to address this challenge using a complex and comprehensive interview strategy that combined one-on-one appreciative interviews with structured group interviews, generative benchmarking, and impromptu conversations. This strategy created options and enabled community members to choose to participate in ways and at times that fit their work schedules, lifestyles, and language preferences.

A group of thirty-four interviewers began the process by conducting one-on-one interviews, in both English and Spanish, with one hundred community catalysts—people identified as informal opinion leaders within the city's many subcommunities. Project leader Dale Rademacher explained how they chose these people: "We imagined the city as a giant web, with influential individuals residing at crossover points. These were the people who knew people—who, if engaged in the process, would attract attention and influence others to join. These were the people we wanted to help us get others to the table later in the process."

Next came structured group interviews, called Community Conversations by the project's leadership. Designed to engage members of existing community groups, these three-hour gatherings involved sixteen to twenty-four people from two, three, or four different clubs or groups. High school soccer players interviewed elders from the senior center. Neighborhood associations from different parts of town came together in "improbable" combined groups, often for the first time ever, in these conversations. As a way of reaching out to Spanish-speaking community members, two Community Conversations were conducted in Spanish. The Community Conversations succeeded in engaging hundreds of community members who might otherwise not have participated in the process. They enhanced interest and involvement in the initiative and built new relationships and partnerships that paved the way for ongoing success when it came time to implement the plan.

Interviewers also conducted what came to be called spot interviews. Interviewers carried individual questions excerpted from the longer Interview Guide with them as they went about their business and lives in the community. Whenever they saw an opportunity, they asked a question. Spot interviews occurred at the local soccer field, in the pharmacy, with the newspaper delivery boy, and with the cashier at the local grocery store. They enabled interviewers to quickly and efficiently engage a larger, even more diverse group of citizens.

Finally, a group of community members conducted what they called best-in-class interviews with other cities to learn about practices that might be adopted or adapted by Longmont. They identified 159 comparable cities across the nation and decided to visit four. Each of the four was a known leader in an area related to one of Longmont's four Appreciative Inquiry Affirmative Topics:

- *One Giant Front Porch.* Warm, comfortable, welcoming, with a strong sense of place.

- *Enhancing Our Environmental Legacy.* Commitment to responsible stewardship of the natural environment.

- *Exciting Living and Business Personality.* Unique, distinct, magnetic character, leading to a strong economic base.

- *Prospering Together in Longmont.* A culture of mutual accountability and respect that helps people reach their full potential.

Best-in-class interviews launched municipal partnerships, stimulated people's creativity, and stretched the boundaries of what people could imagine for Longmont and its future.

What became of all the stories and ideas? Great quotes were recorded on pieces of paper and assembled into a "yellow brick road": the path of entry into the community summit attended by one hundred seventy-five people. Great stories and ideas were assembled into a fifteen-minute slide show that was screened and validated at the gathering. Together, these stories enhanced the city's oral history and paved the way for positive ongoing action.

Outcomes

By all measures—both planned and emergent—the Focus on Long-mont initiative was a stunning success. First and foremost, city leaders achieved their intended purpose: citizens collaboratively identified five strategic directions and endorsed the development of written policies to ensure their implementation. In the years that followed, city leaders used the strategies as a framework for decision making. They consciously sought to leverage strengths that were identified and articulated in their positive core analysis, especially facilitative leadership—that is, an entrepreneurial style combined with a commitment to support and facilitate community action, even when the city has no direct authority. In addition, the city council revisited the strategic directions year after year during their annual goal-setting process. The strategic plan generated by Focus on Longmont, adopted and supported by three city councils and two mayors, continued, four years later, to serve as a unifying force for the city of Longmont.

Just as important, the plan was carried forward not only by the city's formal leadership but also by citizens who have stepped forward to carry out the strategies. Citizens joined many additional community engagement processes as well—for example, choice making related to a public safety tax, public dialogues on immigrant integration, and a visioning process dubbed Reinventing Retirement. In 2006, the Focus on Longmont initiative won the International Association for Public Participation Core Values Award, and the city itself won the National Civic League's All-America City Award.

Good Shepherd Province-Wide Planning

The second case is that of a religious community. The leadership team of the Sisters of the Good Shepherd, Province of Mid-North America (PMNA), sought to engage their whole community in discerning directions for their future. Grounded in the previously established core values of mercy, reconciliation, zeal, and individual worth, the leadership team chose to invite the sisters and Good Shepherd people (that is, lay collaborators who work in partnership to fulfill the order's mission) to take part in an Appreciative Inquiry process to celebrate the good work they had done and determine directions for their next six years. Theirs is a story of wholeness: of how they engaged *every member* of the community in the Appreciative Inquiry 4-D process, of how they ensured that all voices were heard while making meaning of large amounts of data, of how they created community-wide consensus about their future. It is a story of how the Appreciative Inquiry process can be used to engage literally the whole community in ways that strengthen both the community and its members' dedication to their deepest values.

Perhaps more than other communities, religious communities understand what noted author Peter Block means when he writes: "Community offers the promise of belonging and calls for us to acknowledge our interdependence."[77] In 2006 the Sisters of the Good Shepherd PMNA, acknowledging their interdependence, took steps to plan together for their future. At the time, two hundred and fifty apostolic and contemplative sisters were living, working, and worshiping in more than twenty locations in Mid-North America. The community's median age was about seventy-five years old and increasing. At the same time, the number of members was diminishing. The provincial leadership team sought a process that would be in harmony with their vows and that would help them reach out to all two hundred fifty sisters and hundreds of other Good Shepherd people.

They chose Appreciative Inquiry, drawing inspiration from their founder, Saint Mary Euphrasia, who said, "I cannot explain to you, but there is something divine taking place in our mission, and in my soul. Something extraordinary. A river of graces is inundating our Institute." Believing that Appreciative Inquiry could help them once again tap into "a river of graces" and plan for the future of their community, the five-person leadership team took a deep dive. Members of the Apostolic Leadership Team attended four workshops and completed the Corporation for Positive Change Certificate Program: Appreciative Inquiry and the Practice of Positive Change. While in the program, they mapped out an Appreciative Inquiry 4-D process that eventually engaged nearly six hundred people in inquiry and led to an affirmation of their mission and a clear statement of five directions for their future.

The Wholeness Principle in Action

Because the Sisters of the Good Shepherd live and serve in community, it was essential that everyone in the community be given an opportunity to participate in charting the course for their future. This meant that the whole community needed to be involved in every step of the process: on the core team, in the interviews, in making meaning, in envisioning the future, and in crafting directions for the future. And they needed to be involved in ways that would strengthen the fabric of the community.

As One Heart We Weave Our Future

The process was "shepherded" by a Core Team of twenty-seven sisters and eight lay collaborators: a microcosm of the whole community. The first time they came together, they learned about Appreciative Inquiry, determined topics, and created an Interview Guide with four Affirmative Topics:

- Community of Shepherds.
- Exploring the Shepherd's Reach Locally and Globally.
- Shepherding God's Creation.
- Shepherding: A Way of Life.

Their Inquiry Strategy was designed to engage all community members in the Mid-North America province in one-on-one and small-group appreciative interviews.

The interviews were uplifting. They gave every sister an opportunity to be heard, some in English, some in Spanish, and some in Vietnamese. They built bridges throughout the community: among apostolic and contemplative sisters, among those in the "infirmaries" and those still active in ministries, and among sisters and lay collaborators. The appreciative interviews were a great success, enabling the sisters to reaffirm their mission, strengthen their relationships, and share their ideas for the future.

Discovering the Whole Story

After engaging the whole system in appreciative interviews, the Core Team was presented with a classic AI challenge: How could they ensure that the process of making meaning would strengthen people's sense of community and give everyone a sense of having been included, heard, and understood? In other words, how would they make meaning of massive amounts of data to piece together the "whole story" that had been shared by the community? How would they work in service to the whole community to uncover and articulate the community's greatest strengths and hopes for the future?

The interview process yielded 744 pages of stories, quotable quotes, and hopes for the future. When compiled, the documents filled a six-inch binder. The Core Team met to review, interpret, and honor what had been shared, and they chose to divide and conquer the data. Summary sheets were color-coded according to Affirmative Topics. Members of the Core Team self-selected into four topic groups. Each person in a topic group was given one-fourth of the data (between thirty-five and fifty pages) to read and review. In this way, each document was read multiple times, but no one had to read it all. Each reader was asked to summarize her part of the 744 pages onto six Data Summary Worksheets:

1. The positive core of Good Shepherd, PMNA.
2. Areas of positive contribution we should continue.
3. Reflections: the sacred signs I read between the lines.
4. Images for our future: our ministries and our community.
5. Opportunities for action.
6. Priorities for the future.

After two hours of reading, reflection, and prayer, Core Team members entered into dialogue within topic groups. They worked with one clear and essential guiding principle: be sure that the voices of the nearly six hundred people who were interviewed can be heard in your discussions, conclusions, and presentations. Conversations within the small groups and with the entire Core Team went on for three days. The result was a draft set of direction statements illustrated by quotations from some of the nearly six hundred Good Shepherd people who had been interviewed.

When the draft set of directions was shared throughout the province, it was exceedingly well received. People appreciated how well the Core Team had heard and reflected the whole community's ideas, feelings, and hopes for the future. Community dialogues were held to enable all of the sisters to reflect upon and provide suggestions for strengthening the draft. The Core Team gathered and synthesized all of the input, refined the draft, and readied it for community dialogue and ultimately confirmation at their 2008 chapter meeting.

We've Come This Far by Faith, in Faith Our Journey Continues

All sisters were invited to the province's chapter meeting in May 2008, and as many as could travel—more than one hundred eighty—attended for ten days. Among the agenda items were discussion and decision making about the proposed directions, and the election of a new provincial (province leader) and leadership team. By all measures, the chapter meeting was a great success. The direction statements and a list of related action recommendations were approved. A new provincial and leadership team were selected. Sisters enjoyed the positive atmosphere created by Appreciative Inquiry and experienced a deepening of their sense of community. Without question, involvement of the whole community in the Appreciative Inquiry process benefited the community greatly.

The newly elected leadership team immediately got to work carrying out the direction statements. They hired consultants to assess their living needs and properties. They stepped up their use of technology to include Web-based communication, meetings, and learning exchanges. Focusing on their vowed life in community and their mission, they decided to host another gathering of the whole group one year later. And they supported the twenty local communities in continuing dialogue, discernment, and action related to the direction statements. The community and many of its members have been enriched by the process. Although the challenges they face have not grown easier, their ability to be present with each other in compassionate conversations about their future grew stronger.

Boulder County: Greeting Our Future

In the third case, the Aging Services Division of Boulder County joined with community partners to create and implement an Appreciative Inquiry–based countywide strategic plan for aging services. Their goal was "to proactively address the coming challenges of a rapidly expanding aging population, while harnessing and leveraging the growing resources that would be available within the newly configured community." Theirs is an Appreciative Inquiry Design and Destiny story, illustrating how a community translated its vision and plans into concrete action with broad and institutionalized follow-through.

For years, national think tanks have referred to the pending retirement of the Baby Boom generation as a "silver tsunami," but few places in the country have experienced this tsunami more than Boulder County, Colorado. Nestled in the Rocky Mountain foothills northwest of Denver, the area is a prime spot for aging boomers and retirees. A 2006 Colorado Department of Local Affairs report projected a 70 percent increase in the 60+ population between 2000 and 2012. This report and the reality it described raised a significant question for Boulder's health and human services community: How could they best prepare for what was to come?

Soon after the question was raised, local leaders discovered Appreciative Inquiry—and with it, the answer to their question.

Rosemary Williams, retired division manager of aging services, Boulder County Aging Services Division (BCASD), says:

> Appreciative Inquiry was the perfect approach for us to use, as it reinforced and built upon the strengths-based approach to aging services that we had already adopted. It helped us identify and leverage our inherent strengths more broadly and systemically than ever before.

To be successful, aging services leaders had to generate a widely supported long-range plan for approval by the board of county commissioners and individual city councils, along with an ongoing process of engagement that would reinforce the plan and assure its successful implementation.

Getting to the Plan with Appreciative Inquiry

The countywide strategic plan was achieved through months of Appreciative Inquiry interviews, dialogue and consensus building among hundreds of diverse constituents, a two-day AI Summit, and a series of strategic planning sessions. The plan outlined strengths and goals and prioritized activities that would give rise to "vibrant communities in which we all age well." It also articulated principles by which Boulder County would in the future design, develop, deliver, fund, and evaluate aging services.

From Countywide Strategic Plan to Community Action

The thirty-four-page strategic plan was presented to the Boulder County Board of Commissioners in July 2006. Having spent months working toward its completion, seventy community members chose to attend the meeting during which the document was delivered. Rarely had the county commissioners experienced such a groundswell of popular support for what otherwise would have been just another strategic plan. "The presence of so many stakeholders here today clearly shows that this plan reflects the community's vision," said one commissioner. "It ensures that the plan will not just gather dust on a shelf somewhere. We will move forward together to implement it."

But how? How would the community translate its strategic plan into action? How would the initiative's leaders channel the energies of all the service providers, caregivers, community elders, local elected officials, and concerned residents who were now wholly invested in the plan and its implementation?

They did so by forming new inclusive structures that continued to foster high levels of engagement and integrated action. The first of these was a Countywide Leadership Council (CLC), charged with guiding implementation, evaluation, and updating of the plan. Combining broad invitations with targeted recruiting, the CLC attracted one hundred residents with a variety of backgrounds to join. Some of these people had been involved in Greeting Our Future from the start; others were brand new.

After three initial meetings to get to know one another and to outline the work that needed to be done to implement the plan, members of the CLC self-organized into seven work groups. These all-volunteer work groups were moderated by chairs and cochairs elected by group members and were facilitated by Aging Services Division staff, following a previously established precedent of volunteer-staff partnership.

Next the CLC formed a sixteen-member executive committee consisting of the chairs and cochairs of the seven work groups as well as key staff members. The executive committee's job was to partner with the division manager to set the agenda for CLC meetings, coordinate and integrate the CLC's work, and recruit new members at the end of each one-year implementation cycle.

At the same time, the Aging Advisory Council—whose role included dissemination and oversight of state and federal funds—chose to change its criteria for awarding funds. Going forward, grant recipients would have to demonstrate that their initiative or program would further the achievement of one or more of the countywide strategic goals.

Last but not least, the Aging Services Division added a new staff position, a community development specialist whose responsibilities included staffing the CLC, oversight of the CLC work groups, and ongoing relationship maintenance and communication with the community. In addition, she assumed coordination of the previously established Create Our Future grant-making program, thus assuring that county funds would similarly be awarded to programs and organizations whose work demonstrably supported implementation of the strategic plan.

The structures, a natural outgrowth of the plan that had been created, enabled city and county leaders, staff members, and volunteers to remain engaged and in partnership with one another as they gave life to their shared vision. Perhaps as important, the structures provided a vehicle through which a wide range of stakeholders could continue planning, designing, and organizing their activities in ways that were self-organized, strengths-based, and radically inclusive.

Outcomes

The Council's first annual report to the community in 2007 documented six pages of accomplishments, including:

- Implementation of a "visitability" ordinance in one town to ensure that a percentage of all new homes built in that community could be accessed by people using assistance devices such as wheelchairs and walkers.
- Publishing and distribution of a list of countywide food and nutrition resources.
- Launching of an emergency meal distribution plan for community members with great need.
- Initiation of the Any Door Is the Right Door system to standardize consumer-driven, warm, personal, comprehensive, accurate, efficient, consistent, timely, empowering, and strengths-based information and assistance.

- Creation of a guide to transportation services.

Between 2007 and 2008, the Greeting Our Future initiative was recognized locally, regionally, and nationally, receiving three prestigious awards:

- Colorado Parks and Recreation Association Columbine Award (2008).
- Denver Regional Council of Governments Local Government Innovation Award for Planning with Vision (2007).
- National Association of Area Agencies on Aging (n4a) Aging Innovations and Achievement Award (2007).

These awards, as well as the community's powerful and continuing support, led division manager Sherry Leach to comment:

> When we launched this initiative, we did so knowing that we would have to fundamentally change the way we do business. In the end, the plan has transformed every aspect of our work, from funding to grant-making to staffing and more. This brought the plan to life— made it the real and powerful force for change that we'd hoped it would be.

And it continues to be that force for change. Communities throughout Boulder County have completed and adopted their own municipal plans based on the countywide process and document. New and creative partnerships continue to form. The CLC continues to meet and launch new work groups to address new priorities, and the process of "creating vibrant communities in which we all age well" continues throughout Boulder County.

Ten Tips for Using Appreciative Inquiry for Community Planning

Successful community-based Appreciative Inquiry requires creativity and innovation. Each application of Appreciative Inquiry is a unique variation—from the articulation of a compelling Change Agenda that inspires diverse community members and groups to participate, to the ways leaders from many subcultures are brought into alignment to design and support the process; from the wide range of ways that people with many different schedules, interests, and styles are invited to participate and contribute, to the need for outcomes that make sense in policy and in practice. And yet, as the cases in this chapter illustrate, there are certainly best practices for community-based change programs.

The following ten tips offer advice for successfully applying Appreciative Inquiry in community settings. They cannot substitute for a well-considered 4-D process. They are, however, guidelines to make certain that Appreciative Inquiry fits and is appropriately adapted to your community. In short, the tips can help bring out the best of your community members, helping them articulate a future that serves the greater good.

1. *"Communitize" your approach.* Focus the AI process on what matters to the community. Choose a Change Agenda that is broad, compelling, and consistent with your community's overall culture and purpose. Remember that the only right way to do Appreciative Inquiry is a way that will work for your community members. Schedule meetings and projects during "down" times, or link to existing events that are meaningful to your community. Design a variety of processes that are attractive and accessible to the many people you want and need to be involved.

2. *Prepare committed champions.* "You need both the key and the gas to make a car run," said Marietta, citizen leader of Focus on Longmont. Take time up front to build commitment and congruence among your formal leadership (those with authority and resources, or the "key") and the day-to-day project coordinators (those who will bring the process to life, or the "gas"). Cultivate multiple champions from around the organization, so that you'll always have that base of support from both formal and informal leadership. Train them, so they understand both what they're doing and why, so they're com-

fortable discussing the process with others and getting them engaged.

3. *Be purposefully and radically inclusive.* From the very beginning, invite generational, socioeconomic, and cultural diversity into *everything,* from project leadership to advisors to process participants. Intentionally bring subcommunities and subcultures together in the process. And be sure to offer a wide range of ways for people to participate to accommodate different work schedules, lifestyles, interests, languages, and needs.

4. *Fan the affirmative flame.* Never underestimate the power of the positive. It engages people's hearts and sustains their energy. Share the positive stories you collect over and over and over. Keep bringing people back to community strengths and successes. Appreciate and recognize people's efforts as well as results, especially the efforts of the regulars and those who keep the momentum for change alive.

5. *Keep reaching out with information and opportunities.* With communities of hundreds or even thousands of people, never stop reaching out. Communicate everything. Keep experimenting with different ways of imparting information, always focusing on "what it means" and "what's in it for everyone." Create many, many, many different ways and forums for people to participate. Follow up with people who participate, and keep them informed. Engage the local media and create video, still, and written records of key events. Circulate them far and wide. Keep the process front-and-center for as long as possible.

6. *Plan for continuity and transitions.* Before you start the process, ask, If we were gone tomorrow, how would this continue? Then organize your Appreciative Inquiry around the answer. From the beginning, seek out and engage the people who have responsibility for the desired outcomes. Consider in advance what systems, structures, and funding mechanisms will be

needed for the plan to be carried out and lead to positive results. Establish checkpoints in both the planning and the implementation phases. Regularly take inventory of achievements. Celebrate and publicize them.

7. *Invest the time, enjoy the return.* Without question, whole-system community planning using Appreciative Inquiry is time intensive. It takes more time than you think, yet over and over again, community members say it was worth what it took. After three years of leadership with the aging services planning process, Michele Waite reflected, "I had no idea how time-consuming this initiative would be; but still, I wouldn't have changed a thing." The more people you engage, the more time it takes. But the investment of time and energy in appreciative interviews and in having community members share stories and make meaning of their own data yields unimaginable benefits. When people hear the stories from their community, they learn who they are and they see what they can become—personally and as a community.

8. *Be open to what emerges.* It is impossible to predict all the twists and turns you will encounter when using Appreciative Inquiry as a large-scale community-planning process. We have had more people show up than the room could hold. We have had naysayers ask for the microphone. We have had local media show up—sometimes to support, and other times to question a process. Some of these events are challenges to overcome, but most are extraordinary expressions of community support and caring activism, calling forth the need to adapt and innovate. So be open and responsive to the new directions and opportunities that emerge along the way—and the people who bring them. You too may be surprised and in awe of the many gifted people who will work ceaselessly and in surprising ways for a better future in their communities.

9. *Provide ongoing education and training in AI.* Thorough training in Appreciative Inquiry for project leaders and champi-

ons helps them make good choices as they design and lead their planning processes. The need for education does not stop there, however. Ongoing education and training is a key success factor for AI-based community planning. The more people who learn about AI, the better the change process will go. Consider offering educational opportunities tailored to community leaders as well as to various member groups. Throughout the planning process new people will join, and they can also benefit from training. Finally, once the plan is complete, community members will need new and different tools to maintain positive forward movement.

10. *Make Appreciative Inquiry a daily practice.* Appreciative Inquiry–based planning begins a process of community transformation that will continue only as long as it is nurtured. Continue to ask yourselves, How can we apply this to the everyday life of our community? Carmen Ramirez from Longmont said it well: "When we do as much *inside* our departments and organizations as we've done *outside* in the broader community, we'll finally reap the whole benefit that Appreciative Inquiry has to offer."

Conclusion

As the stories in this chapter show, Appreciative Inquiry is a powerful process for meaningful community planning and development. Its unconditionally positive stance is an easy invitation to people who might not otherwise engage or share their ideas and opinions. Its strength-based approach energizes people and builds community confidence in bold futures. From Getting Started through Discovery, Dream, Design, and Destiny, the AI 4-D Cycle can be tailored to address the unique context and challenges of each community. In public communities AI can help expand and uplift the voices of the public, of people in formal leadership roles, as well as those whose voices more often go unheard. In religious communities AI can support "the vowed life" through the choice of topics that reflect the community's deepest values, beliefs, and dedications. In all communities, as in organizations of all types, Appreciative Inquiry fosters openness to learning, a willingness to meet "the other," and a capacity to create life-affirming ways of going forward together.

As you think about your community and its potential use of Appreciative Inquiry, we encourage you to start small. Find a community issue, project, or goal that requires widespread engagement and input, and use it as your ground for learning. Review this book with your project in mind. Invite other concerned community members to join you in your experiment. Now you have your core team and are ready to go. Remember, all that matters is born of relatedness. Use Appreciative Inquiry to build and strengthen relationships in your community, and the results will unfold with ease.

CHAPTER 12

Why Appreciative Inquiry Works

In a decade of using Appreciative Inquiry as a process for organizational change at Hunter Douglas and elsewhere, we have witnessed exciting transformations in the way people work together and in the results they achieve. And we have heard stories, over and over again, about the positive impact of Appreciative Inquiry on people's personal and professional lives. So we began to ask ourselves and those with whom we have worked: What's happening? Why do people get so excited and want to participate in Appreciative Inquiry? Why does participation so readily lead to innovation, productivity, employee satisfaction, and profitability? What is it that creates possibilities for personal transformation and for people to discover and be their best at work? What conditions foster cooperation throughout a whole system of highly diverse groups of people? In short, the central question of our reflection and the question addressed in this chapter is Why Does Appreciative Inquiry Work?

An Inquiry into Appreciative Inquiry

In keeping with the spirit of Appreciative Inquiry, we decided to carry out an inquiry. We created a set of questions and held focus groups with people throughout Hunter Douglas, top to bottom. And we conducted interviews—some formal and some informal—with people in other organizations who had used Appreciative Inquiry. We sought to discover what is it about Appreciative Inquiry that so engages people—and, ultimately, why it works. The interviews were energizing and informative. What we learned was enlightening and, we believe, a significant contribution to the evolving wisdom of Appreciative Inquiry.

Our key finding is that Appreciative Inquiry gives people the experience of personal and collective power. It gives them practice exercising power—and doing so responsibly, for the good of the whole. Once they experience this liberation of power and the effect it has on their lives and the world, people are permanently transformed.

We discovered that for some, Appreciative Inquiry enhanced self-esteem and self-expression. Renee Chavez, an inspector with Hunter Douglas, suggested that participation in Appreciative Inquiry helped her become more fully and powerfully herself:

> I think this is a good job, but I made it that way. The only person who's going to get me what I want is me. Appreciative Inquiry helped me to express myself, and helped me learn to communicate in a better way. It helped me become more of who I've always been.

For others, Appreciative Inquiry permanently and positively affected their careers and career potentials. Tina LaGrange, a customer information representative, told this story:

> Shortly after coming to Hunter Douglas, I applied for a position in the customer information center. I went through the interview process, and was turned down. So I applied again, and was turned down again.

In the past, I might have stopped after this. I might have felt too discouraged to keep trying. But Appreciative Inquiry told me that I was responsible for doing what I needed to do and getting what I needed to be successful. So I found out what I was missing (which turned out to be technical training), got the training, and reapplied one more time. This time, I got the job. I had persisted, because Appreciative Inquiry taught me that's how you get things done.

Another powerful story we heard about the transformational capacity of Appreciative Inquiry came from fabric printer Kathy Mayfield:

Appreciative Inquiry created a complete turnaround for me. I'm painfully shy. Before Appreciative Inquiry, I would go down the hall and wouldn't look at anyone. Now I march! I talk to everyone—even the "suits"! Since this change happened, I'm even getting a little better on the "outside" [i.e., outside of work]. Now I know I'm somebody.

You know, I'm luckier than some people. I don't have to work. But something happened here that changed the way I saw my work. I realized that I didn't have to be here—but that I wanted to be here.

To us, these and similar stories imply that power is like the proverbial genie in the bottle—once liberated, it won't be re-contained. It continues to seek ways of expressing itself. Brian Bassett, shipping coordinator, observed, "As people tried and got results, they gained confidence. That led to five times as much input and the desire to get more involved." The liberation of power creates a self-perpetuating momentum for positive change. Appreciative Inquiry consistently and dramatically liberates people's sense of individual and collective power, adding great value to organizations and communities.

What Is the Value of a Naturally and Comfortably Powerful Person?

Think with us for a moment about this question: What do organizations value about people beyond the inherent worth of every human being? Organizations' answers vary widely. Today, for example, corporations around the globe value people at anything from a few cents per hour to millions of dollars per year, depending on their answers to such questions as Who are the people? What unique skills or background do they bring to the organization? How capable are they of making independent decisions? To what extent can they influence their work environment and the world around them? In essence, how powerful are they?

So let's restate the original question: What is the value of a naturally and comfortably powerful human being? A person who knows that the world is subject to human influence? Who knows that she personally has the power to change the world? Who chooses to exercise that power for the good of the whole? Who encourages and grooms the people around him to similarly exercise their power? Who invites others to cooperate in discovering, dreaming, and designing the future?

"Ah," we hear you say, "now that is a different question! That kind of person is valued much more highly in organizations today than the person who simply shows up and does what he's told." In other words, that kind of person is worth a great deal more in organizational and business terms.

When the members and stakeholders of an organization are naturally and comfortably powerful—when individual and collective power has been unleashed—organizations become more capable of innovation, learning, and contributing to the greater good. They become what we call life centered. A life-centered organization is one in which power—the capacity to create, innovate, and positively influence the future—is an unlimited relational resource. It is an organization in which people care about and work toward being the best they can possibly be, both personally and within the organization. It is an organization guided by spiritual ideals—peace, harmony, justice, love, joy, wisdom, and integrity. It is an organization in which people take responsibility for constructing the world they inhabit and making it good for generations to come.

Our research suggests that Appreciative Inquiry works by generating the conditions that liberate power—by creating life-centered organizations in which naturally and comfortably powerful people thrive.

From Oppression to the Liberation of Power

The journey to liberation—from oppression to power—is one of social emergence. Paulo Freire's work suggests that the "oppressed" are submerged in reality.[78] They are, in a sense, social realists who believe the world is the way it is and there is nothing they can do about it. They experience and describe themselves with neither the position nor the power to change anything. We have heard this organizational lament all too often: "This is how it has always been around here. It has been this way for the twenty years I have worked here. It is never going to change." These are the voices of the organizationally oppressed.

In our experience, organizationally oppressed people live and work in all functions, at all levels, and in all sectors of organizations. No organizational group, level, or function is more receptive to organizational oppression than another. In some organizations, the marketing group doesn't feel heard or able to influence decisions. In others, it is manufacturing. Elsewhere, those at the top express great frustration at being unable to influence the market or shareholders or to motivate employees. In still others, front-line employees experience themselves as invisible and unable to influence the way work—even their own work—gets done. Often, when one group in an organization feels undervalued and unable to influence, so do others.

The first step toward the liberation of power and life-centered organizing begins when people recognize that the world and their organization is open to social change as created by and through human interaction and creativity. At this stage, people often see and describe having a positive impact as an attribute of others: "She is such a great leader. Since she has been here, we have made major improvements." This other-oriented power is a step toward liberation that acknowledges the potential for social change, though still placing the capacity for influence and change with some "other." Generally, the other has more authority or perhaps is more informed, more experienced, or is in some other way more powerful.

When people realize they can and do make a difference in relation to others, they experience true liberation. Theoretically, we call these people social constructionists—people who understand the socially crafted nature of our realities. Appreciative Inquiry, through the Six Freedoms, creates a context rich in relationships and narratives that becomes the path on which the journey to liberation takes place. Following is a more in-depth description of the Six Freedoms, illustrated with quotes and stories from people who have participated in some form of Appreciative Inquiry. These are voices of the organizationally liberated, describing the conditions that bring out their best.

The Appreciative Inquiry 4-D Cycle and the Six Freedoms

So what's the relationship between the Appreciative Inquiry 4-D Cycle and the liberation of power and the establishment of life-centered organizations? Personal and organizational power is unleashed when certain essential conditions are present for people within organizations. Our research suggests that there are at least six of these conditions, which we call the Six Freedoms:

1. Freedom to be known in relationship.
2. Freedom to be heard.
3. Freedom to dream in community.
4. Freedom to choose to contribute.
5. Freedom to act with support.
6. Freedom to be positive.

Any one of these Six Freedoms can significantly alter people's perception of their power within an organizational context. Because individuals learn and are motivated differently, we believe initiatives that provide the opportunity for people to experience multiple freedoms have the potential to make the greatest impact on the largest number of people—and ultimately on the organization as a whole.

The power of Appreciative Inquiry comes, in part, from the way it unleashes all of the Six Freedoms over the course of just one complete 4-D Cycle. Because of this breadth of impact, it has a greater capacity for transforming personal and collective realities than many other organizational change processes.

Freedom to Be Known in Relationship

In work settings, people are often known in roles rather than in relationship. They are vice presidents and operators, doctors and nurses, employees and customers—in short, they are perceived as what they do rather than who they are. However, human identity forms and evolves in relationship. In the words of Sheila McNamee and Kenneth Gergen, "Persons represent the intersection of multiple relationships."[79] The sense of self is a relational identity that thrives in communication with others. According to psychologist Alan Fogel, "Communicative connections to other people are fundamental to the workings of the human mind and self, and to the culture that enriches and sustains our spirits and achievements."[80]

Just as we know and become ourselves in relationship, so also do we contribute to our organizations in relationship. For many people, the quality of their relationships at work is the quality of their work life. Appreciative Inquiry allows us to know one another in relationship rather than in roles. It calls us to know one another not just as unique individuals but also as a part of the web of relationships through which "I" exist.

The more fully we are known in relationship, the more fully we can come to work and contribute. John Cade, a printer with the Window Fashions Division, reflects on the fundamental human need to be known in this way. "I want to be known, and to 'belong,'" says Cade. "The animal takes care of survival, but the heart—the soul—wants to belong."

Being known in relationship includes knowing one another as relational beings—as parents, coaches, artists, bowlers, and so on. The more fully I am known in my world of relationships, the more fully I can come to work and contribute.

Appreciative Inquiry breaks the cycle of depersonalization that masks people's sense of being and belonging. The appreciative interview, which is the core technology of Appreciative Inquiry, is powerfully rooted in the creation of personal relationships. It seeks and explores in depth people's personal peak experiences—times when they were most engaged, most alive, and proudest of themselves, their organizations, and their work. Appreciative interviews ask them to recall those moments in vivid detail and to share their experiences with people they have previously known only in roles—or not at all. The process affirms people in relation to others, enables new relationships to be formed, and enhances respect among people who work together daily. People gain the freedom to understand that to know themselves and others is fundamental to high performance.

Appreciative Inquiry doesn't just build relationships. It also levels the playing field and builds bridges across boundaries of power and authority. As Renee Chavez says, "I did my interviews with people who weren't like me. That helped me meet and get to know people who are very different from me: different jobs, different backgrounds, different races." Mark Maier, a machinist, says it even more succinctly: "Appreciative Inquiry blew the communication gap wide open."

Similarly, John Cade comments on the ways in which Appreciative Inquiry in general—and the interviews in particular—help to make other people and their ideas more accessible: "Appreciative Inquiry gives us opportunities to be known across the boundaries." The contagious spirit of the interviews results in a sense of connection to others: "As our Appreciative Inquiry effort got fully under way, other people became excited, just like me. I didn't feel alone. For the first time, it was 'me with the world.'"

In today's business world, relationships—teams, alliances, partnerships, colleagues—are essential: work gets done through relationships. Management consultant Kevin Kelly claims, "The central economic imperative of the network economy is to amplify relationships."[81] Through Appreciative Inquiry, the freedom to know and be known in relationship liberates people's energy, ideas, and personal and organizational power.

Freedom to Be Heard

When we feel we are not heard, we feel less real, less able to affect our environment. This is the experience of the oppressed. But when another person hears us—when they witness and repeat our ideas and stories—we become tangible, real, significant, somebody who can make a difference. To be heard is to have a recognized and credible voice, to be known as a source of creativity, innovation, and influence. The Reverend Canon Charles Gibbs, executive director of the United Religions Initiative, stated it this way:

> I have seen over and over again—all around the world—what happens when people who are not used to being valued feel heard. The experience of being heard allows them to be present and to offer the best of themselves in a way that could not happen otherwise.

Much has been written on the act of listening, but surprisingly little has been written about the experience of being heard. A person can listen without truly hearing or understanding the person who is speaking. To feel heard, the speaker must recognize that the person listening is attentive, is listening with sincere curiosity, empathy, and a willingness to learn. It requires the listener to hear a person's story and words. In other words, the experience of being heard requires a relationship between speaker and listener. Appreciative interviews encourage this kind of relational hearing. They ask speaker and listener alike to reach beyond the mundane, the theoretical, into personal experience and values. They invite an act of hearing that draws out the best of another person—that encourages the cooperative creation of meaning and identity.

During Appreciative Inquiry, people experience themselves as being heard and as hearing others in powerful, fulfilling, and energizing new ways. Through this act of mutual hearing, employees who are traditionally disenfranchised—the organizationally oppressed—begin to show up, think, and imagine in bold and provocative new ways.

One-on-one appreciative interviews open channels of communication and nurture people's experience of being heard. They do this by unleashing a wealth of stories which, in later phases of the process, spread and multiply throughout the organization. People experience being heard as the ideas and stories they offered during interviews are presented, discussed, and put into action throughout the organization.

When Hunter Douglas first implemented Appreciative Inquiry as a culture change process, Mark Maier was supervising a group that performed technical maintenance on the company's production machinery. He and his staff felt undervalued, not heard, and often ignored—even when it came to their particular area of expertise. Mark decided to put Appreciative Inquiry to the test. He initiated an inquiry among all of the team's internal customers—engineers, technical support staff, and so on. He and his staff collected stories of exceptional support that people had experienced both within Hunter Douglas and at other companies. He invited people to dream about the service they had always wanted and to describe it in detail. What was the result? People felt recognized. They built relationships across functions, in particular between engineering and technical support. Being heard brought the group to life.

Appreciative Inquiry affords people the opportunity to be heard. By setting the stage for the freedom to be heard, it opens doors for people who had felt ignored, without a voice to offer information, ideas, and innovations. It creates a rich context for knowledge creation and exchange, for personal respect, and for employee satisfaction and development.

Freedom to Dream in Community

Visionary leaders have long been recognized as assets to their organizations. Their capacity to propose an image, a dream, a sense of possibility that others can rally around has been regarded highly among the traits of transformational leaders. But what of the dreams of the people? In today's highly diverse world, neither leadership vision nor shared vision alone is enough. We need leaders who invite everyone to dream and to realize their dreams. We need organizations to be safe places where people dream and share dreams in dialogue with one another. We need the freedom to dream in community.

One-on-one interviews and story-based synthesis open people's individual dreams to the whole organization. This capability can change people's work and lives, as it did for Brenda Luebben, a ten-year employee of Hunter Douglas:

> At the end of my interview, I was asked to imagine one thing that would help me do my job even better. I said, "It would be going to Mexico." You see, my sample books, the products which I produce, go to one of our fabricators down in Mexico. Can you believe it? They ended up sending me to Mexico! The trip made me feel like I really knew my job, like my job was really important to the company. Just seeing who they were and what they needed gave me better ways to communicate with those folks.

In cultures that believe in personal revelation, the act of sharing visions and dreams is sacred, in part because of the belief that Spirit speaks through dreams. Through the act of sharing dreams, one person's connection to Spirit can enlighten the whole group. For example, Black Elk—a recognized holy man among the Lakota Sioux—had visions of seven sacred rites.[82] As he shared his visions publicly, the community embraced his dreams as collective guidance and tribal wisdom. Today these seven sacred rites are recognized and carried out by the Lakota Sioux as their seven sacred ceremonies.

One of the most inspiring stories about the freedom to dream in community comes from American Baptist International Ministries. On the heels of several months of interviews with over twelve hundred stakeholders worldwide, two hundred fifty people gathered in an AI Summit to hear people's hopes and dreams for the organization. They gathered to imagine an organization that could deliver on those hopes and dreams to create new ways in which they might serve people in need around the world. They imagined a new kind of service—one that would move from predominantly sending people out to "do good" in the world, to a model of linking people and organizations of similar intent around the globe. This vision was so compelling—and its momentum so great—that by the first anniversary of the summit, close to thirty new initiatives were launched using this "sister organization" model as a template. Then, in the two years that followed, close to two hundred new initiatives unfolded. Consultant Jim Ludema described the power of the community's dream as "unleashing energy that was already there. It was a positive explosion waiting to happen."

Time after time, Appreciative Inquiry invites people at all levels of the organization into the dreaming process. It creates an impetus for doing things better—for realizing dreams, whether they are big or small, personal or organizational. It puts attention on the visionaries rather than the squeaky wheels—on the path ahead rather than the problems of the past. And it enables images of hope, potential, and being the best to rise to the surface of organizational life.

Freedom to Choose to Contribute

Work can separate us from what matters most to us, or it can serve as the vehicle through which we enact and realize our deepest calling. In more patriarchal organizations, some "other" is said to know what is best for us. A manager, supervisor, or employment advisor determines the scope of a job and whether we are suited to it. People are matched to work based on the needs of the organization.

Not so in life-centered organizations, where the freedom to choose one's work and learning opportunities is recognized as essential to creativity, cooperation, and well-being. When people are free to volunteer based on their interests and passions, their capacities to learn and contribute are significantly enhanced. The scope, success, and satisfaction of contributing are directly related to the freedom to choose the nature and extent of the contributions.

In an Appreciative Inquiry process, people can and do join only when they become curious, stimulated, or inspired by a task, activity, or dream. Many people choose only to participate in the interviews—yet even that minimal level of engagement has a liberating effect on those who are involved. Others, like Kathy Mayfield, come on board later in the process. A printer with several years' tenure, she initially refused even to be interviewed. But eight months into the process, someone recruited her into an Action Group—formed at the first AI Summit—that was working on a task that piqued her curiosity and profound interest. Soon she had become one of the strongest supporters of Appreciative Inquiry in the entire organization.

John Cade believes this capacity to choose the nature and extent of one's contribution has a built-in mentoring and developmental quality: "Since some people are more comfortable following than leading," he suggests. "The Appreciative Inquiry process— which is grassroots and designed to engage people in their own time and way—gives them a hand to hold and helps train people to take responsibility for their own lives."

Freedom to choose to contribute leads to commitment, the liberation of power, and learning. When people choose to do a project and commit to others to do it, they become very creative and determined about it. They will do whatever it takes and learn whatever is needed to get the job done. For example, a front-line employee who had volunteered to lead an innovation team went to her personnel department and asked for coaching. She declared that she needed to learn to facilitate meetings and help her team make decisions in order for them to succeed. Her determination paid off for the team, the organization, and herself. The team's project was finished in record time and led to significant process improvements in the company. She was promoted to a supervisory position, and her new team is thriving with her leadership.

In any organizational change process, some people are more committed to, enthusiastic about, and engaged than others. These people become the informal leaders of the change effort. Because Appreciative Inquiry works to locate and channel people's interests and passions, that kind of involvement is nurtured and supported rather than contained. Brian Bassett describes the relationship between this kind of engagement and the liberation of power:

> Because our initial efforts flowed from people's passions, people had energy to do the work. People had success with the work that really mattered to them: work that was so important to them that they were willing to change their old habits and *play*. Once they'd had that experience, they wanted to act elsewhere . . . and continue acting. That's why people at Hunter Douglas kept moving from one Action Group to another. It wasn't because they had to. It was because it felt so good that they didn't want to stop!

Not surprisingly, our research suggests that the more engaged people are in an AI initiative, the greater their experience of personal transformation will be. Joe Sherwood, a manufacturing and fabrication process coordinator, observes:

> I've seen a huge difference in the people who have really embraced Appreciative Inquiry. Those who were more involved, and more willing to become part of the leadership of the process, seemed to grow the most.

Freedom to Act with Support

Much organizational support is limited. To be supported by one part of an organization—one supervisor or one manager—leaves room for doubt, mistrust, and hesitation. It breeds fragmentation. By contrast, when people know that the whole organization is aware of their project and willing to cooperate, they feel safe to experiment, innovate, and learn. In other words, whole-system support stimulates people to take on challenges and draws them into acts of cooperation that bring forth their best.

To act with support is the quintessential act of positive interdependence. In an Appreciative Inquiry, people are invited to act on behalf of the things that passionately inspire them—the things that they know will make a difference in their organization and in the world. They are called to act in the service of the organization, with support from others at all levels of the organization.

The freedom to act with support leads to unprecedented action, and it also raises people's confidence in and hope for the organization. John Deere Harvester Works' highly creative approach to unleashing the freedom to act with support broke through years' worth of apathy and distrust when facilitators designed a five-day summit, the last two days of which were focused exclusively on what they called "tactical implementation." They knew that being able to implement changes right there, while everyone was together, would prove unequivocally to participants that the organization was serious about supporting change.

People dreamed, created an opportunity map, brainstormed projects through which they could accomplish their dream, and selected the ten projects that they believed were most critically important. Then, to their surprise, they were invited to work with one another right there in the summit to plan, line up resources, and initiate the projects! As consultant Jim Ludema says, "This immediate, concrete support reversed over twenty years of history by showing that management was serious about involving the whole system in the changes. In response, employees invested huge amounts of knowledge and creativity into finding innovative solutions." As a result, the plant reduced its new product cycle time from five to three years and gained millions of dollars in new market share.

Hunter Douglas's Appreciative Inquiry was similarly organized to provide both leadership and organizational support—though in a very different form. Business unit managers supported the Action Groups by consistently offering participants access to information, time, resources, skills training, and professional facilitation.

In addition, they served as champions for the Action Groups, and they served on the Appreciative Inquiry Advisory Team.

At the same time, the Advisory Team initiated and maintained a communication network through which the Action Groups' activities and successes were broadcast to the entire organization. This promoted organization-wide support for the work of the Action Groups. When asked to describe what they had done and what they had learned about leading an appreciative change effort, the Advisory Team commented:

> We didn't have to do much, as leaders. Mainly, we provided guidance and the green light for people. We helped build confidence that people's ideas and plans made sense.

Of the initial fourteen Action Groups, eleven either met or exceeded their original goals in ways already described in detail. But what of the three Action Groups that failed to achieve their goals? Surprisingly, our research shows that this freedom to act with support liberated individual and organizational power—even when the actions "failed." Tina LaGrange's story powerfully testifies to that effect:

> I came away from the summit clear that cross-training was very, very important. I just knew that it would solve our mandatory overtime problems and provide people with a career path. But everybody I talked to said, "Sure we need it, but it won't go through. They'll never support it or let it happen."
>
> Still, I joined an Action Group and worked hard. We designed a great program, proposed it to the Advisory Team, and got the go-ahead to test it. Then . . . *nobody signed up!!!*
>
> Once we got over trying to "drive" it through, we stepped back and saw that there was a loud, clear message trying to be heard. "They" weren't the problem—it was the people in the organization. Nobody had much energy for cross-training.
>
> When our program died, I was disappointed—but OK. In the end, the only thing I really accomplished was getting an answer; but that was a big thing. It meant that I had the power to get an answer.

With Appreciative Inquiry, people sense support from one another, from the organization's management, and from the whole system. To take initiative is an adventure and a risk for many. To do so with full knowledge and support of colleagues throughout the organization creates a pathway for self-confidence, learning, and innovation.

Freedom to Be Positive

People and organizations grow and thrive with recognition and appreciation. And yet many organizations today are overrun with deficit discourse. They are habitually prone to problem analysis and hence to fear, blame, and criticism. Their inner dialogue is full of tales of woe and who has done what to whom. In many organizations it even seems chic to be cynical, to be the first to critique new ideas, and to seek to understand and describe causes of failure.

In organizations today, it is simply not the norm to have fun, to be happy, or to be positive. Despite the pain it causes, people allow themselves to be swept away in collective currents of negativity. A long-term employee of an organization mired in deficit discourse shared with dismay: "I have ulcers because of this negative thinking and talking. Every day I come to work and hear nothing but complaints and criticism and blaming. I hate coming to work."

In contrast, Appreciative Inquiry is a bold invitation to be positive. To be positive is more than a freedom—it is a prescription implicit in the process of Appreciative Inquiry. You simply can't participate in an Appreciative Inquiry without focusing on what is positive, what gives life, and what constitutes the positive core. Over and over, people have told us that Appreciative Inquiry works in part because it gives people the freedom to be positive. In the words of someone who first learned about the practice, "The power of Appreciative Inquiry comes, in part, from the permission it gives employees to feel positive and be proud of their working experiences."

People whose dispositions are basically upbeat are the first to celebrate the freedom to be positive. Renee Chavez, for example, deeply valued the opportunity afforded by AI to indulge her natural optimism:

> I don't know if it's me or if it's Appreciative Inquiry—but *I like to be positive.* I liked doing the interviews, because I heard more positive things. Because of my involvement with Appreciative Inquiry, I got people thinking more positively. I think that a lot of the improved morale, the communication, the sense of community with the other departments came from Appreciative Inquiry and its positive approach.

The effect of Appreciative Inquiry is so strong that it can even transform deficit discourse and negative thinking. In the words of one employee:

> I am a very positive thinker, so this suits me very well. But I believe this process is powerful enough to influence all of the staff—not just those of us who are already this way.

What happens to an organization when the freedom to be positive is unleashed? "You know the old adage 'Garbage in / garbage out'?" asks Joe Sherwood. "Well, Appreciative Inquiry replaces the 'garbage in' with positive feelings and positive experiences. It creates instead a cycle of 'energy in / energy out.' It jump-starts organizational change."

The freedom to be positive affected the home life as well as the work life of many Hunter Douglas employees. One employee described what happened when she felt free to be positive and share Appreciative Inquiry with her children: "It worked at home with my kids. It helped get them thinking positively, thinking things through for themselves, and getting what they want." And Rinda Becker, an executive secretary, told us that her use of Appreciative Inquiry on the occasion of her thirtieth wedding anniversary led to "one of the most insightful and meaningful conversations my husband and I have ever had."

How odd to think that people need permission to be positive. And yet so it is today in organization after organization. In its fully affirmative stance, Appreciative Inquiry is a radical departure—a true revolution in positive change.

In Conclusion: An Invitation to Positive Change

One measure of success for an Appreciative Inquiry initiative is whether an organization has enhanced its capacity for positive change. Has the organization's inner dialogue transformed from problem-oriented, deficit discourse to strength-oriented, affirmative discourse? Has knowledge of the organization's positive core expanded? Have members and stakeholders of the organization learned how to learn? Have the level of curiosity and the tendency to inquire increased? Has the organization's mind become an inquiring mind? Have the patterns of conversation, interaction, and relationships become more life centered? On the heels of a successful Appreciative Inquiry, the answer will most often be a resounding yes.

By liberating people's power, Appreciative Inquiry enhances an organization's capacity for positive change. This book is filled with stories that illustrate the power of Appreciative Inquiry, how it works, and why it works. Hunter Douglas's success story is the norm, not the exception, when it comes to getting results with Appreciative Inquiry.

Still, in the midst of growing applications and continued successes, there is much more to be done. Imagine schools around the world where children and teachers discover and learn together—where teachers, parents, and administrators are committed to bringing out the best of every child. Imagine hospitals where doctors ask people to describe their images of health and positive aging and where nurses, doctors, patients, and families gather to cooperatively design the health-care practices for their community. Imagine businesses that are dedicated agents of world benefit—where all stakeholders value the triple bottom line: balancing financial, social, and environmental needs. Imagine a community in which you are known for your unique gifts and strengths—where you choose to work and are supported in areas that interest you. Imagine positive change in your organization.

And so we invite you to join the revolution for positive change. We invite you to experiment with Appreciative Inquiry in new ways and different places and thus to add to the growing body of knowledge about the liberation of power, life-centered organizations, and positive change. In short, we invite you to make our world a better place, one organization at a time.

Notes

Chapter 1
What Is Appreciative Inquiry?

1. David L. Cooperrider and Diana Whitney, *Collaborating for Change: Appreciative Inquiry* (San Francisco: Berrett-Koehler, 1999).

Chapter 2
A Menu of Approaches to Appreciative Inquiry

2. Diana Whitney, Amanda Trosten-Bloom, Jay Cherney, and Ronald Fry, *Appreciative Team Building: Positive Questions to Bring Out the Best of Your Team* (Lincoln, NE: iUniverse, 2004).
3. Sara L. Orem, Jacqueline Binkert, and Ann L. Clancy, *Appreciative Coaching: A Positive Process for Change* (San Francisco: Jossey-Bass, 2007).
4. Diana Whitney, Kae Rader, and Amanda Trosten-Bloom, *Appreciative Leadership* (New York: McGraw-Hill, forthcoming).
5. See www.appreciativeleadershipnow.com.
6. David L. Cooperrider, "The 'Child' As Agent of Inquiry," in *Appreciative Inquiry: An Emerging Direction for Organization Development* (Champaign, IL: Stipes, 2001).
7. Ibid.
8. See http://www.imaginechicago.org/index.html.

Chapter 3
Eight Principles of Appreciative Inquiry

9. Peter L. Berger and Thomas Luckmann, The *Social Construction of Reality: A Treatise in the Sociology of Knowledge, 7th ed.* (London: Pelican Books, 1966).

10. Elise Boulding and Kenneth E. Boulding, *The Future: Images and Processes* (Thousand Oaks, CA: Sage, 1995).

11. Frederik Polak, *The Image of the Future*, trans. from the Dutch *[Die Toekomst Is Verleden Tijd]* and abr. by Elise Boulding (San Francisco: Jossey-Bass, 1973).

12. Suresh Srivastva, David L. Cooperrider, and associates, *Appreciative Management and Leadership* (San Francisco: Jossey-Bass, 1990).

13. Don Miguel Ruiz, *The Four Agreements: A Toltec Wisdom Book* (San Rafael, CA: Amber-Allen, 1997).

14. Joseph Jaworski, *Synchronicity: The Inner Path of Leadership* (San Francisco: Berrett-Koehler, 1996).

15. Kenneth J. Gergen, *Realities and Relationships: Soundings in Social Construction* (Cambridge, MA: Harvard University Press, 1994).

16. Kenneth J. Gergen, *An Invitation to Social Construction* (Thousand Oaks, CA: Sage, 1999).

17. Marilee G. Goldberg, *The Art of the Question: A Guide to Short-Term Question-Centered Therapy* (New York: John Wiley, 1998).

18. Ibid.

19. Viktor E. Frankl, *Man's Search for Meaning* (New York: Washington Square, 1998).

20. Marilee G. Goldberg, *The Art of the Question* (New York: John Wiley, 1998).

21. William Martin, *The Couple's Tao Te Ching* (New York: Marlowe, 2000).

22. Parker Palmer, *Let Your Life Speak: Listening for the Voice of Vocation* (San Francisco: Jossey-Bass, 2000).

23. Rollo May, *The Courage to Create* (New York: Norton, 1994).

24. Frederik Polak, *The Image of the Future*, trans. from the Dutch [*Die Toekomst Is Verleden Tijd*] and abr. by Elise Boulding (San Francisco: Jossey-Bass, 1973).

25. William Bergquist, *The Postmodern Organization: Mastering the Art of Irreversible Change* (San Francisco: Jossey-Bass, 1993).

26. Linda Jones, *The Power of Positive Prophecy* (New York: Hyperion, 1999).

27. Gervase R. Bushe and Graeme H. Coetzer, "Appreciative Inquiry As a Team-Development Intervention: A Controlled Experiment," *Journal of Applied Behavioral Science 31* (March 1995): 13.

28. Diana Whitney and David L. Cooperrider, "The Appreciative Inquiry Summit: Overview and Applications," *Employment Relations Today* 35, no. 2 (1998): 17–28.

29. David Bohm, *Wholeness and the Implicate Order* (New York: Routledge, 1980).

30. Rachel Naomi Remen, *Kitchen Table Wisdom* (New York: Berkley, 1996).

31. Mikhail Gorbachev, *The Search for a New Beginning* (San Francisco: Harper, 1995).
32. James Ludema, "From Deficit Discourse to Vocabularies of Hope: The Power of Appreciation," in *Appreciative Inquiry: Rethinking Human Organization Toward a Positive Theory of Change,* ed. David Cooperrider, P. Sorensen, Diana Whitney, and T. Yaeger (Champaign, IL: Stipes, 2000).
33. Martin Luther King Jr., "The Most Durable Power." Sermon delivered November 6, 1956, in Montgomery, AL.
34. Jon Kabat-Zinn, *Wherever You Go, There You Are: Mindfulness Meditation in Everyday Life* (New York: Hyperion, 1994).
35. Franklin D. Roosevelt, "Second Inaugural Address," delivered January 1937, Washington, DC.
36. Jane Galloway Seiling, *The Membership Organization: Achieving Top Performance Through the New Workplace Community* (Mountain View, CA: Davies-Black, 1997).
37. Tom McGehee, *Whoosh: Business in the Fast Lane* (Cambridge, MA: Perseus Books, 2001).
38. Rollo May, *The Courage to Create* (New York: Norton, 1994).
39. Geoffrey M. Bellman, *Your Signature Path: Gaining New Perspectives on Life and Work* (San Francisco: Berrett-Koehler, 1996).
40. Max DePree, *Leading Without Power: Finding Hope in Serving Community* (San Francisco: Jossey-Bass, 1997).

Chapter 4
Appreciative Inquiry in Action: From Origins to Current Practice

41. David L. Cooperrider, Frank Barrett, and Suresh Srivastva, "Social Construction and Appreciative Inquiry: A Journey in Organizational Theory," in *Management and Organization: Relational Alternatives to Individualism,* ed. Dian Marie Hosking, H. Peter Dachler, and Kenneth J. Gergen (Brookfield USA: Avebury, 1995).
42. Ibid.
43. Diana Whitney, David L. Cooperrider, M. Garrison, and J. Moore, "Appreciative Inquiry and Culture Change at GTE: Launching a Positive Revolution," in *Appreciative Inquiry and Organization Transformation: Reports from the Field,* ed. Ronald Fry, Diana Whitney, Jane Seiling, and Frank Barrett (Westport, CT: Quorum Books, 2001).
44. Martin Seligman, "Speech at Lincoln Summit," September 1999, Positive Psychology Center, University of Pennsylvania, http://www.ppc.sas.upenn.edu/lincspeech.htm (retrieved October 18, 2009).
45. Ibid.

46. Martin Seligman, *Authentic Happiness: Using the New Positive Psychology to Realize Your Potential for Lasting Fulfillment* (New York: Free Press, 2004).

47. http://www.ppc.sas.upenn.edu/.

48. http://www.sas.upenn.edu/lps/graduate/mapp/.

49. http://www.mentorcoach.com/AHC/index.htm.

50. Jerry Sternin and R. Choo, "The Power of Positive Deviancy," *Harvard Business Review*, January 1999.

51. Ibid.

52. Charles Gibbs, "The United Religions Initiative at Work: Interfaith Dialogue Through Appreciative Inquiry, Sowing Seeds of Transformation," in *Interfaith Dialogue and Peacebuilding* (Washington, DC: United States Institute of Peace, 2002).

53. Jane E. Dutton, Robert E. Quinn, and Kim S. Cameron, eds., *Positive Organizational Scholarship* (San Francisco: Berrett-Koehler, 2003).

54. Gervase R. Bushe and Robert J. Marshak, *Revisioning Organization Development: Diagnostic and Dialogic Premises and Patterns of Practice* (forthcoming).

55. http://appreciativeinquiry.case.edu.

Chapter 7
Discovery: Appreciative Interviews and More

56. Diana Whitney, David L. Cooperrider, Amanda Trosten-Bloom, and Brian Kaplin, *Encyclopedia of Positive Questions*, vol. 1 (Euclid, OH: Lakeshore Communications. 2002).

57. Diana Whitney, David L. Cooperrider, Amanda Trosten-Bloom, and Brian Kaplin, *Encyclopedia of Positive Questions*, vol. 1, *Using AI to Bring Out the Best in Your Organization* (Brunswick, OH: Crown Custom Publishing, 2001).

58. Diana Whitney, Amanda Trosten-Bloom, Jay Cherney, and Ronald Fry, *Appreciative Team Building: Positive Questions to Bring Out the Best of Your Team* (Lincoln, NE: iUniverse, 2004).

59. Dawn C. Dole, Jen Hetzel Silbert, Ada Jo Mann, and Diana Whitney, *Positive Family Dynamics: Appreciative Questions to Bring Out the Best in Families* (Chagrin Falls, OH: Taos Institute Publications, 2008).

60. Davis Taylor, Reflections on work with the *San Jose Mercury News* national advertising team.

61. Karl E. Weick, *Sensemaking in Organizations* (Thousand Oaks, CA: Sage, 1995).

62. Jerome Brunner, *Acts of Meaning: Four Lectures on Mind and Culture* (Cambridge, MA: Harvard University Press, 1990).

63. H. Paul Grice, *Studies in the Way of Words* (Cambridge, MA: Harvard University Press, 1989).

64. David L. Cooperrider and Diana Whitney, *Appreciative Inquiry: A Positive Revolution in Change* (San Francisco, Berrett-Koehler, 2005).

Chapter 8
Dream: Visions and Voices of the Future

65. David L. Cooperrider, "Positive Image, Positive Action: The Affirmative Basic of Organizing," in *Appreciative Management and Leadership* (San Francisco: Jossey-Bass, 1990).

66. Jim C. Collins and Jerry I. Porras, *Built to Last: Successful Habits of Visionary Leaders* (New York: Harper-Collins, 1994).

67. Ibid.

68. Richard Strauss, "Einleitung" ("Introduction") from *Also Sprach Zarathustra,* op. 30, 1896.

Chapter 9
Design: Giving Form to Values and Ideals

69. Margaret Mead, ed., *Cultural Patterns and Technical Change* (New York: Mentor Books, 1955).

70. Thomas J. Peters and Robert H. Waterman, *In Search of Excellence* (New York: Harper & Row, 1982).

71. David Korten, *The Post-Corporate World: Life After Capitalism* (San Francisco: Berrett-Koehler, 2000).

72. Dee Hock, *Birth of the Chaordic Age* (San Francisco: Berrett-Koehler, 1999).

73. Diana Whitney, "Designing Organizations As If Life Matters: Principles of Appreciative Organizing," in *Designing Information and Organizations with a Positive Lens: Advances in Appreciative Inquiry,* vol. 2, ed. Michel Avital, Richard J. Boland, and David L. Cooperrider (Oxford: Elsevier Science, 2007).

74. Jane Watkins and Bernard Mohr, *Appreciative Inquiry: Change at the Speed of Imagination* (San Francisco: Jossey-Bass/Pfeiffer, 2001).

Chapter 10
Destiny: Inspired Action and Improvisation

75. Diana Whitney, Kae Rader, and Amanda Trosten-Bloom, *Appreciative Leadership* (New York: McGraw-Hill, 2010).

76. Jim Anthony, *Ette Gazette,* Twentieth Anniversary Edition, October 2009, 13.

Chapter 11
Appreciative Inquiry: A Process for Community Planning

77. Peter Block, *Community: The Structure of Belonging* (San Francisco: Berrett-Koehler, 2008).

Chapter 12
Why Appreciative Inquiry Works

78. Paulo Freire, *Pedagogy of the Oppressed* (New York: Continuum, 1970).
79. Sheila McNamee and Kenneth J. Gergen, eds., *Relational Responsibility* (Thousand Oaks, CA: Sage, 1999).
80. Alan Fogel, *Developing Through Relationships* (Chicago: University of Chicago Press, 1993).
81. Kevin Kelly, *New Rules for the New Economy* (New York: Penguin, 1998).
82. Wallace Black Elk and Joseph Epes Brown, *The Sacred Pipe: Black Elk's Account of the Seven Rites of the Oglala Sioux* (Norman: University of Oklahoma Press, 1989).

Index

About the Authors

Diana Whitney and Amanda Trosten-Bloom have been friends and colleagues for thirty years. They initially met in Philadelphia working for the Hay Group. They now lead Corporation for Positive Change, an international consultancy whose mission is to bring Appreciative Inquiry to the most pressing issues of our time. Diana and Amanda are highly regarded by clients and colleagues alike for their abilities to design and facilitate large-scale positive change. They are wise advisors, inspiring keynote speakers, and compelling educa-

tors dedicated to supporting executives and consultants in the pursuit of Appreciative Inquiry knowledge and skills. Their clients include Fortune 500 corporations, government agencies, religious organizations, health-care systems, and communities.

Dedicated to advancing the field of positive change through practical innovations, they offer public and customized in-house workshops specifically designed to build capacity in Appreciative Inquiry and positive change. They have also created a series of CDs and DVDs on Appreciative Inquiry, and the first fully strength-based process to deepen leadership self-awareness and appreciative intelligence, titled the *Appreciative Leadership Development Program*.

Diana is a founder and director emeritus of the Taos Institute, a Fellow of the World Business Academy, and a Distinguished Consulting Faculty member at Saybrook University. She lives in Chapel Hill, North Carolina, where she offers workshops and writes. She has two grown children. She can be reached at Diana@positivechange.org.

Amanda is a certified consultant with Associated Consultants International (ACI), an associate with the Taos Institute, and an active participant in organization development and appreciative inquiry learning communities around the globe. She lives in Golden, Colorado, with her husband and daughter. There she hosts and mentors other Appreciative Inquiry consultants, teaches workshops, and works with local school systems, cities, and her Unitarian-Universalist community. She can be reached at Amanda@positivechange.org.

Diana and Amanda share a common spiritual practice based on Lakota traditions and Taoist philosophy, and they seek to integrate these principles and practices into their work. This commitment has led them to volunteer their time and talents to support the formation of the United Religions Initiative, a global interfaith organization dedicated to peace.

About Corporation for Positive Change

We are the premier Appreciative Inquiry consulting firm—a community of pioneering consultants dedicated to positive change in all sectors of work and life. We offer large-scale consulting, executive coaching, keynote speeches, and workshops on a range of topics related to Appreciative Inquiry. We partner with our clients, supporting them with leading-edge Appreciative Inquiry processes, practices, tools, and research. We can be reached at www.positivechange.org.

Berrett–Koehler
Publishers

Berrett-Koehler is an independent publisher dedicated to an ambitious mission: *Creating a World That Works for All*.

We believe that to truly create a better world, action is needed at all levels—individual, organizational, and societal. At the individual level, our publications help people align their lives with their values and with their aspirations for a better world. At the organizational level, our publications promote progressive leadership and management practices, socially respon-sible approaches to business, and humane and effective organizations. At the societal level, our publications advance social and economic justice, shared prosperity, sustainability, and new solutions to national and global issues.

A major theme of our publications is "Opening Up New Space." Berrett-Koehler titles challenge conventional thinking, introduce new ideas, and foster positive change. Their common quest is changing the underlying beliefs, mindsets, institutions, and structures that keep generating the same cycles of problems, no matter who our leaders are or what improvement programs we adopt.

We strive to practice what we preach—to operate our publishing company in line with the ideas in our books. At the core of our approach is steward-ship, which we define as a deep sense of responsibility to administer the company for the benefit of all of our "stakeholder" groups: authors, cus-tomers, employees, investors, service providers, and the communities and environment around us.

We are grateful to the thousands of readers, authors, and other friends of the company who consider themselves to be part of the "BK Community." We hope that you, too, will join us in our mission.

A BK Business Book

This book is part of our BK Business series. BK Business titles pioneer new and progressive leadership and management practices in all types of public, private, and nonprofit organizations. They promote socially responsible ap-proaches to business, innovative organizational change methods, and more humane and effective organizations.

Berrett–Koehler
Publishers

A community dedicated to creating
a world that works for all

Visit Our Website: www.bkconnection.com

Read book excerpts, see author videos and Internet movies, read our
authors' blogs, join discussion groups, download book apps, find out about
the BK Affiliate Network, browse subject-area libraries of books, get special
discounts, and more!

Subscribe to Our Free E-Newsletter, the *BK Communiqué*

Be the first to hear about new publications, special discount offers, exclu-
sive articles, news about bestsellers, and more! Get on the list for our free
e-newsletter by going to **www.bkconnection.com**.

Get Quantity Discounts

Berrett-Koehler books are available at quantity discounts for orders of ten or
more copies. Please call us toll-free at (800) 929-2929 or email us at **bkp**
.orders@aidcvt.com.

Join the BK Community

BKcommunity.com is a virtual meeting place where people from around
the world can engage with kindred spirits to create a world that works for
all. BKcommunity.com members may create their own profiles, blog, start
and participate in forums and discussion groups, post photos and videos,
answer surveys, announce and register for upcoming events, and chat with
others online in real time. Please join the conversation!

MIX
Paper from
responsible sources
FSC® C012752